# Escape from Tyranny

The Story of Four Brothers

Geoff Trigg

A catalogue record for this book is available from the National Library of Australia

Copyright © 2020 Geoff Trigg
All rights reserved.
ISBN-13: 978-1-922343-43-7

Linellen Press
265 Boomerang Road
Oldbury, Western Australia
www.linellenpress.com.au

# Dedication

To JANE TRIGG, nee SAX
13.12.1948 – 11.8.1997

Beloved Wife, Mother
Teacher & Friend
May her memory bear testament to
the Vitality, Insight & Fortitude
which influenced so many

*Jane Trigg*

# Contents

Dedication ..................................................................................... iii
Contents ......................................................................................... v
Acknowledgements ..................................................................... ix
Forward ......................................................................................... 1
Names List for people mentioned ............................................. 4
Chapter 1 ...................................................................................... 9
   *Background: An Introduction to the Australian Sax Family* ............... 9
Chapter 2 .................................................................................... 14
   *The Early Years at Novy Hrosenkov, Czechoslovakia* ..................... 14
Chapter 3 .................................................................................... 26
   *Escape by Sea* ............................................................................. 26
Chapter 4 .................................................................................... 55
   *Life in "The Promised Land"* ..................................................... 55
Chapter 5 .................................................................................... 64
   *Prisoners of War – Greece to Poland* ........................................... 64
Chapter 6 .................................................................................... 92
   *Terezin: World War II Ghetto and Concentration Camp* ............. 92
Chapter 7 .................................................................................. 102
   *After the War – Rebuild or Relocate. Australia and Israel* ......... 102
Chapter 8 .................................................................................. 115
   *Growing Up in Katanning and Perth, Western Australia* ........... 115

Chapter 9 ................................................................................................ 161
   *Martha Sax nee Weinstein* ............................................................... 161
Chapter 10 .............................................................................................. 173
   *Walter's Story by Mary Hunt* .......................................................... 173
Chapter 11 .............................................................................................. 207
   *Bruno Sax: A Gynecologist in Israel* ................................................ 207
Chapter 12 .............................................................................................. 214
   *John Sax: A Canadian Citizen* ........................................................ 214
Chapter 13 .............................................................................................. 219
   *Edith/Eva: The Sister who Survived and Stayed* ............................ 219
Chapter 14 .............................................................................................. 231
   *Origins* ............................................................................................ 231
Chapter 15 .............................................................................................. 245
   *A Collection of Sax Humour, Facts and Oddities* ........................... 245
Chapter 16 .............................................................................................. 253
   *Conclusion – Survive and Thrive* ................................................... 253
Appendix 1 - *Interview with Bruno Sax* ............................................... 257
Appendix 2 - *Timeline –Significant Dates for the Sax Family* ........... 260
Appendix 3 - *European Political History Impacting the Sax Family* . 270
Appendix 4 - *The Split of Czechoslovakia* ........................................... 273
Appendix 5 - *North Moravia* ................................................................ 275
Appendix 6 - *Australia and a background to its immigration policies* 277
Appendix 7 - *Letter from Walter Sax to Erwin Sax* ............................ 282
Appendix 8 - *Letter from Bruno Sax to Kathe Trigg* .......................... 284
Appendix 9 - *Letter to Jane Trigg from Bruno Sax* ............................ 287
Appendix 10 - *Letter from Walter Sax to Jane Trigg* ......................... 289

Appendix 11 - *Sax family notes* ......................................................... 293
Appendix 12 - *Poems by Jane Trigg* .................................................... 295
        *Viktor* ............................................................................ 295
        *Prague* .......................................................................... 297
        *Full Circle* .................................................................... 300
        *Aftermath* .................................................................... 301
        *Across the Street* ......................................................... 302
Appendix 13 - *Sax Family Photo Gallery* ............................................ 304
About the Author .............................................................................. 314

# Acknowledgements

This book was to have originally covered the life story of Irwin Erwin Sax. It quickly became obvious that it had to also include his three brothers – Walter, John and Bruno.

The background information came from many sources, from around the world.

Jane Trigg, nee Sax, wrote so much about her experiences growing up in Western Australia, particularly in Katanning, the lives of her parents and her discoveries of her Jewish inheritance. She wrote to and received letters from her three uncles, Chagit (Bruno's wife) and from her aunt Eva and family in the Czech Republic. Some of her poems have been included, up to the time she passed away from cancer in 1997. This book would not have been written without her substantial input.

The Australian Sax family photos provided a wealth of original information, including specific photos of the brothers' experiences in Lamsdorf POW camp.

Information and photos from Zohar Sax in Israel, Sol Sax in Canada plus both Tina Ho and Jana Sax in America, added great depth to the story. Approval from his family to include the total document "Walter's Story" written by Mary Hunt, giving the life story of Walter Sax from Czechoslovakia to Los Angeles, is very much appreciated.

Martha Sax, Erwin's wife, provided her memories, as recorded by Jane and Rachel Trigg, from the escape before World War II, her time as a fashion model in Palestine, through to retirement in Western Australia.

Andrew Trigg provided technical advice on copyright and found access to internet sites relating to factual details on various aspects of the story.

A personal description of John's life and its impact on his family by Sol Sax was a document of high praise, love and appreciation for his father.

A similar document written by Ruth Harith, Bruno's daughter, is a wonderful expression of admiration and love for her father and the role he played in the life of every member of the Israeli Sax family.

Photos from Tina Sax covered both Walter's life in the US and some World War II historical shots. Tina also provided photos of Sax cemetery monuments going back generations in the Czech Republic, taken when she went on a pilgrimage there to explore her Sax background.

These aided the deepening of the knowledge pool about four extraordinary brothers.

Internet access to official documents, Wikipedia and Google systems of data provision made the search for background details infinitely more productive than would otherwise be possible.

Several translators were used to convert to English a number of Czech letters and documents. Jane Trigg developed her Czech knowledge with translation books in order to convert from Czech to English, letters from Eva and her family. Zohar arranged translations to cover several Czech letters from Bruno's life and Sol Sax arranged several translations by his Czech family connections. These were all insights into personal aspects of the brothers' lives and I was very thankful to have them for inclusion. I have no knowledge of how accurate the translations were but all appear to fit into the general subject and tone of each letter.

My wife, Anne, whose word knowledge in suggesting formatting and spelling improvements, while working through several edits, made the reading much smoother and more easily understood. She also had to suffer me going on about the Sax family, much of which she had heard before.

Members of the Karrinyup Writers Club, which I joined to improve my writing skills, provided much support and proof reading of my draft work. Their combined wisdom and word-smith experience were greatly appreciated.

To all who are mentioned and those I have not named, I am hugely grateful for your help. I can only hope the result is judged as adequate and useful as an aid for future generations to understand their family history.

*Sol Sax, 2014*

*Tina Ho and Jana Sax*

*From the left: Kathe, Jane and Rachel Trigg*

*Zohar Sax*

# Foreward

The content of this book is based on written memoirs, letters to and between the brothers and Martha Sax, stories, documents and newspaper articles, photos and background information derived from the internet.

Most of the original details supplied from the brothers and Martha were written many years after the war and so their recollections sometimes differ in minor aspects.

There was an abundance of photos from which to choose for inclusion and many were included, without creating a picture book or photo album. Those chosen were an attempt to balance examples covering the four brothers and their immediate families, as well as adding quality content to each chapter.

Most chapters begin with several pages to 'set the scene', including details explaining the background of what was to follow with the personal accounts. These detail pages can sometimes seem to be duplications but are provided to present the chapter content in the best light for ease of understanding.

By far the most personal details are about Erwin and Martha Sax, as remembered and written by their daughter, Jane, my first wife.

Jane's recollections were exceedingly well written and easily readable while dealing with strong emotions and feelings.

The stories about her father showed the stress Erwin had been subjected to for a large part of his life, during momentous times that impacted on the whole world. Starting after World War II with a new family, and moving once more, again with nothing, to a foreign land on the other side of the world, required a huge commitment and great flexibility. Having to develop his second language of English to become his prime language, while rebuilding his life and caring for his family late in life, asked even more from him. Running an Australian farm, then becoming a shop keeper in a small country town, when all of his training was as a forester and timber mill manager must have required all of his survival skills. This he undertook and conquered, to enjoy a comfortable retirement with his daughter and grandchildren. Few men could achieve more from that background.

His three brothers; Walter, John and Bruno, achieved similar results from their lives, each of them with significant burdens from the past, but they all left a solid legacy for their families – life and prosperity in another land.

The names of people involved in this account varied, depending on the English, Czech or German equivalents. Sometimes only a couple of letters changed. With Erwin Sax, the name Irwin was interchangeable. Sometimes a "v" replaced the "w". His Australian formal name was Irwin Erwin Sax and the business name was "I.E.Sax & Co".

The majority of what they went through they kept to themselves, wanting to put the past behind them while working for the future. So much of this book was a positioning of fragments, like jigsaw pieces, to provide a true and as-accurate-as-possible account of their stories.

These were exceptional men during extreme times.

*Erwin Sax*          *Bruno Sax*

*John Sax*

*Walter Sax*

# Names List for people mentioned

## First known generation

Herman/Heinrich Sax: Grandfather of Erwin and his siblings

Cecilia Sax: Wife of Herman Sax

Adolf Sax: Brother of Herman Sax

## Second Generation: Children of Herman and Cecilia Sax

Karolina/Carolina Sax: Daughter. Aunt of Erwin and siblings

Jakob Sax: Son. Uncle of Erwin and siblings

Karl Sax: Son. As above

Sigmund/Zigmund Sax: Father of Erwin Sax and siblings. Married to Yohanna/Johanna/Jana Sax, nee Buchler

Jacob Sax: Son. Uncle of Erwin and siblings.

Marcus Sax: Son. As above

David Sax: Son. As above

**Third Generation: Children of Sigmund/Zigmund Sax and Yohanna/Johanna/Jana Sax, also David Sax and Jacob Sax**

| | |
|---|---|
| **Irwin/Erwin/Ervin Sax**: | Son. Married Gabriella/Gaby/Gabi Sax – divorced. Married **Martha/Marta Weinstein.** |
| **John/Jan/Yan/Hanus Sax**: | Son. Married Jarmila/Jarka Bozkova |
| **Walter/Valter Sax**: | Son. Married Charlotte/Chari/Shari Juszkovic |
| **Bruno Sax**: | Son. Married Chargit/Hagit Horovitz |
| Otto/Ota Sax: | Son. Died in WW II |
| Ernest/Ernst Sax: | Son. Died in WW II |
| Eva/Edith/Edit Sax: | Daughter. Married Joseph Konarik. Survived the war. |
| Irene/Ady Sax: | Daughter. Married Hugo Zwilinger. Died in WW II |
| Ada Sax: | Daughter. Died in WW II |
| Ruth/Ruti Sax: | Daughter. Died in WW II |
| Martha Sax: | Daughter. Married Mr Nussbaum. Died in WW II |
| Robert Sax: | Son of Jacob Sax. Cousin of Erwin Sax and siblings |
| Walter Sax: | As above |

| | |
|---|---|
| Irma Sax: | Daughter of David Sax. Cousin of Erwin Sax and siblings |
| Hilda Sax: | As above |

## Fourth Generation: Children of previous generation

| | |
|---|---|
| Judith Sax: | Daughter of Erwin and Gabriella Sax. Died in WW II |
| Jane/Jana Trigg, nee Sax: | Daughter of Erwin and Martha Sax. Wife of Geoff Trigg |
| Solly/Sol Sax: | Son of John and Jarmila Sax. Married Dominique Riccio |
| Ruti/Ruth Sax: | Daughter of Bruno and Chagit Sax |
| Yifat Sax: | Daughter of Bruno and Chagit Sax |
| Zohar Sax: | Son of Bruno and Chagit Sax |
| Paul Sax: | Son of Walter and Charlotte Sax. Married Tina Ho |
| Robert Sax: | Son of Walter and Charlotte Sax. Married Adienne |
| Alenka Konarik: | Daughter of Edith/Eva Sax and Josef Konarik |
| Evanka Konarik: | As above |
| Josef Konarik: | Son of Edith/Eva Sax and Josef Konarik |

| | |
|---|---|
| Kurt Zwilinger: | Son of Irene Sax and Hugo Zwilinger. Died in WW II |
| Lilly Zwilinger: | Daughter of Irene Sax and Hugo Zwilinger. Died in WW II |
| Ingaborg Nussbaum: | Daughter of Martha Sax and Mr Nussbaum. Died in WW II |
| Eva Nussbaum: | Daughter of Martha Sax and Mr Nussbaum. Died in WW II |

**Others**

| | |
|---|---|
| Karel Werner: | First husband of Martha Weinstein |

Note: The Sax family tree is shown on pages 234 – 236.

# Chapter 1

# Background: An Introduction to the Australian Sax Family

## The Old Cigar Tin

It sits there, a thread of memory but incongruous on a pile of neat, Chinese-made, plastic carrying cases. They contain multi-coloured plastic plugs, screwdriver sets and small, modern, electrical tools. The item of my focus is a rusty metal tin, with "Willem II Half Corona 10 cigars Made in Holland" on the front in faded letters. It now contains old electrical drill bits but had been used for storing wood-turning cutting tools by its original owner, then a collection of fishhooks, but originally, mini cigars.

Until he moved into a Busselton retirement village, the old metal tin, along with a collection of rusty nuts, bolts, and screws, plus a few surviving hand tools, belonged to my father-in-law, Irwin Erwin Sax. He and his wife, Martha, were originally from Czechoslovakia and arrived in Fremantle as World War II and Czechoslovakian communist regime refugees in 1949.

He had been a heavy smoker most of his life but had moved from cigarettes to a pipe soon after we met in 1971. The pipe was replaced with mini cigars and finally, Tic Tac mints; so many that he often rattled when he walked, one vice progressively replacing another.

My first experiences with the Sax family began in a fairly normal way. I met their daughter, Jane, when working as an engineer in Bunbury, Western Australia, where she was an English Literature teacher at the local High School, and a friendship developed. That friendship grew, to the point where we drove up to Perth for the first time to stay at the Sax family house through the weekend for their assessment as to whether I was good enough for their daughter.

Erwin and Martha, his wife, had recently moved from the Western Australian country town of Katanning, where they owned and ran a shop, to Rossmoyne, a suburb of Perth. Erwin had found a part-time job as a night watchman at the factory of *Western Glass* factory, but was close to full-time retirement.

That weekend transformed me, a conservative Australian 20-year-old, originally from a Victorian country town where adventurous food meant the local Italian or Chinese restaurants and home cooking included mashed potato, three vegetables, and chops or sausages. Cold meat and cheese were polony and Kraft Cheddar, with Vegemite spread on white bread thrown in as a treat.

I tasted for the first time Jewish/Czechoslovakian cooking, including Jewish chicken soup, potato latkes, German seven-layer Schwarzwalder Kirschtorte (Black Forest gateau), strange-smelling cheeses and an array of cold meat sausage slices. I hadn't known flavours like them before or even that they existed, although I had seen such exotic foods in the local delicatessen.

The strong Czech accents were also new to me, with no recently-arrived central Europeans experienced in a Victorian country schoolyard in the 1950s and 60s, or at the local Institute of Advanced Education. Had I lived in a suburb of Melbourne or Sydney, my education regarding non-British foods and accents could have been much more advanced. Australian food tastes and knowledge of the world were still limited in those times, particularly away from the major cities.

Jane and I soon married, and her family became a central point of my life and, eventually, our children's lives.

Erwin quickly found uses for his new son-in-law. I had learned to play chess at school in a limited way. He was a Grand Master and also a very proficient card player. My main role was to try hard but get beaten, every time. My card-playing did not last long. It ended when I understood how competitive he could be, which removed the enjoyment of playing.

With chess, by pure luck, I eventually won a game. He then immediately set up both sides of the board and played both until he worked out what he thought was my 'strategy'. I could not convince him it was by luck only. We played several more games where he beat me convincingly, his satisfaction restored. The problem of finding quality, chess-playing opponents for him was removed, several years in the future, when chess computers first became available. They made ideal gifts for him, and over five to ten years, he burnt out three of them, each one more developed with more capacity than the last. They filled large parts of his spare time and finally let me off the hook!

The history of Jane's parents was also a revelation to a conservative, sheltered young Australian, knowing little of the refugee's new life in Australia. I also had no personal understanding of the disastrous impact of the Nazi, criminally insane slaughter of millions of Jewish Europeans during World War II.

Erwin had fled from the German occupation of Czechoslovakia in 1939 with his three brothers, to eventually join the British Army in Palestine, but was captured by the Germans in Greece. During the rest of the war, they were POWs in a German camp, close to the Czechoslovakian border. He found, after the war, on his return to his home town, that the majority of his family members and relatives were dead. Erwin and his second wife, Martha, made a final sea trip to Australia, with their baby daughter, Jane, to eventually settle into a new life in a West Australian wheat belt country town, far from the life they had experienced in the old-world but war-ravaged civilisation of central Europe.

For me, these stories, very reluctantly let go by my father-in-law, but greatly expanded by his wife Martha and his brothers, were from another world, acted out by imaginary figures. To have them now as part of mine and my children's family stories led me to investigate more fully, and particularly for my children's sake, the background of the wider Sax history.

Years after their deaths, and indeed, after Jane's early and tragic death due to cancer in 1997, I visited Prague after a river cruise on the Danube. The visit was part of an organised tour, but I felt as if there were old ghosts to acknowledge and placate on behalf of Jane's family.

After the obligatory and included tour of the tourist and historical spots of Prague, a side trip to the old fortress of Terezin, outside of the city, was arranged. This fortress was used by the Nazis to hold hundreds of thousands of Jews from the region, for a short while, before they were moved off to Auschwitz – "The

Final Solution". A number of the Sax family members were 'processed' at Terezin during the war by the Nazis, never to be seen again.

I spoke very little on that tour due to the horror of what had taken place there.

The visit to Prague also included time in the old Jewish Quarter and a viewing of the Pinkas Synagogue which has a permanent memorial to the Czech/Jewish citizens who were sent to the Nazi death camps. Nearly 80,000 names are painted on the walls and ceilings of the building, arranged in order of their villages, towns, and cities. The names included the lost Sax family members.

How was it possible? I thought a lot about this visit after I returned home to Australia.

I suspect large parts of soldiers' war memories become locked away, and they have refused to talk about their horrific experiences in battle or as prisoners. Survivors often stay silent – not wanting to pass on their pain to family members or acknowledge what they had seen or had been forced to do or endure. They might also feel guilty that they survived, and so many others died.

That old cigar tin is already connected to each of my three children, as I have helped one daughter renovate her house, and the drill bits from the case have enabled renewal of her home and a new future. For my other daughter, many holes were drilled in the walls of her newly-purchased flat to allow for bookshelves to be installed and cups to be hung on hooks.

The cigar tin was almost picked up by my son at one time when he was 'into' a collection of old but interesting tins. It may also have gone with him on a road trip to the north of the state for a year, along with his grandfather's old fishing tackle and rods. I still remember how much Erwin hated the taste of fish because his family were helped to survive with carp caught in the farm pond during the First World War. All available farm products were sent off to support the fighting troops. He loved fishing but gave the fish away.

Surprisingly some of that fishing equipment my son took came back to Perth from his 'year out' after his university course. I still use Erwin's fish scaling and gutting knife in the garden to cut up vegetables.

This story may give the cigar tin a greater function of connecting grandparents to grandchildren and to the wider family spread over several continents. Hopefully, it will help to explain the memories and burdens carried in the past to enable new beginnings for future generations.

# Chapter 2

# The Early Years at Novy Hrosenkov, Czechoslovakia

*Early Sax Family photo,
with young children, before Sigmund died.
From the left: Ernst, Otto, Sigmund/Ziegmund (standing), Jana
(seated), Eva, Martha, Irna/Irene*

The Jewish Sax family had lived in the southern Czechoslovakian town of Novy Hrosenkov for a number of generations. The town was in Moravia, close to the regional boundary with Slovakia.

The lives of the four brothers followed in this book – Erwin, Walter, John and Bruno – were part of a large family of eleven siblings, plus their father, Zigmund Sax, and mother, Jana (Yohanna). Two older brothers, Otto and Ernest, completed the six brothers, while the five sisters were Irene, Martha, Edith, Ada, and Ruth.

The town had a population of about 7000 people prior to World War II and exists in the Beskid Mountains. It was and still is, a popular summer holiday spot, and in winter, it attracted tourists and city people for skiing. A climb of 4000 feet would allow a two-hour ski, ending up near the Sax's house.

Novy Hrosenkov had little industry, comprising just a glass factory and three timber sawmills, the Sax's being the largest. All three were owned by Jewish families. The family sawmill was originally run by their father and his brother David. After Zigmund's death, his wife, Jana, took control with help from the oldest children.

*Sax Brothers sawmill. Early days.*
*Sigmund on the left, and his brother David on the right.*

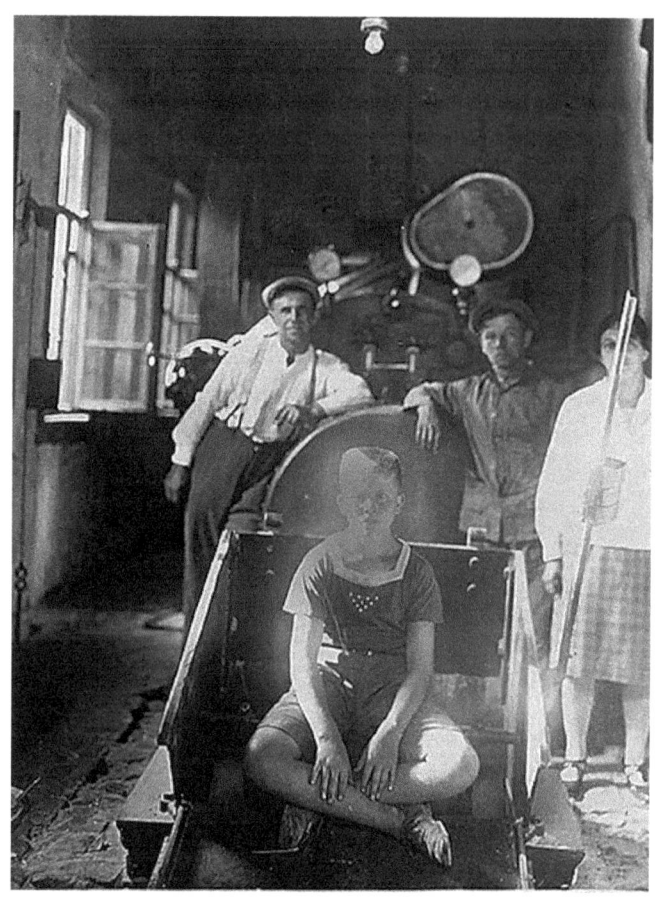

*Sax Bros. sawmill. Young Bruno at the front.*

In summer, the residents could go hiking, fishing, swimming, and boating, or play football and volleyball. In winter it was skiing, skating, dancing lessons, chess, and card games. There was no local hospital in the town, but because of the adjacent forest areas, there were many mill workers and foresters living in the town. Other residents included farmers and schoolteachers. All would take advantage of the entertainment, sporting activities, forests, and ski slopes. The nearby mountains also attracted walkers and mountain climbers.

The Sax family worked hard to establish the sawmill and house sites, some farmland and areas of forest from which they would cut softwood timber, particularly pine, for milling and sale.

*Father, Sigmund Sax and mother, Jana Sax*

At around 13 or 14 years of age, each of the children would leave their quiet country town and spend time in a big Czech city, normally with the family of a relative. There they would receive a better education than in the small, local school. Like many others, Walter went to a German-speaking town and attended a German commercial school for bookkeeping, accounting, and learning the German language. Ernest went to Vienna to attend a high commercial school. He was intelligent enough to have completed a commerce doctorate or become a professor if he had been given the chance.

Many Czech Jews in Bohemia and Moravia identified with a German heritage. This showed in the desire to acquire higher education in German schools and universities. For Czechs trying to promote a national identity, the German-oriented Jews were an obstacle to their efforts. This higher education attracted children from both language groups toward the opposite side of politics, away from the promotion of Czech pride and confidence in a national Czech future in the world.

For the Sax family, such lofty considerations were of little interest. A good education, particularly a higher education, could only be achieved in recognised and long-established German schools and colleges.

*Map 1: showing significant locations for the Sax family and Martha Sax, nee Weinstein: Bortice, where Martha was born, Novy Hrosenkov, where the brothers were born and Jihlava, where Jane Trigg, nee Sax was born.*

This was all interrupted when their father, Zigmund, unexpectedly died of a heart attack in 1925. It meant Ernest had to return to Novy Hrosenkov to help manage the sawmill. Otto, who was the oldest brother, had tertiary qualifications in timber milling and so became the business manager for the mill. One of their sisters also worked in the office. The name then became "The Jana Sax Sawmill", with their mother as owner.

Once Walter completed his accountancy qualifications, he worked in Prague for six years as an accountant in a division of a large company. Bruno, the youngest brother, also went to live in Prague to undertake university training to become a qualified doctor.

Several of the Sax brothers, including Otto, Walter, John, and Erwin, served in the Czechoslovakian Army. Erwin came home on leave in 1936. Both Erwin and John attended a special forestry school and gained tertiary qualifications in the operation of sawmills and the qualities of different timbers. Their training was aimed at complementing the family sawmill operation. Erwin completed his forestry course between 1926 and 1928.

Everything changed when, under the Munich Agreement worked out by Britain, France, Germany, and Italy on the 29th September 1938, Czechoslovakia's German-speaking border regions were sliced off and ceded to the German Nazi Third Reich. Other areas were taken by Poland and Hungary. This had an immediate impact on millions of Czechoslovak citizens. Thousands were forced to relocate away from these areas.

The population movement from the frontier regions was already underway by May 1938, as a first wave. By October 1st, this relocation of refugee Czechs forced out of their homes was immense in scale as the German Army started to take over the areas surrendered. That land takeover was forced on the Czechoslovak government by the four nations of the Munich Agreement. Initially, the people fleeing from the Germans were Social Democrats, Communists, Jews, and anti-fascist Sudeten Germans.

These refugees included Germans who had already fled from Nazi Germany, including opposition politicians, writers, artists, intellectuals, and journalists. They had travelled over the mountainous borders into Czechoslovakia where the German language was still spoken, education and culture were heavily influenced by Germans, the press was still free, and there were no visa restrictions. These people were forced onto the roads once more.

The second wave was made up of government employees, then those who did not wish to live in a country controlled by the foreign Germans, fearing what they would do when they had full control. A Czechoslovakian law, passed in February 1939, stated that a refugee was anyone who had left an area ceded to Germany, Poland, or Hungary after May 20th 1938, but was a citizen of Czechoslovakia.

This huge movement of people quickly filled towns and country villages in the country's interior, bringing with them all they could carry or transport. Czech charitable organisations like the Red Cross and regional youth groups treated it as a humanitarian crisis. By early October, relatives, friends, and even strangers had taken in whoever they could shelter. Schools, old factories, warehouses, and guesthouses were filled, but the people kept coming.

Discrimination against Jews in Czechoslovakia had been minimal and one of the lowest for any European country before the rise of Hitler and his Nazi Party. That started to change as Germany built up power and influence. When people fled into Czechoslovakia from Germany, discrimination against Jewish refugees in contrast to non-Jewish refugees became obvious. One reason was the government adopted policies that required Jewish refugees to be moved into country districts, particularly the Bohemian-Moravian highlands. The Sax family had direct experience of this Jewish movement when distant relatives arrived in their region.

From the end of March 1939, Germany controlled all of Czechoslovakia and absorbed it into the Third Reich. This was six months after the Munich Agreement allowed for only the German-speaking regions to be occupied. A few kilometres away from Novy Hrosenkov, over the internal border into Slovakia, its fascist leadership created an 'independent state', with permission from and subservient to Nazi Germany.

In September, World War II started, after Poland was invaded.

*German soldiers march into Prague in March, 1939*

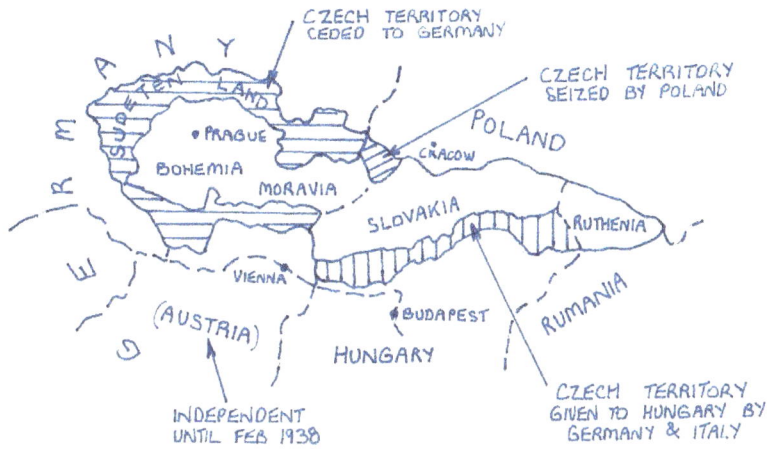

*Map 2a: showing Czechoslovakia in 1938 and the lost territories with land taken by Germany, Poland, and Hungary.*

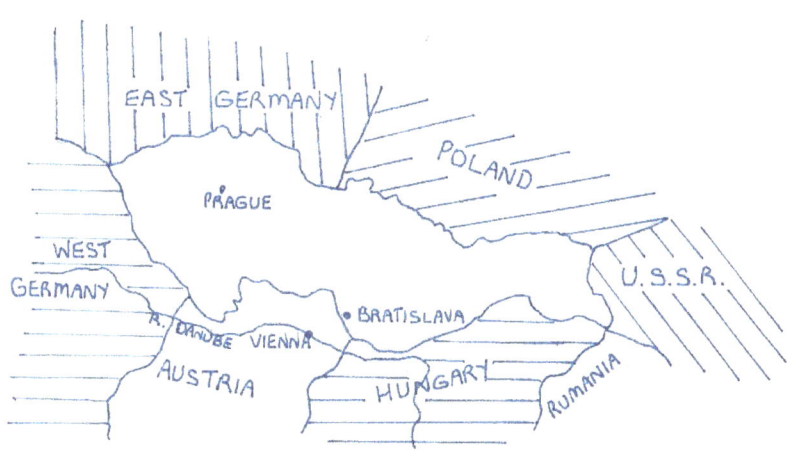

*Map 2b: showing Czechoslovakia in 1968 (controlled by the USSR), including Slovakia, Ruthenia taken by USSR/Ukraine and Germany split into West Germany and East Germany (controlled by USSR)*

Erwin attended his forestry school from 1926 to 1928, with the following translated school report:

## *Osobni Doklady* – **Personal Documents**

State/Government/National Forest Sawmill School of Valasske Mezirici

Catalogue / Register *Number* 13

School Year  1927/28

## Course Certificate

Mr  *Sax Ervin*
Born on the  *1 November 1907*
At  *Novem Hrozenkove (Novy Hrozenkov)* in *Moravia*

Attended the state forestry sawmill school of Valasske Mezirici from
*1 September 1926 to 28 June 1928*
and was assessed in this way:

*renowned/ commended*

### Compulsory Subjects Taught

| | | |
|---|---|---|
| Czech Language | ............ | Commended |
| Writing (written Czech?) | ............ | Commended |
| Honesty? and Calculation | ............ | Excellent |
| Geometry and ... | ............ | Excellent |
| Accounting | ............ | Excellent |
| Business Theory | ............ | Excellent |
| Citizenship ? Theory | ............ | Excellent |
| Technology | ............ | Excellent |
| Machine? | ............ | Excellent |
| Machine ...? | ............ | Excellent |
| Training/Practice in Diligence/Industry and in Workshop | ............ | Excellent |
| Health | ............ | Excellent |
| National Economy | ............ | Excellent |
| German | ............ | Excellent |

**Leisure classes**

Shorthand
Typing?

Family life continued in Novy Hrosenkov prior to the war, including a forthcoming wedding message written under a Sax business letterhead, by Bruno, in 1933, probably for the marriage of his sister, Edith:

"*DAMPFSAGE, HOLZHANDLUNG, UND*

*HOLZWOLL – ERZEUGUNG*

*Johanna Sax*
*New Hrosenkov, Czechoslovak Republic*
*Postparkasse Brunn, No. 104.226*
*Bank-Konto bei der Bank of Moravia in Vzetin*
*TELEFON NR. 3*

*New Hrosenkov, September 5th, 1933*

*My dears!*

*The time of your long-awaited marriage has finally arrived. It's a time when you will carry all of your choices together, and unfortunately difficult moments of life as well. This is why I wish you both as many joyful moments as possible so that happiness may emerge victoriously out of every struggle in life. And may this happiness be with you all your lives. I also wish that you will always be healthy and united, because only a unified marriage can be a beautiful one. Once more I wish you all the best and I am calling three cheers to your marriage. Zdar, zdar, zdar* (means success).

*Yours*

*Bruno*"

Another letter from Bruno covered typical minor family issues of the time:

"Dear Edith,

As you wished, I had your shoes repaired and then packed everything. I also added two of mum's photos. I am also sending some flowers (what you have sown, you should also keep). Please forgive me, I've forgotten to take care of your dress because it's been raining the last couple of days and it's impossible to ride a bike. Rutka (Ruth) said that she will bring it in the morning but I don't know. I am also sending you a small glass from our shop. You see, Erno (Ernest) has taken over your place and we have already sold one. Tetka can wait. Mother is planning on buying a new coat from the earnings. She has quite a lot to do these days, after all we are at school and those boys (except for me) are no help. Today we are doing laundry. Therefore, we will most likely not have any lunch. Mother is looking forward to seeing Ada and Ada is looking forward to seeing us. It's already 9 o'clock, so I have to conclude my letter. Send my greetings to Jozka.

Warm greetings from mother and the others as well.

Edith, don't forget to thank...

Edith, mother is sending you those... CZK from aunt Hermina. Please confirm everything. Mum slaughtered the rooster on Tuesday. She thought that a car would come, and since then it's already starting to smell, so she can't send it."

*Sax Family portrait, 1918.*
*Back Row-L to R: Martha, Irene, Otto, Ernest, Edith.*
*Middle: Ruth, Jana, Bruno, Sigmund, Ada.*
*Front: John, Erwin, Walter.*

*Part Sax family, prior to WW II*

# Chapter 3

# Escape by Sea

History is littered with the stories of major movements of refugees over long distances, trying to survive with their families. Those movements were often caused by invasion, oppression, famine, disease, natural disasters, or dramatic changes in governmental policies or attitudes.

In the last 50 years, refugees from Vietnam fleeing from the communists arrived in Australia, the US, or Canada by the boat or plane load. At the time of writing this book, Afghans, Syrians, and Iraqis are still moving from war zones in their home countries or from fanatical religious attitudes. Africans from several countries have flooded across the Mediterranean, trying to access Italy, Greece, France, and Spain, with many dying in the attempt. They have then moved through those countries into northern Europe, away from warlords, gang activity or violence, into a region of perceived peace and economic improvement.

All these people, and many more, have risked everything for a new life, and their movements have attracted profiteers, like sharks to blood in the water. Even now, the controversial Australian political policy towards refugees is to prevent the boats from Indonesia and Malaysia reaching Australian shores. The stated objective is to stop the profiteers and human smugglers as well as saving lives from being lost at sea in leaking or ill-equipped boats. Over generations, refugees have been stripped of any remaining wealth they possessed for the promise of safe delivery to a receiving shore. People have become rich on the suffering of others. It has happened throughout history, and there is little to make us believe it won't be happening in the future.

So it was with the Jews trying to escape Hitler in World War II. Every step on the road to safety had a price: for government official fees, people arranging boats to illegally try to get to Palestine, inflated costs of rail fares, food, clothing, 'under-the-counter' payments to officials looking the other way or stamping documents even when there were reasons not to.

For the Jews in Czechoslovakia, it started in Germany between 1933 and 1938, with the extreme Nazi attitudes towards all Jewish people. The Jews were to be removed by all means possible, from all land controlled by Germany or from life itself. This attitude and policy was adopted by Austria as Germany annexed that country, (the "Anschluss"), with few Austrian complaints.

With this came the flight of Jews into neighbouring countries. Germany occupied the north-western part of Czechoslovakia, the Sudetenland, with active support from the majority German-background residents living there. Czech Jews joined German and Austrian Jews moving east and south into the central, less-populated areas of Czechoslovakia, away from the immediate impact of Nazi policies and actions. Relatives of the Sax family arrived in Novy Hrosenkov and neighbouring villages from these countries and the Sudetenland, looking for refuge.

Conditions were getting worse by the start of 1939. Stories, both real and rumoured, were being told of camps for Jews, few knowing what the camps involved, but with the knowledge that nothing good came from the Nazis for the Jewish people.

The brothers wrote of relatives who had become refugees arriving in the district around Novy Hrosenkov. The family helped their relatives by hiding a lot of valuable silver items they had carried with them in the roof beams of the Sax house. That silver was never found again after the war.

Things further tightened on 15 March 1939, when German troops marched through the streets of Prague, and all universities ejected Jewish students as required by Nazi policy. This included Bruno from his studies in medicine at Prague University.

Of the four brothers, Erwin was the oldest and most interested in politics. He somehow arranged Japanese passports for his three brothers and wife, Gaby. The only connection found, so far, linking Japan to the granting of Japanese visas to Jews trying to escape Hitler and the concentration camps is the vice-consul of the Japanese Consulate in Kaunas, Lithuania, Mr Chiune Sugihara. He disobeyed his government's orders and started issuing travel visas to Japan for Jews he knew were in great danger, with few other ways of escape. Lithuanian and Polish Jews were the main recipients, but he also spent a short time in Prague, still writing out and stamping visa documents. The numbers of people saved by his hand vary in reports between 4,500 and 10,000. Even these large numbers were tiny when compared with the millions who were killed. In 1940, the outlet using these documents to travel into the Mediterranean and beyond was closed. How Erwin found out about the possibility of Japanese documents being available and how he made the arrangements will probably never be known.

Their inquiries located an illegal ship leaving from the Black Sea for Palestine, accessed by riverboats down the Danube River from Vienna. This operation, run by a small organisation called *Black Rose Transport*, was established by several young men who had set up an office in a passageway close to Wenceslas Square in Prague. The purpose of the organisation was to arrange the movement of Jews away to safety from the Nazis, particularly by using the Danube as an escape route. Exit permits for 650 people had been arranged from German authorities, and many more applications were received than could be accommodated. Long lines of people formed in the street waiting to get to the *Black Rose* offices to obtain a permit. Somehow the brothers, Martha and her then-husband, were successful. The payment for each name on the departure list was expensive at the time, 10,000 Czech koruna, to get them from Prague to Vienna, then to the Black Sea down the Danube and finally to Palestine.

Erwin and Gaby had nothing from the past to indicate what the Germans would do to peaceful Jewish families living in the more rural parts of Czechoslovakia. World War I had only affected such communities regarding all available food going to support the troops and army-aged men being required to join up. Civilians living away from the battlefronts were left alone. Also, there had been no government policy then directed at targeting Jews for extreme treatment by any of the warring nations.

The Sax family had enjoyed several generations of peaceful operation of their farm and saw-mill. They had coexisted well with their mostly Catholic neighbors and were respected there. However, it appeared that this was going to be a different war. Hitler and his Nazi Party were extremely anti-Jew, anti-Gypsy, and anti-

Communist, with policies already acted on in Germany.

*Grandmother Jana Sax with granddaughter Judith Sax, Erwin's daughter.*

An elderly mother, their sisters, very young nieces, nephews, and Erwin's infant daughter should have been safe there, at least safer than being on an old ship travelling thousands of kilometres over the sea to Palestine. They might not even be allowed to get on that ship in the first place or be allowed to enter Palestine. Many such refugees perished on that journey when their ships sank, or were interned by the British on Cyprus. The remaining two older brothers in the family, Otto and Ernest, would stay with their mother and the rest of the family to run the sawmill and farm, their major possessions and source of income.

Able-bodied men were being taken by the Germans from the conquered countries and forced into labour in mines and factories, to maximise the growth of German industry and the armed forces while German men became soldiers, sailors or airmen. If not immediately killed, the men of the Sax family could expect no easy future under the Nazis. It would not have helped matters that several of the Sax brothers had served in the Czech Army, including Otto, Walter, John, and Erwin. Erwin was on leave from the army in 1936 when he first met his future wife, Gaby.

Judith Sax, only one and a half years old, was judged as being too young to go on the trip, and so was left with her grandmother and Erwin's sister, Ruti, with the idea of them joining the brothers at the first opportunity. That idea may also have applied to other family members, but to no avail. Time was already running out for the remaining family.

Leaving Novy Hrosenkov would have been hard, with many tears and long embraces. The four brothers would have made sure the house and mill were left in good repair and their family secure, as much as was possible.

The brothers made their final preparations for departure: their dealings with Czech Government agencies were completed; their belongings packed, and their passports stamped with immigration and transit visas; the essential train and boat tickets were safe in wallets, and all qualification documents or proof of experience letters were collected. They had obtained essential items, including Marseille soap for use with seawater, a medicine kit, Vasano pills for seasickness, and canned food. Between them, a number of foreign languages could be spoken, so they were ready to join one of the largest population movements from Europe in modern history.

Then came the time for leaving on the special train, from Masaryk Station in Prague to Vienna, just before midnight. Austria had been absorbed by Germany a year earlier, and the Nazis had not yet closed the borders to prevent Jews escaping. All those leaving would never be allowed back, their possessions, including land and businesses, having to be left behind. The Nazis had not then fully organised the gathering of Jews into concentration and extermination camps.

Erwin, his wife Gaby, and his three brothers took the train to Vienna to board a riverboat. There were two available then for the escape voyage, named *Car Dusan* (*Tzar Dusan*) and *Kralica Marija* (*Queen Maria*) – both were large, powered, river barges, and inadequate for the journey in peaceful times. Each could normally carry 320 people. Everyone slept wherever there was room, with some wooden booths built for use as toilets.

*Mother Jana Sax with son, daughters, and granddaughter, approx. 1938/39.*
*Note the Jewish star on daughter's blouse which indicates Nazi control of the country by that time.*

Also, on one of the boats, the *Kralica Marija*, was Martha Werner, nee Weinstein and her husband Karel Werner, a wealthy young man from a Jewish family. They were fleeing the Nazis for the same reasons as the Sax brothers. Martha was well travelled around Europe with her husband. She was born and grew up in Boritice, near the Czech-German border. Because of growing up with three brothers, she was a bit of a tomboy when young, with inner strength that would serve her well over the war years and beyond.

She already knew the Sax brothers, having been introduced by Walter, who met her at the department store in Prague where they both worked. Martha had worked in a different department at the store, which was owned by her Uncle.

To get to the boat, Martha and Karel had travelled separately by train to Vienna from Czechoslovakia, but it is unknown whether they were on the same riverboat as the Saxes.

The Jews boarding boats for the trip to the Black Sea would have been conspicuous, particularly to German and Austrian Nazis or regular soldiers noting those leaving. So many were trying to escape, loaded with all they could carry but unsure of what they needed for the trip – clothes, food, goods to trade, and money to pay the extortionate cost of everything. All along the river, the movement of refugee Jews would have been a unique opportunity to cash in on their suffering and panic. The boats would have been full to overflowing, carrying many more than the normal number. They would have resembled the refugee boats trying to get to Australia from Indonesia, or from Africa to Europe across the Mediterranean in recent years.

At least the weather would have been on their side. The journey started at the end of April 1939, the European Spring, with rising temperatures. From the boat, the surrounding country would have displayed the colours and lush growth of a well-watered land. Their intended destination was Palestine, a hot land suffering from a lack of water with little development until future generations could convert a new Israel into productive farms and orchards.

The river took them from Austria, through Yugoslavia and along the border between Bulgaria and Romania, then cut across the eastern edge of Romania to Sulina, fronting the Black Sea on the Danube River Delta. At that time, Sulina was a town of about 7000 people. The views from the boats included cities and villages, ancient castles and fortresses, particularly through Hungary. Marshland and farms took up most of the river frontage, with tributary rivers and smaller streams along its length feeding the main volume of water flowing to the Black Sea. Now, the same voyage is taken by very long, modern tourist ships, with all amenities and no concerns for the wealthy foreign visitors, other than to have a good time.

The movement of the Danube was fast in its early reaches through Germany and Austria but progressively slowed down as the country flattened out to the east and south. It seemed even the river rushed to be away from the Nazis and relaxed when beyond the threat. Silt dropped by the slowing river created islands as it neared the sea. When its course approached the end, it branched into three channels, with only the Sulina branch being navigable for river traffic.

In the end, the river journey took only a few days, with minimal hold-ups. The riverboats finally deposited their cargoes of humanity onto the wharves of Sulina. The town was never more than a small and uninspiring Black Sea port south of Odessa, already starting to lose its population due to the increasing threat of war and its impact on waterborne trade.

The Jewish refugees expected to board a ship ready to leave for Palestine, but it had not yet arrived and didn't arrive for a few weeks. During that time, better consideration was given to the most appropriate things to take on board, with a limit of 40 kilograms in one suitcase or backpack per passenger, the basis of a new life away from tyranny. That weight limit included the required food for the expected few days journey to their destination of Palestine.

Martha planned well, using their remaining money to buy quality clothes, shoes, and their required food. She couldn't know her good shoes would be stolen at the first opportunity on the ship. The prices in Sulina were exorbitant as the locals took the opportunity to benefit from the desperate needs of refugees while they waited for their ship to arrive. No money was to be taken on board, possibly because it would have been useless trying to use Czech money in British-controlled Palestine. Travellers had to guess how long the sea voyage would take, even though they had been told it would be a few days with no problems. That could easily become weeks or even months if the countries they passed gave problems or British Navy ships intervened.

The ship finally arrived – the *Frossula* – an old, dirty steamer probably built over 50 years before and most recently used to transport cattle. It sailed under the Panamanian flag. Weeks passed as hundreds of small, narrow, four-storey high bunks were installed, enough for 650 passengers. The boat originally carried coal, and the large empty coal storage space under the deck was fitted out for that purpose. This was slow work, with the final boarding being unhurried. Up the gangway streamed doctors and lawyers, musicians and operatic performers, businessmen and housewives, labourers and politicians, Czechs, Slovaks, Germans, Austrians, and Poles – all fleeing for their lives.

The *Frossula* was crewed by a rough mixture of sailors from all over the world, a riffraff crew hired to operate a ship that had been purchased because it was cheap and adequate for the task, but only barely. It was intended for one trip and no return, to be beached in Palestine.

Once on board, the wealthier passengers found ways to benefit, as always in every society. Better sleeping quarters under cover in the cargo hold with improved bedding could be arranged. The rest lay on metal-plated decks wherever there was room, side-by-side. Sailors had quantities of food and access to bread from the ship's ovens, which were sold at a premium while their stocks lasted. Clothes and body washing could only be done with seawater, and little soap was available. Martha quickly found that washing in seawater wrecked the better-quality clothes she had invested in, but there was no alternative. Toilet needs were met with basic arrangements using metal slides, emptying their material over the side before being sluiced off with seawater.

Once the ship was underway, its old systems groaning in distress, the initial feeling was one of escape to freedom, fresh sea air and sunshine. Within a few days, after the inevitable seasickness suffered by the majority of people who had never been to sea on a tossing and pitching ship, the mood turned to boredom.

Progress was made from the Black Sea and past the Dardanelles, the place of great loss to Anzac troops during the Gallipoli campaign of World War I. Then into the Sea of Marmara and finally into the Mediterranean itself.

The route to a beach in Palestine would have been an easy, few days journey in peacetime, with good weather, but the British Government had other ideas. Navy destroyers and gunboats were positioned to prevent ships like the *Frossula* making it to their chosen destination. All such Jewish refugee-bearing vessels, no matter what size, were to be forced to sail to Cyprus, with Jewish refugee passengers to be interned in one of several fenced camps there. German camps for Jews meant death. At least British camps for the same people preserved their lives but with no clarity on their future. This was a few months before the major shooting war of Germany against England and France began, but all on board knew that it would commence in the near future.

It seemed British restrictions were unknown on the boat. The first interception by gunboats came as a surprise on the densely-packed decks. One warship quickly became three, all equipped with a cannon and machine guns, which increased anxiety levels for both the crew and passengers. When the first coloured rockets burst overhead followed by a red rocket, the captain of the *Frossula* took the obvious decision to alter course and turn away from his southern track towards Palestine.

The old ship, with ominous noises coming from the engine and the hull, then drifted for weeks with no firm decisions on the next move being made. British military aircraft and ships kept an eye on progress, or the lack of it, knowing that more attempts could be made to land illegally.

Water was still available onboard, but the quality of food was deteriorating and in short supply. Boredom and frustration grew amongst the passengers. The brothers played endless games of cards while the waiting continued. The ship stayed out to sea, and passengers enjoyed the sunshine and calm of the ocean while it lasted. A violent storm darkened the mood, and the labouring engines added to concerns. A number of attempts were made to land, all ending in failure due to interception, adding to the mood of hopelessness and depression.

They tried to stay out of sight as much as possible, away from the English patrolling aircraft and gunboats. Sweaty, mostly unwashed bodies were pushed below deck to hide every time aircraft passed overhead, even though the British must have known the old boat's cargo.

The British Navy sailors and captains of the destroyers and gunboats had their orders, laboriously argued through by the British Parliament in London. Strife in Palestine, from outraged Arabs, sometimes breaking out into riots, threatened the British protectorate control of the area. An officially-approved annual quota had been rigorously adhered to by officials, for the number of Jews being allowed into the existing community. Jewish leaders in Palestine were worried about illegal arrivals upsetting the fine balance of these quotas. Other organisations battled to save European Jews by whatever means possible, paying little attention to the arrangements made by the British Government.

One last attempt to land resulted in, yet again, detection by the British, and a gunboat came so close that passengers could see the individual faces of sailors as they manned the cannon and machine guns, while operating searchlights, with a red flare being fired over the ship. A machine gun opened fire and two men were shot and killed. Immediately the *Frossula* changed course and under full power moved back out to sea.

Both the passengers and crew were shocked by the incident. Food and water were almost exhausted and the ship finally pulled into Beirut for supplies in the early morning. The rising sun showed the port to be now on a military footing before a major fighting war had been declared. A German ship, flying the swastika, was already in the harbour and soon another gunboat, this time from Turkey, appeared and directed the *Frossula* out to sea. Under the view of Turkish sailors manning guns, the anchor was raised, with objections from young men on board. The ship again headed away from land. Water and provisions were still desperately needed.

Distress telegraphs from the ship to all potential avenues for help resulted in no offers of aid. The increasing possibility of war in Europe seemed to have made countries deaf to the needs of foreign Jews, with no interest in arguing against the military might of Germany. Best to stay silent and not get into a dispute.

Finally, with a sick woman on board needing urgent attention, the *Frossula* was reluctantly allowed to dock at Tripoli, Syria. Early moves to force the ship out of the harbour ceased when the urgent need for medical attention for the ill woman was accepted by authorities.

The ship docked, and all on board waited to see what would happen. The ill woman was attended to, and then the first positive surprise for the entire trip took place. Arab women of the Red Crescent arranged for fruit, food, medicines, and water to be brought to the port. As soon as these supplies were loaded the ship had to move out onto the high seas once more. Four months had now gone by since leaving Sulina, and hope was fading of ever reaching Palestine. The British Navy continued to monitor the vessel.

Unknown to the passengers, arrangements had commenced between the captain and another ship at sea for a change in tactics.

The *Tiger Hill* was a similar old ship carrying Jewish refugees which had been travelling for only a few days from the Black Sea. Arrangements were made by radio between the two ships to meet up at sea. Both ships steamed towards the rendezvous point, somewhere in the Mediterranean away from any coast and this time without British observation. The *Tiger Hill* had kept its cargo secret and had not been bothered by gunboats.

The *Frossula* immigrants transferred in high seas to the *Tiger Hill* in groups using the lifeboats. Rope ladders had to be climbed down into the boats and then climbed up into the new ship. No one was injured or drowned in the transfer. For the whole trip, two men didn't make it – both shot by the British, and the ill woman still in a Tripoli hospital.

*Memorial for two men killed on the ship Tiger Hill, on Tel Aviv beach*

In two days, the *Tiger Hill* reached Palestine, without any obstruction, and the ship was rammed up onto the beach with passengers climbing over the sides on rope ladders into the water or the lifeboats. Many Jews, residents of Tel Aviv, were gathered on the shore, trying to hide the new arrivals in the crowd, but all of the Sax brothers plus Gaby, Martha, and Karel were caught by British soldiers. They were then placed in a fenced camp near the Arab village of Sarafand in the nearby desert. Eight days later, after being fed only minimal rations, they were all released into Tel Aviv, free to live by whatever means they could manage.

*Map 3: showing escape route from Vienna, Austria, down the Danube to the Black Sea then to the Mediterranean Sea, to Mersin in Turkey, Tripoli in Syria and ending at Tel Aviv, Palestine. Transfer from the 'Frossula' to the 'Tiger Hill' occurred somewhere unknown in the Mediterranean.*

Files had been created for every prisoner in detention when they were admitted into the Sarafand Detention Camp. These 'Palestine, Illegal Immigration from German-Occupied Europe, 1938-1945' documents compiled by the British administration were available for Erwin, Walter, and Bruno. Their parents' names were all the same, as was the route taken to reach Palestine: Sulina to Beirut on board *SS Frosulla,* to Tel Aviv on board *SS Tiger Hill.* Novy Hrosenkov was their birthplace. Ervin/Irwin's address in 'Country of Origin' was Vsetin, CSR, 970 Hovlinkova Str. His occupation was given as 'Carpenter'. Walter's address was given as Prague. Klemenska 26, CSR and his occupation as 'Clerk'. Bruno's address was Novy Hrozenkov, 278 CSR; his occupation recorded as 'Student'. All of their circumstances were recorded as 'Destitute'. John's document for detention could not be found.

So much time had been spent trying to break the British blockade by *Frossula*, but the *Tiger Hill* made it on the first attempt, one of only a few ships to succeed, before, during, or after the war while the British had control of Palestine. This was out of more than a hundred ships to make the attempt, the most well-known being the *Exodus 47*, which became famous through the book and movie of the same name years later.

The following true account from Martha Sax, the second wife of Erwin Sax, regarding the 1939 escape from Czechoslovakia and her early life in Palestine, was recorded many years later in Western Australia:

*"We went from Czechoslovakia to Vienna on April 30th, 1939. There were two boats on the River Danube, each with 330 passengers and one was called "Kralica Marija" (Queen Maria). It took us to Sulina in Romania. From there we got onto the "Frossula" to go to Israel. On board there were around 600 to 610 adults and 40 children. People were only allowed to take one suitcase weighing 40 kg, with that suitcase to contain clothes and food for the journey. We didn't know how long we were going to be on board.*

*I was married to my first husband Karel (Karl) Werner. We could not take money out so I spent my money buying good quality food, shoes and clothes. On board the ship, the men were separated from the women. Water was rationed and only for drinking. Washing was done in seawater. I was high up on the boat. The washing system involved putting a container over the side for water. By the time it had bounced its way to the top, a lot had been spilled. It took a long time to get enough water for a wash. There was little soap and it was used sparingly. When you washed, grease came off in little balls. Clothes were also washed in saltwater which made all of my clothes fall apart at the seams.*

*A guard was put over the drinking water to make sure it was* rationed fairly. One woman bribed the guards to get a lot of water to use to wash her hair! My good shoes were stolen and I arrived in Israel wearing my brother in law's shoes which were much too big.

The four Sax brothers and Erwin's first wife Gaby were also on the ship. I had worked in the same store as Walter in Brno and Knevhin. I also knew lots of Erwin's cousins who were working in the Jepa, a large department store, the first department store in Czechoslovakia, in 1939.

The "Frossula" cruised around the Mediterranean. The British would not allow the ship to land in Tel Aviv. They fired on them when they tried. Two people were killed. A lawyer who had a two-year-old son was shot. The son survived. The other person killed was a Polish youth of about 18. The ship then went back out to sea. The "Czerna Ruze" - the Black Rose organisation - was involved in helping Czech Jews leave the country. When Bruno went to Czechoslovakia in 1990, he had some photos taken outside the Czerna Ruze offices.

*Two Photos of Bruno Sax at the "Cerna Ruze" (Black Rose) Prague office entrance and upstairs beside the "Cerna Ruze" symbol, 1990*

The Greek captain of the Frossula did not want to risk his ship, so we got in contact with another ship, a Polish ship called "Tiger Hill". 650 people transferred in the middle of the night in rough seas. No one drowned. This took place about two weeks before the attempted landing.

The second time the captain decided to go in, he went in and landed in the early morning, on the beach at Tel Aviv. The police came to arrest him. There had already been 1400 people on the Tiger Hill so now there were 2000 people. They arrived the day before war broke out in Europe, probably 2nd September 1939.

When we arrived in Palestine, we were taken to a place where a lot of food was given to us in a big smorgasbord meal. I took a babovka (a cake) to Karl who asked why I had done that. I told him "you never know what will happen later". Later we were *taken to prison for eight days and were given very little food.*

*On release, the Sax brothers set up a store and made shoes. They made themselves into a production line and did quite well. From there they enlisted in the British Army.*

*My brother Viktor was there too. He went in January. He was working in an orange grove. Karel and I got accommodation with a lady and looked for work. Karl wasn't trained for anything. He was a lawyer and wasn't used to manual work. I started as a cleaning lady. Karl studied English!! I worked for a rich German family. The lady for whom I worked was very kind.*

*Afterwards I worked for another lady, too, a Mrs Levi, on Thursdays. One Thursday it was raining. I took rubber boots and an umbrella and went to work. When I arrived there, the lady said "Oh, it's raining, we don't clean." I went home drenched, with no pay. Mrs Levi gave me aniseed tea.*

*On the ship, I had a few friends. One was a friend of my husband for whom I sewed on buttons and did some washing for payment. Karl got a job. He had a friend from Brno who had done some gold refining for dental work and fillings. Karl worked there and hated it. He suggested that we start a laundry. Together we did the washing. I ironed. One of my feet was swollen and the Doctor said to stop.*

*Twice a year in Israel, especially in Tel Aviv, buyers from Lebanon and Egypt (Arab states) used to buy clothes - coats, costumes (suits) and dresses. France was out of it because of the war so it was concentrated in Palestine. One day a friend of Karl's came and said his brother-in-law was looking for girls to model clothes and thought of me. The brother-in-law was a lawyer whom Karl's brother knew in Prague. I went to see him and got the job. So, I went from laundry lady to model.*

*Martha Werner/Sax modelling in Palestine, 1940-1945*

*I was told to go to a firm of English sisters who wanted to show a collection to an Egyptian customer. I was told I couldn't model because I only had flat-heeled shoes. I had to go and buy high heels. I got known and did a lot of fashion parades. I went to Haifa, Jerusalem and Tel Aviv.*

*When we left Czechoslovakia, Erwin and Gabi decided to leave Judith with grandma Sax because they thought there would be no or few children on the trip to Israel and that Judith would be safer in Czechoslovakia. There were children on the Frossula and they all arrived in Israel safely."*

## Press Clipping: Fashion News in Jerusalem, 1945

The more wealthy and fashionable people of Palestine and neighbouring countries appeared lightly affected by the war, as the following social article shows. Martha modelled in front of this level of society, at the following display, probably held in late 1945:

*New Paris Fashions in Jerusalem*

*That Paris is losing no time in establishing herself again as the world's fashion centre was felt in Jerusalem yesterday, when a large collection, which included models from Maggy Rouff, Lanvin, Paquin, Patou and Worth were shown at the King David Hotel.*

*This collection from the Salon Djeny of Beirut, together with the latest model fur coats from the Salon Scharf of Jerusalem, were shown to nearly 400 interested spectators, with the male sex well represented. The Red Cross shared in the success of the Fashion Show as a fur coat donated by the Salon Scharf was auctioned, netting LP50.*

*Liberated Paris has not been able to show any new materials or colours but has, it seems, been able to unearth considerable quantities of plain blacks, greys and browns and quite a startling amount of taffeta and more – materials which have not been seen here for most of the duration.*

*In styles, Paris still presents the front emphasis - frills, pleats, gathers and shirring, whether on the skirt or blouse. For decoration there is much jet embroidery, spangles in all colours, sequins and even hand-painted and embroidered flowers on evening dresses.*

*There were two notably attractive dresses – a brown moire with short tunic, fastened with two gold buttons, wide bell sleeves…But the piece de resistance was undoubtably the Patou …*

*Mr. Scharf's fur coats were all of a beautiful cut, with the Canadian mink running away with the show.*

## Notes on the 1939 movement of refugee ships to Palestine:

Over 100,000 people tried to illegally enter Palestine before, during, and after World War II on 142 voyages involving 120 ships. Well over half of the ships were stopped by British patrols. The Royal Navy had eight warships on station in Palestine, and additional ships were used for tracking suspicious vessels heading in that direction. Most of the immigrants intercepted were sent to internment camps in Cyprus. Some were sent to a detention camp in Palestine and others to Mauritius. The British held up to 50,000 people in these camps. Over 1,600 drowned at sea, and only a few thousand actually entered Palestine.

It is recorded that, as early as 1934, the first attempt to bring a large number of illegal immigrants by sea to Palestine happened when 350 Jews sailed on a chartered ship, the *Vallos*, without the permission of the Jewish agency. It was feared that such illegal movements would cause the British to restrict legal immigration. The ship arrived off the coast of Palestine on August 25, and the passengers disembarked with the help of the Haganah.

The *Tiger Hill*, the ship the Saxes arrived in Palestine on, is recorded as a 1499-ton ship built in 1887 which sailed from Constanta on August 3, 1939, with about 750 immigrants on board. Passengers from the *Frossoula*, another illegal immigrant ship that was marooned off Lebanon, were taken on board. On September 1, the first day of World War II, the *Tiger Hill* was intercepted and fired on by British Navy gunboats off Tel Aviv, and beached.

European Jews were desperate for ways to leave Europe, but there were few options. Jewish immigrants were not accepted legally and willingly by any country at that time. Some countries would give them transit visas. One was Romania, which was an ally of Germany but had a lenient policy for Jews, and its officials could be bribed, until it was invaded by Germany. Romanian Jews and those from all over Europe, if they could, got to Black Sea ports in various ways using different agencies. These included those who only sought profit and offered transportation on overcrowded, dangerous ships to Istanbul. From there, it was hoped to get further transport to Palestine.

On May 28, 1939, the ship *Atrato* was caught by the British Navy. It had already brought 2,400 Jewish immigrants to Palestine in seven voyages. On August 22, the ship *Parita* with over 850 passengers arrived in Palestine and offloaded its passengers. On September 1, the ship *Tiger Hill*, with the Saxes on board, brought over 1,400 passengers. Every ship was greeted by a large crowd, allowing some immigrants to be hidden. World War II had begun, and up to the beginning of the war, this form of migration had rescued about 21,000 Jews from Europe, not all of whom made it to Palestine.

In England, during a House of Commons debate in July 1939, the colonial secretary admitted that destroyers and small launches had been used by the Royal Navy to find and turn back or capture those who had escaped the Nazis in Europe. This meant that Jews who had escaped death by the Germans were now hunted by five destroyers of the British Royal Navy, plus a number of gunboats and launches. British warships were authorised to fire at any ship that was suspected of having illegal immigrants on board and was on the way to Palestine, if it did not obey issued warnings. This was in international waters and before the war started. It applied to ships under any flag.

Because of this approval to fire on Jewish immigrant ships, on the very first day of World War II, September 1, 1939, while Warsaw and other Polish cities were being bombed by the Nazis, HMS *Lorna* fired on the old, overcrowded refugee ship *Tiger Hill*. This occurred as she neared the Palestine coast ready to unload over 1400 refugees from the Nazi onslaught. The ship did not turn back, and the encounter with the British destroyer ended in a victory for the Royal Navy.

*The ship 'Tiger Hill' beached on Tel Aviv beach, 1939*

The first two persons killed by British bullets or shells during World War II may well not have been German soldiers but Jewish civilian escapees from Nazi Europe trying to enter Palestine.

The *Tiger Hill* was one of a few ships that tried to break the

British blockade of Jews into Palestine before World War II began. It was one of only a few ships that succeeded in its mission. The British Navy was successful in turning back the majority of ships or re-directing them to Cyprus. The most famous of ships attempting this illegal journey was the *Exodus*, which in midsummer of 1947 after the war had ended, inspired the author Leon Uris to write his best-selling historical novel on which the Hollywood box office hit *Exodus* in the 1960s was based. The British intercepted the ship and, in attempting to send a strong message to those on board and to others who would attempt the same journey, sent the 4,530 Jewish displaced persons back to Europe. Press reports of this incident dramatized the plight of surviving European Jews. The passengers refused to disembark and resisted deportation. In the end, they were forced to leave the ship in Germany after spending weeks in the stifling holds with little food or water remaining.

In addition to Martha Sax's memories, the following is a story from another passenger who travelled on both the *Frossula* and the *Tiger Hill*:

> *"After a few days sailing down the Danube River we reached the Romanian port of Sulina, lying on the Danube Delta where the river spills into the Black Sea. It was a small, dirty and utterly uninspiring town. For several days we waited for the steamer that would take us on board and deliver us to the Palestinian shore, a few days later. The ship was nowhere in sight but we were told it was on its way and then when it arrived, sleeping facilities would be installed for all passengers.*
>
> *A few more days of waiting went past. Finally, an old 3,000 tonne freighter named the Frossula sailed into the harbour and dropped anchor. We soon met the captain, who was most unimpressive. So too were the crew with every deckhand covered in tattoos.*
>
> *The time came to go on board. No one felt the urge to hurry because there was no reason. Slowly, with backpacks, we all climbed the gangway. Doctors, authors, symphonic orchestra and*

opera conductors, businessmen, lawyers, union and political party officials, Czechs and Slovaks, Germans and Austrians and many others. We were all fleeing from fascism.

The newly constructed sleeping accommodation on board the Frossula looked miserable. The rich found ways to corrupt the crew. They got sleeping quarters below deck, in the cargo hold, with some thin sheets and pillows. The other passengers had to make up their bedding on the deck metal sheet plates, with one small pillow. We lay on deck, side-by-side, next to some galleys or toilet closet slides that stuck overboard. When your business was done, the slide was washed down with seawater that was hoisted up in a bucket fastened to the railing with a rope.

The quarter deck was under the rule of a mess steward. While he had the supplies, he sold all kinds of sweets and even bread fresh from the oven to anyone who had money, until he ran out. The ship was probably built towards the end of the 1800s or the beginning of the 1900s. It was a Greek ship sailing under a Panamanian flag of convenience.

At last all passengers were on board and the ship weighed anchor and eventually left Sulina. For most on board the first couple of days were an experience. The sea was clear and calm with a full sun and the passengers were given the chance to see life at sea. The ship left behind the Bosporus and the Dardanelles and moved through the Sea of Marmara and out into the Mediterranean.

The ship remained on a southward course, heading for the beaches of Palestine. The shoreline was still out of sight and everything was calm when we noticed an English patrol boat coming closer. It was equipped with a cannon and machine guns. A second and third boat appeared with the same armament. We were surrounded and they must have known we were there. We suspected nothing and some waved to the sailors on patrol boats. Suddenly, out of the blue, a bang and then another bang was heard and the air above our heads had the shining blaze of coloured rockets. The last one, the warning signal, was red and it meant that unless we changed course at once and turned back we would be shot at.

The Captain kept his cool and we immediately changed direction with the old ship turning heavily with noises coming from her engine and machinery.

The British patrol boats swung around and sailed away from us, making for the coast. For us it was a failure of our first attempt without even being able to see the Palestinian coast, and not even landing illegally. No one felt like celebrating but we were still hopeful of success, possibly the next day. We still had drinking water, but we were beginning to lose weight because of the poor food.

In an out-of-the-way area in the middle of the Mediterranean away from military ships and aircraft, the Frossoula manoeuvred, waiting for a suitable time when the ship could be taken to a Palestinian beach to finally offload passengers.

The ship drifted around aimlessly on the sea for two months. Seasickness affected practically everybody. The telegraph operator let some of the passengers listen to news from Czechoslovakia for a few minutes if paid for with clothing. Some of the women had sex with the sailors in exchange for food. The drinking water and food ration had shrunk noticeably from what they were a month ago. No one knew when or where they would be able to leave the ship. We stayed away from the coast and enjoyed the view of the sea in the sunshine, with nothing else to do.

Things changed because of a violent storm and a rough sea so the ship got thrown around with lots of disturbing sounds with forward and side rocking and pitching. Many times we attempted to land along the Palestinian coast and each time the English patrol boats chased us out to sea again. They were watching us, day and night. In the afternoons, all passengers had to stay crammed below deck, because an English warplane would come every day to reconnoitre the ship's position and the lookout was not supposed to be able to see there were people on board. Therefore, we had to hide. This went on for many days.

This went on into the third month and once more in desperation, we approached the Palestinian coast. At dusk the patrol boat drew near with all its lights and projectors shining on us. In the dark we could see the cannon and machine guns and even the faces of the English sailors. A red flare soared into the sky and a machine gun was fired at our ship. Three men were killed, the fathers of six children. They were buried at sea.

The drinking water was all but gone and the food reserves were practically used up. The telegrapher put out a call for help to request permission to enter a port to take on supplies. No answers or offers of help were received and the people on board the Frossoula struggled to stay alive.

The Captain, as a desperate act, set course for the Turkish port of Messina. We found out it had recently been turned into a garrison town and a wartime harbour. When we cast anchor outside the port entrance in the early dawn light we found out that a German ship, the Levante, flying the swastika astern, lay on our starboard side. A military patrol boat quickly appeared with its cannons and machine guns, a Turkish ship, and we were warned to immediately leave or be fired on.

Young men surrounded the anchor to try and stop the Captain from leaving the port. After discussion, with the patrol boat aiming machine-guns at us, we gave in. The anchor was raised and we left the port.

The ship sent telegraphs of distress addressed to the League of Nations in Geneva. We needed to enter a port somewhere except Germany. We were in desperate need of drinking water, food and medicine. Our desperate calls were received by all European states and the rest of the world.

The situation was desperate. Hungry rats were coming out of hiding places as time went on. Also, there was a seriously ill woman on board. We decided to go into the Syrian port of Tripolis. They tried to chase us out again but the sick patient turned out to be our salvation. She had to be taken to hospital and so we docked and waited to see what would happen.

We had a totally unexpected surprise. Arab women from the Red Crescent, the equivalent to the Red Cross, arranged for fruit, food, medicines and drinking water to be brought on board the ship.

But then we had to leave Tripolis again. We had been on our voyage for over four months. The British followed the ship's movements step by step. It seemed there was no chance of landing in Palestine.

We don't know how our captain heard of the "Tiger Hill", another Greek freighter just like our ship, sailing under the Panamanian convenience flag. She was also carrying a cargo of emigrants but she had only been underway for a few days and it was not known that she carried refugees. Over the radio, the two captains made a deal to solve the problem.

Somewhere in the middle of the Mediterranean, the Tiger Hill waited for us and the Frossoula went to that location as fast as the old ship would travel. We left our ship in the lifeboats and, in high seas, climbed rope ladders to board the Tiger Hill. We all changed ships, except for the three men who were shot and the woman who stayed in the hospital in Tripolis.

It took the Tiger Hill two days to reach the Palestinian coast. We climbed into lifeboats and steered toward the beach. The English caught us, to the last man, in no time at all, but we were not returned to Germany. We were placed in the English refugee camp in the desert near Sarafand. That was the day that World War II broke out. We had to stay in the concentration camp for about a fortnight then we were released."

# Chapter 4

# Life in "The Promised Land"

On arrival, with their feet finally on the sand of Tel Aviv Beach in Palestine, the passengers from the *Tiger Hill* were rounded up by British soldiers. They had to be separated from hundreds of civilian Jews trying to hide them in their numbers on the beach. Initially, all who landed were held within a fenced camp near the Arab village of Sarafand-al-Amar. The camp was part of the largest British military base in the Middle East. The prison within the base was called Sarafand, and the *Tiger Hill* passengers were held there for less than two weeks before being released into Palestine with residency permits.

Tel Aviv was then growing quickly, with the Jewish population increasing faster than the British administration wanted, regardless of the tight controls on the number of immigrants each year. Apart from illegal immigration by land or sea, a variety of schemes undermined British restrictions. Jewish students from other countries arrived to study at the University but never left. Fictitious marriages were arranged, with the intended groom or bride being permitted to stay.

For Martha and Karel, Gaby and the brothers, their initial life free from the Nazis started in tents in a field, with a form of Kibbutz arrangement where everything was shared. All were expected to find work but were given bedding and a start towards self-sufficiency by a labour organisation set up to help new arrivals. Those with family already in Palestine immediately left to join them. The remaining group, now shrunk to about 100, arranged their camp for the short term. The brothers showed their organisational skills and became part of the governing group tasked with finding paid work, keeping the camp in order, and providing meals.

*A main street of Tel Aviv, 1939*

The income from paid work started to make a positive difference but the camp had to be relocated once the rainy season started. The cities of Palestine were growing fast. Stone and concrete multi-storied buildings fronted well-made streets with electrical power and drainage systems. The population was dominated by Arabs, with Jews being a small but growing minority. Some cities and towns, however, had a greater percentage of Jews, and this growth caused concerns for the local Arab residents. Intermittent outbreaks of agitation over years by troublemakers regularly resulted in riots. Arabs, Jews, and some British soldiers were injured or killed, and buildings were blown up.

The brothers and Gaby settled into a rented house and became citizens of Palestine, not yet Israel, working in a land that so many could only dream of or died pursuing that dream. Vegetables were grown at the house, and various members found work to contribute to the budget, with Erwin and John using their knowledge of timber and sawmilling to undertake carpentry work. They were ready to take on anything involving labour – ditch-digging, road construction, concrete floor construction and labouring on farms or orchards, as well as more exacting tasks. Walter also learned how to work with locks and machines.

A chance inquiry to Gaby while walking on the Tel Aviv Beach started the brothers on a new business of shoemaking. Gaby had needed new sandals, and, with spare money tight, the brothers put together make-shift replacements, each taking on the various steps of production. With others wanting to buy them, within months their new business grew, requiring more staff to be employed. Sales of their products even spread to the city of Haifa.

In February 1940, while the brothers were still in Palestine, Bruno received correspondence from his sister Ruth in Novy Hrosenkov, for his birthday:

*"N.H. February 24, 1940*

*Dearest Bruno,*

*I've never wished more than in this moment to be with you, to be with all of you. It is caused by sadness and also my desire for those I love, and desire to see unknown lands. You must be thinking…(illegible). If only you were right. I leave such moments to the will of fate. I am sending this faithful intermediary of my effusions and emotions to you on my behalf. Do with it what you will but give it at least a moment of silence and attention. In my mind, I think back to our childhood over and over. I cherish every shared moment. No, dear Bruno (Brunicku), providence can't be punishing us like this, after all I know that we belong together. And on the day of your birthday, when the moon crawls lazily across the sky, step outside and that will be a sign that I'm seeing it from the threshold of our birth cabin. I am sending you the most… greeting which a human heart could ever feel and the sweetest kiss of a sister's love… Hold your head high proudly, just like we are not afraid, and believe with us. My wishes here come to an end. Enjoy the wonders of your 20 years of age to the fullest and be very happy.*

*With a kiss, your sincere…*

*Rutka (Ruth)*

Another letter from Ruth without a date, but sent to the four brothers and Erwin's wife Gabi, was on a happy note, without any sad overtone:

> "Dear Gabi and boys!
>
> We are sending Ervinek (Erwin) and Gabi a small substitute for their borrowed happiness. I agree with the opinion of our newpher (nephew?) that the original is prettier than all the pictures put together. In the afternoon, me and Lilka will go to Jankova...(illegible) so that he gets to enjoy himself, I hope he will add a note for you too. I don't know what to do for little Walter. Last week I visited Ditka and the week before Marka. Both of them and their families are doing well, but they are so lazy that they are sending their greetings through me. That's it for today, with a kiss to all,
>
> Rutka"

And another letter to Bruno from Judith:

> "Dear Brunek,
>
> I too wish you everything you desire for your birthday. I hope the gods will be favourable to us and we will celebrate your next birthday as well as mine together, with a snifter of...(illegible) schnapps. I wish I could send you a gulp right now.
>
> Waving to you and sending you a... kiss.
>
> Judith"

Nothing was mentioned by the brothers or Martha in their writings about the Arab/Jewish unrest. They were newcomers, working hard to make a living and wanted to keep out of trouble. British soldiers held the lid on the growing tension as much as possible. The League of Nations had given the British a mandate to govern Palestine, and that duty became increasingly difficult and violent. The Arabs continued to see more Jews arriving from Europe, with no intention of ever leaving. New settlements were being built, and Arab land was being purchased for additional Kibbutz developments. Cities were growing, with construction being in the European style, not traditional Palestinian.

Martha and Karel also had to find employment. No social welfare payments existed so they had to work to be able to live. Karel was not a great help when it came to hard manual labour. Initially, they tried to run a laundrette, washing and ironing clothes, with Karel collecting and returning the clean washing. At this time, Martha complained of a lump on the back of her neck. Doctors told her she should not attempt to have it removed from such a vital location. Their diagnosis of it being a fatty lump eventually was proven wrong when it activated years later as a cancer and caused her early death in Perth, Western Australia.

As already noted, Martha went through a period of working as a cleaning lady in Tel Aviv. She was a hard worker and was not put off by the menial drudgery of house and office cleaning. Karel tried his hand working for a dental firm doing gold refining and tooth fillings, but he hated it. Martha's big break came from a friend who designed clothes and asked Martha to model them for her. The garment industry was growing, partly because European countries were being either occupied or involved in fighting against German armies. Paris and other major design centres were closed during the German occupation, and so the Middle East became an alternative, with wealthy Lebanese and Egyptian buyers attending fashion shows in Tel Aviv, Haifa, Jerusalem and other large cities in the region.

Martha's modelling career quickly grew into a way of life for her in Palestine. Her photos and press clippings depicted high-class establishments, young women parading the latest fashions, and society clientele in modern suits and dresses. One location of note was the King David Hotel in Jerusalem, a large, modern, multi-story building with restaurants and provision for fashion modelling, seminars, and conferences. Martha was involved in parading there and in other similar locations in 1944/45. It was also the British Administrative Headquarters for Palestine, taking up the entire southern wing of the hotel.

*King David Hotel, Tel Aviv, Palestine, 1940*

Martha's life could have ended in that hotel because less than a year later, on 22 July, 1946, after she and the brothers had left Palestine, the southern wing was blown up. This action was taken by an extremist right-wing Jewish underground organisation, *Irgun*, causing many deaths and injuries. The group was one of a number working against the British mandate and the forced restriction of Jewish settlement. They tried to stop the internment of thousands of Jews in camps on Cyprus and to meet the desperate needs of holocaust survivors in Europe looking for a new home after the war.

The Sax brothers continued to run a successful small company making shoes and sandals, while Martha was involved in her new modelling career. At that time, the war in Europe was going badly for the Allies, with Germany overwhelming most of Europe and attacking Britain in an air war, the Battle of Britain. German submarines were sinking many allied ships in the Atlantic, and the future seemed grim. The US had not yet entered the war, and fascist Italian forces held large areas of North Africa, Albania, Abyssinia, and Greece.

Jews living in Palestine, a location originally thought to be far away from the fighting in Europe and Russia, must have become increasingly nervous. It was possible that German armies might even eventually invade the Palestinian region, such were their successes through Europe. The remaining Jewish families in the home countries could not be contacted or saved. Nothing seemed to stand against the German war machine.

Erwin, again more interested in following politics and the war's progress than the others, discussed the situation with his brothers. They decided to put aside their new life in Palestine and join the army. The Czech government-in-exile had a contingent of soldiers based in Palestine. It had been reconstituted as the 11th Infantry Battalion and was based at Gedera, near Tel Aviv. The brothers applied there but were told that no further recruits could be accepted. Instead, on 14th November 1940, they joined the British Army and went into training. The foreign-sounding *Sax* name was unusual to the British recruiting staff, particularly with four of the same name joining together on the same day.

*Four British soldiers in Palestine, 1940, in front of camp medical staff. From left: John, Walter, Erwin, Bruno.*

*L to R, Back Row: Walter, Bruno, John.*
*Front Row: Gaby, Erwin, in Palestine*

In the photos, they looked young, fit and suntanned, ready for this new adventure. The unit was first sent to Egypt and then to Tobruk in early January 1941, to occupy an area captured by Australian units from the Italians. Their group ensured the delivery of processed or canned food, cigarettes, and other non-perishable goods to the various British units holding the front line. The work was not without risks because of regular German air raids, with many bombs being dropped in the harbour and near their barracks to try to disrupt or sink allied shipping.

After a short time there, they were sent to Greece by ship. The Germans were moving 400,000 troops into the Balkans, and Greece was endangered. Their unit was part of the build-up by the Allies in

Greece to defend the country, with forces being sent there, including the Australian 6th Division. Before much British support artillery, tanks and aircraft could be relocated to Greece, the Germans attacked and rapidly moved south through the country. Being caught unprepared, the Allies withdrew what they could of their forces, beginning on 25 April 1941, to Crete. Once Greece was mostly secured by the Germans, they organised to attack Crete, using thousands of parachute soldiers as a spearhead, many of whom were killed before they hit the ground. By the start of June, the Allies were losing the fight and desperately evacuating their forces from Crete. However, thousands of soldiers were captured by the Germans, including many Australians, on both Greece and Crete.

It made sense that the best fighting troops and their officers were evacuated first, to be followed by support forces if time permitted. Time did not permit, and unfortunately, those support forces included the four brothers. They were captured but not injured.

*In Palestine, 1940.*
*John and Bruno standing at each end.*
*Walter in middle on RHS. Erwin sitting on LHS.*

# Chapter 5

# Prisoners of War – Greece to Poland

How the brothers came to be captured is a story on its own, within the main story covering the conquest of Greece by the Germans. It connects their whirlwind move to Greece, their capture and the start of their years as POW's.

They arrived in Greece with their unit, poorly equipped for any real fighting, but expecting more heavy equipment to follow. Less than one rifle for ten men meant, even on guard duty, weapons had to be exchanged at the end of each shift. They had arrived at a time when German forces were beginning to move south rapidly, aided by air attacks and the use of armoured vehicles, including tanks. The mixed Allied units, many of them non-combatant, fought a rearguard action as they retreated south, with few heavy weapons and no armour. Once the airfield at Maleme was captured, the Germans flew in reinforcement troops.

*Under German attack, southern Greece, April, 1941*

For many, the retreat in Greece ended at the southern port of Kalamata, where British flying boats and ships tried to evacuate as many troops as possible to Crete and beyond. The Germans were moving so fast that the British commanding officers were both panicked and undecided as to whether to rally their forces and fight with heavy casualties or surrender to save the lives of the maximum numbers of soldiers. This was not a shining moment in British military history. Small groups of soldiers hid in the hills or tried to walk along the coast to find a boat to escape, but most were captured. The remaining British forces were pushed into the area around the port.

Supplies were quickly used up, with aerial bombing further demoralising the troops. All of this occurred around the 28$^{th}$ and 29$^{th}$ of April 1941. Weak leadership finally took its toll, and surrender became inevitable.

Walter, as a corporal, remembered an officer giving him orders to take charge of a group of soldiers and to board a ship at dawn for an escape to Crete. He found himself alone early the next morning because the others had decided to escape in their own ways. He finally met up with his brothers, found a lorry and they moved still further south to try to arrange a boat at a seaside village that would take them to Crete. Escape, if successful, would have only put off the time of capture by a few weeks. The battle for Crete started on the 20$^{th}$ of May and ended by the 30th of the month.

Their plan came to an end when all were captured before the end of the day by German para-troopers.

Thousands of British, Australian, New Zealand, and Palestinian soldiers (both Jews and Arabs), were captured by the Germans. Over the following days, extra individuals and small groups of soldiers were picked up by German units through the surrounding hills and along the coast.

Those Jews from Palestine, although under British command and in British uniforms, had a major concern. The German attitude toward Jews had been demonstrated already in the conquered countries of Europe and in Germany itself. Would they be separated and killed, as had happened in their home countries? Some thought of suicide rather than be captured, tortured and killed. Others stayed with British units to act as fellow countrymen for protection.

*Map 4: showing movement of German troops through Greece in April 1941 and the probable capture area, around Kalamata, where the four brothers became Prisoners of War.*

The brothers did not write of any prejudicial attitudes towards them by regular German fighting soldiers. Sketchy comments covered their movement as prisoners from one small camp to another after capture. These camps were makeshift and quickly thrown together to control over 8,000 Allied prisoners.

Initially, the Fifth German Panzer Division was in charge of the largest POW camp in the south of Greece but was quickly replaced with other less important support units. A Greek army camp close to Kalamata became a more stable base for POW control. Captives were demoralised, sick, hungry, and in shock, the process from freedom to captivity being so fast. Lack of food became a problem, with starvation starting to become possible. Greek peddlers were allowed to sell food and water to the prisoners for a short time, and the German guards arranged for an inadequate thin soup to be distributed as a temporary solution.

Groups of POWs were progressively moved north by ship to Salonika, towards Germany. The Palestinians, including the Sax brothers, were not separated or their Jewish origins referred to. The movements north took time, with prisoners being transferred from one short-term camp to another. Old Greek army barracks or bases were often used. The German invasion of Russia in June 1941 required massive use of trains to transport their armies, weapons, and provisions to the new eastern front. POW relocation had to be held up until transportation became available by train, and then only by using sealed cattle wagons, with up to 50 men per wagon. With Greece and Crete captured, the German 12$^{th}$ Army was also moving north, and transport routes were dominated by military trains and convoys.

The brothers' turn finally came, and they were taken by train from Greece through Yugoslavia to Austria, where they were transferred to a work camp in the Tyrol area near Innsbruck for three weeks. Photos of Bruno visiting a typical group of WW II barracks or POW camp buildings in 1971, in Lienz, Austria, were labelled: *"Not to forget. Alone in memories. Today we are smiling. We were not in 1941"*. These photos suggest that this was the location of their temporary work base before they arrived at their permanent POW camp.

The train journey from Greece was extremely difficult, with only one day's rations of bread provided. From Greece and Crete, right along the route of prisoner-of-war movement into Germany and Poland, POWs escaped when they could. The German guards became increasingly frustrated by the scale of prisoner disappearances. To minimise any external help they might get to escape, no contact was allowed with locals at the work camps along the way.

Thirst, hunger, cramped conditions, overcrowding, harsh treatment, and lack of toilet facilities were constants. With so many in each wagon, only half had room to sit. Later they would swap, and those seated would then have to stand. One soldier described the ordeal:

*"A week in cattle trucks in the height of sweltering summer...No seats or other amenities. All of us weak and suffering from diarrhoea, many with bleeding bowels and no sanitary arrangements whatsoever."*

*Bruno revisiting Austrian work camp barracks in 1971, in the Tyrol area, near Lienz. The brothers were forced to work there in 1941, during the train journey from Greece to Lamsdorf POW camp in Poland.*

Finally, by the end of July, all POWs from Greece and Crete had arrived at their permanent camps, ending their time of travel between temporary, transit, and work sites. The brothers' home for the rest of the war was Stalag VIIIB, at a town called Lamsdorf, in Upper Silesia, Poland.

Lamsdorf camp was subject to Red Cross supervision and international treaties, although feelings of apprehension, uncertainty, and lack of rights were keenly felt. There was a large range of nationalities already in the camp, with the earliest arrivals coming from the British evacuation at Dunkirk.

*Map 5, of Poland showing Lamsdorf POW camp location and Novy Hrosenkov in Czechoslovakia/Czech Republic*

Their arrival at Lamsdorf was not before time. They had been badly affected by the terrible train journey. All prisoners had to slowly learn to walk properly again, such were the cramped conditions. However, they still had to move, or march if possible, the three-mile distance to the actual camp from the rail yards, where they had been taken from their sealed cattle wagons. They were then photographed, fingerprinted, given a number, and a dog tag. They received a spoon and fork, a mess tin, two blankets, a straw-filled paillasse, with boards for the base of their bunk. They soon found that the straw bag they slept on was a home for fleas. Their few belongings were fumigated, and they were showered upon arrival.

*Brothers in uniform, as POWs at Lamsdorf POW camp.
From left: John, Erwin, Walter, Bruno.*

One big positive benefit from being held at the camp was that Red Cross parcels became available, with each parcel containing 5 to 6 pounds of different foods and useful items. They varied in content, depending on whether they came from Britain, America, Australia, New Zealand, Canada, or Scotland. Typical contents were powdered milk, biscuits, butter, chocolate, jam, raisins, tea, marmalade, canned meat or sardines, soap and cheese. Often the cheese or chocolate had already deteriorated.

A system developed where each parcel would be shared amongst a small group of men, to make them last longer and provide more to look forward to. The Red Cross parcels made a huge difference because the camp food was poor quality and in small amounts.

When combined, they were adequately provided for.

The single-storey barracks they lived in were rectangular, with showers and a 'copper' – a metal, built-in vat to boil water for tea and coffee in the centre. There were three-tiered H bunks in each unit. These were joined, and about 6 m apart. Up to 360 men could sleep in each building if the three tiers were occupied, but normally only two tiers were used by 240 men. There were ten tables with timber bench seats on one side of each barrack building, with ten men to a table. Not everyone could be seated at one time.

Lights were turned out at 9 pm and doors closed. A night bucket was available for any nocturnal toilet needs. No toilet paper was ever made available.

Each day, guards would take two men per barrack to gather firewood from the nearby woods. This was used to heat the copper twice a day to provide for tea, in a cup made from a tin can. Every morning, the Germans served mint tea with sweetening, but it made men nauseous on an empty stomach. For lunch, there would be a 6-ounce ladle of soup – in summer it might be a tasty pea or barley soup. In winter, it was always turnip soup, with a piece of horse or even rat meat. At times the soup was replaced with a delicious oatmeal.

Late in the afternoon, all would receive an eighth of a rye bread loaf, a potato, a dab of butter, and a piece of sausage. It was close to a starvation diet, but the food from the Red Cross parcels lifted the quality of their meals above survival level. These parcels came regularly in summer, but, in winter, when they were most needed, their arrival was spasmodic, possibly due to the intense cold and deep snow on roads. Also, the German rail system was busy moving soldiers and equipment to and from the Russian front. With both the Red Cross parcels and packages from home, the Germans stabbed the parcels with knives to ensure that they could not be hoarded and used in escapes.

Prisoners received some articles in the Red Cross parcels that were of a lower value to them, so small shops existed to exchange them for more useful products. Cigarettes were the currency used and the items 'on sale' could include razor blades, Army forks and spoons, clothing, books, and tins of jam. Different items had different prices in cigarettes. They were all displayed on tables under a barracks window.

*British unit photo, Lamsdorf POW camp. All brothers included. Erwin, front row RHS. Walter 2nd from his RHS. John and Bruno on back row.*

In summer, the prisoners developed good suntans with little to do, other than playing sports like soccer and cricket, or gymnastics with exercise balls. Inside the barracks, cards were played, as well as chess, cribbage, and other board games. The brothers, who had been brought up on chess and cards, spent a lot of time playing. A Bridge tournament was run once or twice a year, and they were always well represented in the finals.

The POWs were sent out on work parties which brought them into contact with local civilians. These work parties numbered in the hundreds, and some were a long distance from the camp. Cigarettes were often traded between POWs and civilians, along with items from Red Cross parcels for books and even small radios. Walter obtained a quality German watch by bartering with local Polish residents.

Chocolate and cigarettes were high-value items for trade and even for better medical or dental treatment, which could be arranged with local doctors and dentists.

With over 25,000 POWs in the camp and on work parties, many

programs were developed to absorb free time, including a choir, a band, Sunday church services, an acting group, and a variety of sporting teams. A large range of classes were run by POWs who could teach. Walter wrote of attending classes to learn English, both elementary and advanced, French, diesel engine repairs, and hotel management. They all helped pass the time and keep their minds active.

Many work parties were arranged using prisoners as labourers for a large number of work sites, with groups entering and leaving the fenced campsite every day, always under guard. Non-commissioned officers, which the brothers had become, and those of higher rank, were able to choose or reject work, as determined by the Geneva Convention. The work parties were often taken by lorry or train to their work location, which could be in a forest, sawmill, mine, rail yard, factory, or in repairing roads, bridges, and buildings.

In all of these movements, opportunities were taken to trade with local civilians for items not available in the camp. The main food item wanted by the prisoners was always fresh bread.

POWs could send and receive heavily censored letters to and from people outside the camp, even in England. Walter's girlfriend and future wife, Charlotte, was in England when the war began and stayed there. A friend of hers wanted to write to a POW, and so Walter was suggested. From then on, he received parcels, often with many cigarettes and other useful or tradable goods.

The Red Cross ensured their parcels got through to all camps, including Lamsdorf. The Germans stayed with the convention because German POWs in England and elsewhere also received parcels.

When the brothers were first captured, because of their Jewish backgrounds, they had great concerns for their safety. They had left Czechoslovakia because of the Nazis, and now they had been captured and taken back to almost where they had started. But after an initial issue with the Germans on how they would deal with Jews in British Army uniform, they were treated like any other prisoner. The Germans had considered depriving all Jewish soldiers of their Red Cross parcels, keeping these prisoners in a separate area within the camp and making them wear yellow star badges. However, the strong attitude by the Allied officers that, regardless of background, all British POWs were to be treated equally, forced the Germans to give up the idea of any difference in treatment.

Because of how the Russians had treated German POWs during World War I, the German guards in Lamsdorf and other camps took retribution on Russian prisoners and treated them very badly.

Where the camp was situated, the summers were tolerable compared to the bitterly cold winters. Soup rations improved in quality, and more summer vegetables were available. The delivery of Red Cross parcels and packages from home was more reliable.

As the war rolled on, German manpower for the war effort became critical, particularly because of losses on the Eastern front. The number of guards was reduced, with only the outer perimeter of the camp being patrolled. The balance of the conflict changed, with the Russians moving closer and the Western front being established, initially in Italy and later in France. The continued loss to Germany of men and war materials was becoming more obvious. The constant day and night Allied bombing of German targets had an impact on the camp. The extensive system of Stalag Lufts (camps holding captured flying crews) overflowed with airmen from downed bombers. Those overflows meant that more flyers ended up at Lamsdorf, and the camp population number continued to expand.

After the brothers had been in the camp for some time, they were able to find a foreign worker who came from Moravia in Czechoslovakia, at a factory during a working party. He agreed to take a package of Red Cross food to mail it back to the Sax family. A letter was also sent to their sister, Ruti, who wrote back, using a form of code so that the true message was hidden. That one letter sent and replied to was the only successful correspondence while they were in Lamsdorf. Later, they learnt that soon after the letter was sent, the family was taken away to a concentration camp.

The fear of extermination by the Nazis was always with the brothers and other Jews in British uniforms. The camp had regular surprise visits by SS men with dogs, and the Jewish POWs were always first to be paraded for inspection before the rest of the camp was called out.

At times, as NCOs, the brothers chose to go with work parties, just to get out of the camp or to trade with local civilians. They sometimes worked in a forest felling trees, with minimal guard control. Erwin chose to push scrap metal into the softwood logs whenever he could, to try to sabotage the logs and eventually the mill saws. If discovered, he would probably have been shot, along with the rest of the workgroup, including his brothers.

During their work in the forest, they were once very close to the forest keeper's house and duck yard. After a short effort, a duck was caught and taken back to camp by one brother who made out he was ill. The roast duck dinner that night was memorable. Foreign Polish workers nearby were blamed for the duck's disappearance. The brothers joked that they would never have stolen the bird because the punishments were so severe.

They all kept their knowledge of the German language secret, to be able to listen in to the guards' discussions. Once while enjoying the peace and physical activity of working in the forest, they witnessed a large number of ragged people walking through the trees, under guard. A conversation between nearby POW guards revealed that they had been Jews, who were being moved to a concentration camp. Speaking in German, the guards commented that Jewish POWs, including the brothers in the Lamsdorf camp, might eventually be the only Jews left alive. Bruno later said no one could then tell him that the normal German soldier knew nothing about the extermination camps.

At times, a German agent would be put into the camp, speaking and acting as a captured English soldier or airman. It was assumed that a body found in a large water-filled pit at the end of a barrack building was such a spy. It had been there through winter and was only found when the ice melted in spring. These prisoner-dug holes were a low-cost provision for fire-fighting, with drainage water being directed to the pits and reserved for easy access if a building caught fire.

They had been POWs since July 1941. In 1943, Erwin received a letter from a friend in Palestine. He found out that his wife, Gaby, the mother of his daughter Judith, was involved in an affair. The man was a friend of theirs who had been on board the *Frossula* and the *Tiger Hill*, when they arrived by sea to Palestine. Gaby was apparently happy with the affair. Erwin was devastated and spent days wandering around, talking to himself, and trying to decide what to do. Weeks went by, then he finally decided to forgive her.

In August 1942, a limited raid was staged by the Allies at Dieppe, on the French coast. In October, another small raid occurred on the Channel Island of Sark, the only British territory, apart from Guernsy Island, to be occupied by the Germans. The Dieppe raid used thousands of seaborne commandos and special forces, with air cover and warship protection. Many of the soldiers involved were from Canada. The mission was to capture prisoners, collect intelligence, and do major damage to coastal defences to lift morale for the Allies. The operation was a failure, with thousands captured and little damage done.

The Sark raid was much smaller, to gather intelligence and capture prisoners for questioning. When all fighting ended, the Germans found instructions on captured soldiers that covered directions on how to tie up prisoners to stop them escaping. The Allies said, with the gunfire from both sides, some German prisoners were shot in the crossfire and were found later to be tied up. The Germans believed that prisoners were tied up and shot by the British on purpose.

In response and retaliation, Berlin ordered that 1,376 Allied prisoners, mostly Canadians from the Dieppe raid, were to be bound the same way – a painful knotting around the thumbs with hands behind the back. Initially, 1,500 POWs were shackled in Lamsdorf alone, plus in many other camps.

The Canadians responded with similar shackling of German prisoners held in Canada. This went on for some time until an agreement was arranged by the Swiss in December for the Canadians, British and Germans to end the practice, once assurances had been given.

The guards at Lamsdorf had been involved in shackling prisoners. They were put in chains 18 inches long between the arms and behind their back. The prisoners soon learned how to take them off. If caught without them, out of the barracks, they would be chained again. There were not enough chains and so Red Cross package strings were eventually used.

Walter wrote that Germans tied up prisoners by the hundreds for weeks, mostly with a rank (not privates), from morning to night, apart from a break at lunch. To go to the toilet, they had to have permission. It went on for six months. In winter, because their hands were tied up, they could not be kept warm in pockets. For the rest of his life, Bruno had marks on his wrists where he had been tied.

During this time, the camp authorities decided they would settle old scores with the prisoners. Regular mail, Red Cross parcels, and cigarettes were stopped. Then all sports, concerts, and classes were forbidden. With only the camp rations to live on, a shortage of blankets, no fuel allowance and the increasing winter cold, conditions in the camp became the worst of the war. In some camps, German staff disclaimed all obligations under the Geneva Convention and talked of continuing collective punishment with no appeal. A few sadistic guards kicked and prodded prisoners with bayonets. Those found smoking in barracks while wearing loose shackles received brutal punishments.

As time went on, conditions relaxed and tight shackles were replaced with more comfortable restrictions. It was found that the keys from the top of old corn beef tins would open shackles or handcuffs. The restrictions were finally abandoned as early as December.

Like the four brothers, there had been hundreds of men from Palestine who enlisted in the British Army. When many were captured, mostly in Greece and Crete, the Arab Palestinian prisoners were separated from the rest in Germany. These men were sent to a particular camp where they were given intense propaganda to try and turn them towards supporting Germany, under the control of the Grand Mufti of Jerusalem. Some volunteered and joined the Arab Legion to return to the Middle East where they would fight against the British mandate and Jewish expansion in Palestine. The rest who refused were sent to Lamsdorf and joined the prisoners there, causing no unrest and joining in normal activities.

With the work parties, the guards were initially very strict and tough on the POWs but slowly they relaxed the working groups as the camp settled down for what was to be a long, drawn-out war.

NCOs were first required to work, along with normal soldiers. This was against the Geneva Convention and a few months later, the orders were cancelled. During that initial time, the brothers had to work in the forest about two miles from the camp. While they marched to the work-site, they saw a camp filled with Jewish civilians. They sang Jewish songs as they marched past and received applause from behind the fences from the prisoners, who recognised the songs. Within a few months, the civilians were moved away, probably to a concentration camp.

The POW camp had a dental clinic included, but it only performed extractions, not any other care. Walter had been having tooth problems and so he switched positions with a prisoner who worked in a town with a dentist. Walter paid two packs of cigarettes and a container of cocoa to have a good quality tooth implant installed. Similar arrangements were made by other prisoners for better quality medical and dental care than what they could get in the camp.

By 1944, with the Germans fighting on two fronts and the bombing campaign building up, a painting showing all of Europe was made by prisoners to show the relative locations of the Allied and German lines. This was destroyed as soon as it was discovered. After several such maps were destroyed, a large version was painted on a barracks wall, and regular adjustments were made regarding the front lines as they changed. The hidden radios in the barracks gave more accurate information than the official German broadcasts. Instead of removing the map, even German officers came to inspect and comment on the lines. This showed how relaxed the camp had become, the guards believing they were well away from fighting, particularly from the Russian front.

At a worksite, in this case, a sand quarry with a lake, Walter had the idea of fishing for extra food. He asked men working in a large machine maintenance building to make him some fishhooks. The manager got involved and helped with the design of the hooks, instead of ordering Walter back to work. Walter eventually was successful catching trout – twelve fish in one day. One fish was cooked in the camp for the manager to thank him for his help.

Another time, during a long work project of several months, the idea was raised to breed rabbits for extra meat. Male and female rabbits were purchased through the guards, with prisoners making cages. The breeding was very successful, and they eventually started eating rabbit meat. The man who looked after them got so attached to his pets that he couldn't think of eating them.

The brothers were involved in various 'projects' while in the camp, as were many other prisoners. POW life was very different to the concentration camps dedicated to removing unwanted groups from the future society planned by the Nazis. No international controls applied to these 'death camps', with the majority of activities and scale of the operations being kept secret until the end of the war. On the other hand, POW camps were well known and checked by Red Cross and Geneva Convention inspectors. The same rules applied to similar camps run by the Allies in England, Canada and even in distant locations like Australia, for German, Italian and Japanese POWs.

Only Erwin had been married when they were captured, with his wife Gaby still in Palestine and his daughter Judith probably dead in a concentration camp by the end of 1943. Walter had a girlfriend, Charlotte, who was in England. Bruno and John had no commitments other than the rest of their family back in Novy Hrosenkov.

Lamsdorf was full of men who had been forcibly removed from their loved ones, with little to occupy their time other than survival. At the meal tables, depressed young men talked about the loss of their best years to establish themselves in jobs, marry and have a family. Older men missed girlfriends, wives and children and their wider family life. Many worried about how their families were able to support themselves while they remained prisoners and the war continued. Another issue was whether their wives or girlfriends were still being faithful to them, several years after they were captured.

Erwin had to put off the day when he would be able to speak face-to-face with Gaby, to make a final decision on their future together.

By November 1943, the German armies were retreating from Russia and Italy. POW camps were being relocated from the outer boundaries of German-controlled territory to the interior of Germany, Austria, and Poland. There was a reorganisation which affected Lamsdorf, with the main camp being renamed Stalag 344, and the name Stalag VIIIB allocated to the Teschen annex camp. The reorganisation brought with it a deterioration in the guards' attitude towards POWs. The Russian army was advancing, which made the Germans tighten security and become nervous and suspicious of anything happening in the camp.

The brothers continued to pick which working parties they would join, while retaining the right to refuse to be involved. The war closed in on Germany, and its forces were pushed back while losing many thousands of troops. Captured flight crew members from shot down Allied bombers continued to be delivered to the air force section of the camp. The four months before the end of the war in Europe on 8 May 1945 were dangerous and confusing for both prisoners and guards.

The Germans received orders to evacuate the camp and move the prisoners away from the advancing front line of fighting. There was general disorder, and prisoners in the various work groups were moved in many directions. Some prisoners escaped to the Russian lines and a number of camps had already been liberated. Many prisoners were made to clear landslides or repair war damage to roads and bridges to keep the transport routes open.

Some escaped, either west to Allied lines, or towards Turkey. A few even arrived back in Palestine. Others joined partisan groups in Yugoslavia and Greece to fight the Germans.

In the months of 1945, before the war ended, Bruno had been in a fight with a German guard and had been sent to the Zagan penal camp to serve a sentence. Held south of Berlin, Bruno was eventually evacuated before his other brothers who were located further to the southeast. He was near a French camp where the POWs were even freer to go out working without guards. His decision to escape then was because of growing indications that the war would end soon, and he was desperate to go back to Novy Hrosenkov in Moravia to discover what had happened to the family. He went out with a French work party. They provided civilian clothes, the equivalent of $50, and put him on a train, which travelled for several days to arrive at Breslau (Wroclaw) in Poland. There, others organised the next step of his escape, with Red Cross packages but no water. He could only drink by putting his handkerchief in the falling rain and sucking on it.

A bucket was found by guards in the wagon where he had been first hiding, put there for toilet use, and a search eventually revealed him to the Germans. He was taken back to the French camp and slept in another prisoner's bed overnight without his real identity as an escaping POW from another camp becoming known. His true identity was eventually discovered and reported by a civilian after a few days. This short-lived freedom had lasted ten days, and his trial by the Germans for escaping resulted in a penal camp sentence of one month. He eventually gave the $50 back to the surprised French man, who was not able to understand how he had hidden it during body searches. The money would have been less acceptable if he had known that it would have been rolled up in a pouch and inserted into Bruno's rear end, to be expelled later.

John was in the camp where Bruno had been, a few days travel west of where Erwin and Walter were held. He was then closer to home at the end of the war.

At Lamsdorf, word filtered through that an evacuation of all guards and prisoners would be carried out to move them away from the Russian front. Everyone tried to make bags or backpacks and hoard cans or containers of biscuits and any other food available. Some work parties further out were already on the move. On the night of January 22, 1945, the camp prisoners were formed up and marched out, with everyone receiving a Red Cross parcel. The parcels were mostly dropped on the roadsides as the marchers battled through the deep snow-covered roads during an extremely cold winter. Men, in poor condition due to malnutrition and with low stamina, staggered out of the line as their strength gave up, never to be seen again.

The lines broke up into groups, which gathered in barns or wherever shelter could be found each night. Boots got wet while marching and froze at night if they were taken off. They also froze if left on, along with their feet. Prisoners found they could stop their boots freezing by removing them and sleeping on top of them in the straw. Their feet were kept warm by cutting strips off their long greatcoats to wrap their feet in. The march was not meant to be cruel or to kill prisoners, but it was badly organised in the middle of winter, with little to no planning. They were taken by back roads, away from main villages and towns, trying to keep away from the inhabitants. Those civilians, when they saw the prisoners, sometimes threw bricks or stones at them, while others gave them whatever food they could spare.

Food provided by the camp controllers was sparse, and communal cooking was for both prisoners and their guards. Some Red Cross parcels got through, but the supply was disrupted. The groups, now split into 250 to 300 men, diverted through different locations because of blocked roads in winter conditions. Most could cover twenty to forty kilometres in a day, always away from where the Russian lines were advancing.

Many prisoners died due to the lack of proper planning and because of the appalling winter conditions, in some areas the worst in fifty years. About 30,000 Allied prisoners were force-marched across Germany and Poland for about four months. Temperatures went below minus 20°C. Hundreds of thousands of civilian refugees were also moving, trying to keep out of Russian hands knowing the extent of retribution they would take on any German caught, particularly the women.

Walter and Erwin were not part of this panicked relocation. They had been working at a saw-mill in the Sudetenland, the North West area of Czechoslovakia, occupied by a large German-origin population before the war. The work camp received an evacuation order, and so the guards with twenty-five POWs were moved by train to the west. Walter thought the now depressed guards reminded him of when they had arrived at Lamsdorf as POWs in 1941. The guards were having to accept that Germany would be defeated, with massive damage having been done to German cities and towns. They lacked information on the conditions for their families back home and how the extreme Nazi extermination of millions of Jews and other groups might impact on their individual lives as German soldiers, once investigations revealed the horrific facts.

One night, while still in Czechoslovakia, the train stopped at a village and both Walter and Erwin jumped off the train and hid in a pigsty. They were found the next morning by a Czech woman who took them in. The village leaders provided food and drink and cared for them for three or four days. They were then given more food and civilian clothes for their trip to Prague. This was just before the war ended, so they had to get a lift from any passing vehicle, mostly trucks. They were temporarily separated but finally arrived in Prague.

## Note: Stalag VIIIB Lamsdorf

This was a large prisoner of war camp, later renumbered Stalag 344. It was located near the small town of Lamsdorf (now called Lambinowice, in Poland) in what was then known as Upper Silesia.

In 1939, the camp housed Polish prisoners from the German September 1939 Polish offensive. Later on, more than 100,000 prisoners from Australia, Belgium, Britain, Canada, France, Greece, New Zealand, the Netherlands, Poland, South Africa, the Soviet Union, Yugoslavia, Czechoslovakia and the United States passed through this camp. In 1941, a separate camp, Stalag VIIIF, was set up close by to house Soviet and Polish prisoners.

In 1943, the Lamsdorf camp was split up, and many of the prisoners, with the Working Parties/Arbeitskommandos, were transferred to new base camps; Stalag VIIIC Sagan (now modern Zagan) and Stalag VIIID Teschen. The Soviet army reached the camp on 17 March 1945.

Straight after the war, the Lamsdorf camp was used by the Soviets to house Germans, both prisoners of war and civilians. Polish army personnel being repatriated from POW camps were also processed through Lamsdorf and sometimes held there as prisoners for several months. Some were later released while others were sent to Gulags (labour camps) in Siberia.

By 1943, the famous camp for Allied flight personnel in Sagan-Stalag Luft III had become so overcrowded that about 1,000 prisoners, mostly non-commissioned aircrew, were transferred to Lamsdorf. A part of Stalag VIIIB was separated by new barbed wire fences to create a camp within a camp. All food was still provided from kitchens operated by Army personnel in the camp proper.

The hospital facilities at Stalag VIIIB were amongst the best in all Stalags. The hospital was set up on a separate site with eleven concrete buildings. Six of them were self-contained wards, with space for about 100 patients. The others served as treatment blocks with operating theatres, x-ray and laboratory facilities, as well as kitchens, plus accommodation for medical staff.

**Jewish/Palestinian POWs at Lamsdorf**

At the beginning of August 1941, over 1,100 Palestinian/Jewish POWs in two groups arrived at Stalag VIIIB Lamsdorf.

The veteran prisoners, taken at Dunkirk, told them that the German staff had no idea how to deal with them. The Germans initially decided that the Palestinians would not share in the distribution of Red Cross parcels sent from Britain. The British declared that in such a case, the British, too, would refuse to get their parcels. The Germans were alarmed, and the parcels were then distributed amongst all the prisoners.

The Palestinians discussed the parcel problem with an inspection team from the Swiss embassy. A Red Cross representative in the camp informed the new prisoners of the Geneva Treaty rules and emphasised the rule permitting non-commissioned officers the right to refuse to work. The Germans were sensitive to this problem of NCO work, since the prisoners regarded work as a contribution to the German war effort, and did their best to avoid it.

*Watch Tower overlooking POW washing lines, Lamsdorf*

## The Long March

In January 1945, as the Soviet armies resumed their offensive and advanced into Germany, many of the prisoners were marched westward in groups of 200 to 300 in the so-called "Long March". Many of them died from the bitter cold and exhaustion. The lucky ones got far enough to the west to be liberated by the American or British armies. The unlucky ones were 'liberated' by the Soviets. They, instead of turning them over quickly to the Western Allies, held them as virtual hostages for several more months, until the British agreed to release the POWs of Soviet origin. These soldiers had been fighting on the German side, which left the British government with little choice in the matter. They were understandably reluctant to hand these men over to the Soviet Union for their inevitable execution. Soldiers from states such as Latvia, Lithuania, and Estonia had fought with the Germans in an effort to release their homelands from Soviet occupation and oppression.

This Long March was not a death march, as occurred in other areas of World War II, although it was a horrific experience, and many died. On this mass movement, there were some instances of cruelty, but most of the deaths were caused by illness, the cold, malnutrition, and the action of Allied aircraft. The whole situation was created, not by the deliberate mishandling of the captors, but by a totally mismanaged evacuation that should never have happened.

The POWs marched in small columns following side roads to villages where they could find accommodation in barns at the end of each day. Some accounts mention that at the end of each day's march, they would identify their billet, usually a barn, by the number of the Arbeitskommando chalked on the door, confirming that they remained in the same working party throughout that trek. Food was sparse, the guards themselves were hungry, and cooking was done communally. The delivery of Red Cross parcels was disrupted but remained a vital source of additional food, as well as cigarettes.

In most camps, the POWs were actually broken up into groups of 250 to 300 men and because of the inadequate roads, the flow of battle, and the location of the front line, not all the prisoners followed the same route. The groups would march twenty to forty kilometres a day – resting in factories, churches, barns, and even in the open. Soon, long columns of POWs were wandering over the northern part of Germany with little or nothing in the way of food, shelter, or medical care.

Prisoners from different camps had different experiences: sometimes, the Germans provided farm wagons for those unable to walk. Seldom were horses available, so teams of POWs pulled the wagons through the snow.

## Dr. Bruno's Memoirs of German Captivity

"Since 1940, four brothers of the British Army have joined the illegal immigrants from the Czech Republic, after spending a year in Israel. The British initially opposed the mobilisation of four brothers into one unit, but they had to agree, and in captivity they did not succeed in separating us. When someone called the family name Sax, all four of us, three corporals and I, Bruno, a sergeant, answered.

In captivity, after various troubles, we reached Lamsdorf, Germany. After a while, for two weeks a large group was sent to work in a paper factory in Cardiff. The factory was about 250 km from the house in Moravia, so close but so far away. There were also many foreign workers, including one from Slovakia. When he went on Christmas holidays in 1941, he agreed to take a package from us (mainly food from the Red Cross) and mail it to our family in the Czech Republic. In a letter in the package, my brother Walter wrote that he was reading a book about four brothers who had passed the marathon runway, but in the opposite direction, as well as all that had happened to us since we left the house. Our sister Ruth understood the hint and in a reply letter she sent with the Slovakian, she wrote that she too was reading a book about two girlfriends, one of whom was infected with an epidemic that broke out at the time. They were not allowed to meet, so they met only at night on the hill behind the house. She also wrote about the difficult situation of all those who were affected by the disease. In fact, it was the only and last connection we had with our extended family. After the war we learned that two months later they were sent to a camp from which they did not return. Since 1942, a group of about 20 people had been sent to work in the forest. Since we were of a rank, we did not have to work, only as volunteers, but we wanted to go out into the free air. We cut down trees and sawed them up. My brother Erwin, with every opportunity he had, found a piece of iron and pushed it into the tree, sabotaging it.

We lived in a building where there had been a tavern.

There was an English group before us. In the corner of the room was a pile of potatoes. In the evening, to our amazement, mice with coloured ribbons on their necks appeared. It was from a gambling game of the English. The first thing we did was to clear the potatoes from our room.

In our work near the forest keeper's house we saw ducks. Our mouths were drooling. It was decided to create Operation Duck. After a serious chase we caught one. One of the brothers announced that he was not feeling well and returned to the camp, with the duck hidden in his shirt. The king's dinner that awaited us that evening would not shame the Hilton kitchen. The next day the forest guard told us that the foreign Polish workers had apparently stolen a duck, prisoners, that is. We would certainly not do so because the punishment was severe.

Working in the forest was our most beautiful period of activity, both physically and mentally. One day we saw a mass of ragged people walking like shadows in exhaustion. This was the only encounter with concentration camp prisoners. Later on, we heard a conversation between two Germans, that if we were to survive, we would be the only Jews. The Germans, of course, did not know that we understood the language. So, no one can tell me that the Germans did not know what was being done in the camps.

The fear for our lives as Jews accompanied us throughout the four years of captivity. On several occasions there was a surprise visit by SS men in the camp accompanied by dogs and shouting. We Jews were always the first group to be called out of the houses, and only an hour later the others were called.

*After the failure of the invasion of Dive, German POWs were found bound with their hands behind their backs. As a reaction and retaliation, the Germans tied up prisoners by the hundreds for weeks, mostly with ranks. The tie was made from morning to night with a short break for lunch. Even to go to a lavatory we had to ask to be allowed to leave, so we went for half a year like this. In the winter it was cold and you couldn't heat the tips of your hands in your pockets. To this day I have marks on my wrists."*

**Note**: This refers to the British raid on Dieppe, France, on 19th August, 1942, where instructions on how to tie up German prisoners were left after the raiding party retreated back to England. The Germans issued propaganda that their soldiers had been shot resisting being tied up and that the hand-tying method used at Dieppe would apply to POWs held in Germany.

*"One day we heard that a Czech pilot was in the hospital in the camp. We went to visit him but after the anti-Semitic expression we heard from him we left him. A few days later, the representative of the committee of the Bericha contacted me."* (Note: The Bericha was an organised effort to help Jewish survivors, mainly from Eastern Europe, to reach safety, particularly in Palestine) *"He asked me to change my identity with the pilot, because I was like him. He wanted to run away. At first, I refused, but after he asked for my forgiveness, we stayed for a few days in the hospital and he was sent to the officer's camp. The commander of the German camp invited me on a trip and he already knew that the Czech pilot had escaped and had been caught. During the trip he told me that my German had improved a lot since our last conversation. In short, after a few days I was sent back to my camp and received a week in prison. As compensation, I received a very cordial welcome when I was*

*released.*

At the Christmas party, a conversation developed at the table. A young man of about 18 was stuck in longing and said, "I'm losing my best years here." Two older people who left a girlfriend at home, a third who got engaged, a married fourth, a married fifth plus a child. Each of them lamented that he was losing his most beautiful years and everyone agreed. In the camp, outside the counting tables twice a day, we had practically nothing to do. We four brothers loved to play bridge. In fact, we participated in the game for four months on the sea on our way to Israel on the illegal immigrant ship. Bridge was also a social card game. The development of competitions and their conclusion had the names of winners announced. At the end of the order, our names were mentioned a lot.

The chess game was common and I also took part. Nine countries participated in the competition and each country played four players. The German camp commander was enthusiastic about the idea and contributed chess to the conductor. In the middle of the competition, he was interested in the situation, which informed him that the leading Palestinians had stopped taking an interest.

Of 36 games, we received 34 points, one loss and two points, to the chagrin of the German commander, we received the chess prize.

One of the curiosities of the camp was the presence of 'shops'. The dealer had cigarettes. The most wanted item was bread, as well as the other items of the Red Cross packages that we received every week. In fact, these packages saved our health and perhaps our lives. The bread was obtained by one of the shop owners who agreed with the Germans when the bread was brought into the camp in a truck. Even German officers came to buy cigarettes for *socks, etc.*

*I spent the last months of captivity in the Sagen penal camp south of Berlin, near a French camp. I made friends with the French. They were freer and went out to work without a guard. We felt that the end of the war was approaching and I decided to try to escape. I wanted to go home to Moravia to see what the family was up to. I did not know then that everyone had already perished. I went out with the French to work. They took care of suitable clothes and even gave me $50. They brought me to a train that travelled four days to Breslau. The French made sure someone was waiting for me when I arrived.*

*Everything was very organised. The train had packages of Red Cross products and I didn't lack food, but there was no drinking water. It rained and I reached out with a handkerchief to wet my throat a little. There was also a bucket for the carriage. To my dismay, the Germans later found the bucket and thought that someone was probably important and rushed to search. When they found me they brought me to the French camp. I slept in a prisoner's bed who worked at night. A German inspector was in my room that night near my bed but did not suspect me. After a few days I was sent to the French camp, but unfortunately, I was caught by a citizen who suspected me. I was outside for about 10 days. After the trial and the desired sentence (one month in prison) I met with the Frenchman who organised my escape and gave him back the $50. He was very surprised how I managed to hide the money despite all the inspections I went through. I showed him the patent-mother used to roll knitting thread over a piece of paper and so I did the same with sewing thread on the money. After a few years, in Paris, I searched for him but I learned that he had already died."*

*Bruno Sax and two local officials, Lamsdorf POW camp (closed down), years after the war.*

# Chapter 6

## Terezin: World War II Ghetto and Concentration Camp –

### A visit in 2008.

Our 2008 Danube River cruise was filled with the experiences of good food and wine, great people, music, dance, poetry, and the history of ancient cities and towns. A waltz on the Blue Danube. Our boat was named *MS Avalon Poetry*, and it was decked out with all the mod cons expected of a modern 'space ship' fit for European river cruising.

Our mid-summer holiday itinerary included a long list of historic locations – Budapest, Vienna, Durnstein, Litz, Passau, Regensberg, a one-day side visit to Salzburg and a wander through a number of villages chosen as stopovers, and then, as a conclusion to the cruise, Nuremburg.

My personal and family interest with this river originated from my departed first wife, Jane Trigg, nee Sax, the mother of my children. She did not have the chance to undertake this trip, having died of cancer in 1997. I was here in 2008 for both personal enjoyment as a tourist but also to try to understand the drama of World War II and its impact on the Sax family.

The Danube River was very important at that time, more than 70 years in the past when it became an escape route for Jews and non-Jews from a half dozen European countries threatened or invaded by the German Nazi armies. They were all trying to save themselves and their families from the beginning of Hitler's madness in 1938/39, before international conflict closed off this major channel to freedom.

It was impossible to understand the feelings and worries of the four Sax brothers on that river in 1938 heading for Palestine. They were trying to plan for the future while looking back, fearful of pursuit by Nazi-sympathising local military or police units in Germany or Austria.

The worry about the safety of the remaining family members in their country town of Novy Hrozenkov in Czechoslovakia would have been constant. Had they done the right thing? The choice to stay or to go, if wrong, could be a disaster. Erwin Sax and his wife had decided to leave their daughter Judith with her grandmother, Erwin's mother, because of their fears for her safety on this illegal attempt to get to Palestine. This must have been matched with their fears for her life if the Nazis acted against the Czechoslovakian Jews as they had in Germany and Austria.

Our cruise ended. Nuremberg's main history from the war centred on the post-war Nazi war crimes trials and its location as the National Shrine-city of the Nazi party, the scene of vast political and military rallies before and during the war. These were held to consolidate and ferment the resolve of the German people to conquer much of the world and remove obstructions to the expansion of the nation while cleansing it of undesirable people, particularly the Jewish race.

In 1935, the Nuremberg laws were passed depriving all Jews of German citizenship and civic rights, a forerunner of similar laws in all countries to be conquered by the Nazis during the war. Less than ten years later, the city was mostly destroyed by Allied bombing and then rebuilt after the war.

In Nuremberg, we inspected the war crimes courtroom and listened to explanations on the legal processing of Nazi war criminals. We travelled by motorcoach through the German countryside, on modern highways into Czechoslovakia through Pilsen to Prague, the capital. The coach driver remarked on the Russian post-war architecture established in the old city of Pilsen, the heart of Pilsener beer-making. The architecture resembled a series of old bricks, with no defining feature other than mottled grey colours and the need for long-overdue maintenance.

We had seen the same style of depressing buildings in Budapest, which were now slowly being replaced. Pilsen had a similar look, tired, basic, and boring. A relatively short distance later, we arrived at the Czechoslovakian capital. The existing centre of Prague would probably have been recognisable hundreds of years ago, with little to no damage done to it during war. All of the most noteworthy sites had been cleaned and repaired, to maximise the flow of tourist income. The excesses of communist architecture seemed to have been reserved for the suburbs, with many standard concrete apartment boxes being obvious there.

We spent as much time as our sore feet would allow, due to the ubiquitous cobblestone streets, particularly in the small portion of Prague known as the Jewish quarter. In Josefov, the *Old Ghetto*, a few hundred metres from Wenceslas Square, the reduced remains of a pre-war, busy Jewish life remained – only six synagogues, a town hall and a cemetery, plus a few street signs.

The Jewish cemetery was different from anything we had seen around the world, about 12,000 tombstones marking 20,000 graves on up to 12 levels, within the area of an Australian house block! The piles of small pebbles on top of many of the grave memorials were a reminder of the culture or traditions already ancient before Australia had come to the attention of Europeans, with the cemetery being closed since 1787. The ancient stones were tilted in all directions, some half-sunken into the ground. This had been the only burial ground permitted for the Jews in over three centuries.

*Ancient Jewish cemetery in 'the Old Ghetto', Josefov, Prague*

The one place we visited that could compare in tragedy with what we would see at Terezin was the Pinkas Synagogue, memorable because of the 80,000 names of Moravian and Bohemian communities, families and individual people murdered by the Nazis, mostly in concentration camps.

The words on the walls and ceiling were written in red for the town or village, the family name, and also the first letter of each person's name. These swam across the length and width of the large ceiling and down the walls, in a sea of black words on a white background. You could easily damage your neck if you let yourself get too involved while looking up. We were told the Russians painted out the whole room in white as soon as they arrived when the war ended, to remove the names, following that government's anti-Jewish policies of the past. The names we saw were reproductions of an earlier creation. So much loss and destruction. Whole villages and family lines coming to an end early in the 1940s. These 80,000 names were only from Czechoslovakia. What about Poland, Ukraine, Germany, Austria? The list went on.

Here and there, you could hear a startled exclamation. Someone had found a name, looking for it but hoping for it not to be there. Maybe it had been thought that the person had survived, somewhere. Hopes now destroyed.

The lady who was one of the few guides in the building looked old enough to have survived World War II concentration camps, if she had been a child at the time. She could only speak Czech and our tour guide took her to one side to explain in her language our need to find the Sax names. They both looked the other way. What we were photographing was against the rules – why, we didn't know. All too soon, she was whispering one of the few English words she probably knew, "Please, please." It was time to go, to leave this tomb of names. It resembled the weird Bone Chapel of the Sedlac Ossuary we visited the next day, the walls covered with the bones of the dead from the plague, hundreds of years ago. The Pinkas Synagogue replaced the bones with the names of the dead from another form of plague, stacked for the many to view.

Another day was spent on a coach trip visit to Kutna Hora. The city, built from 1142, showed us how old and developed the region had been, even if the most recent exploitation by the Russians, who replaced the Germans, was still obvious in parts.

Then came the day trip from Prague to the old fortress town and World War II Nazi/Jewish ghetto of Terezin. I knew of its existence from notes about the Sax family that my wife Jane had written, but not much more than a name and a dark past.

The drive through the countryside from Prague was enjoyable and similar to agricultural areas around the world, through grain fields ready for harvest and past old farmhouses and sheds or barns – many in need of overdue maintenance. The energy seemed washed out of the place, things moving at the slower pace of a past era. Maybe it was just the hot summer season.

Then we drove through the entrance gates and into an old massively-built fortress from the past, a protected town within thick stone or concrete walls, still solid as if waiting for a battle that never came. The bus passed three and four-storey buildings built before World War I, some painted up in muted yellow, orange, light blue, and green, most in need of attention, but still occupied. The cars parked on the stone kerbside were older models, some from the Soviet days but none new or in a clean condition. Again, the energy seemed to have flowed away.

We got off the bus at a relatively nondescript entrance, obviously not an original main door. Entry fees were paid and English translation brochures selected. Enough effort was obvious in the presentation of the displays for tourist consumption. The visitors were quiet, almost reverent. Some came from more wealthy countries with their modern clothing and cameras, some with restricted means or from the poorer areas of Europe. A fair proportion of Jewish people were probably there because of its infamous past and the possible connections to their family history.

The first impression as we entered was that many of the original floors, walls, and built-in features appeared not to have been upgraded for generations, workable but poorly maintained. All were worn with the place not attracting the hordes of tourists needed to fund extensive improvements and replacements, or new technology displays. Maybe that was what suited such a place. This was the site of dreadful suffering and death for the Jews, while the German occupiers, even the non-SS soldiers, committed inhumane acts of atrocity.

*Jewish Cemetery & Memorial for those murdered in Terezin*

We watched a flickering black and white archival film showing scenes of the fortress and ghetto through the war years. For the most brutal events, no film was shown. The seats and stage appeared to have been salvaged from another place, maybe an old movie theatre. We stayed silent and let it wash over us, then went upstairs to see the exhibits, including samples of captive children's drawings and writings. Many expressed hopes of sunny days and normal life drawn in the variety of coloured crayons and pencils made available, some of them possibly staged for the single Red Cross inspection during the war years.

Most of their original efforts had been destroyed during the war, just as the children who made them were destroyed. A sizable remainder had been hidden in unobserved corners, pushed through holes in floors and walls or behind furniture, like prayers into the Wailing Wall in Jerusalem.

The rest of the exhibits were more photos, a scale model of the fortress, copies of Nazi rules for prisoners written in Czech and

German, with lists of particular punishments for offenders. We eventually moved out and followed the directions leading to kitchens, laundries, a surgery and medical facility, the many rabbit warrens of sleeping areas, children's classrooms, a large crematorium, and even an area for theatre productions.

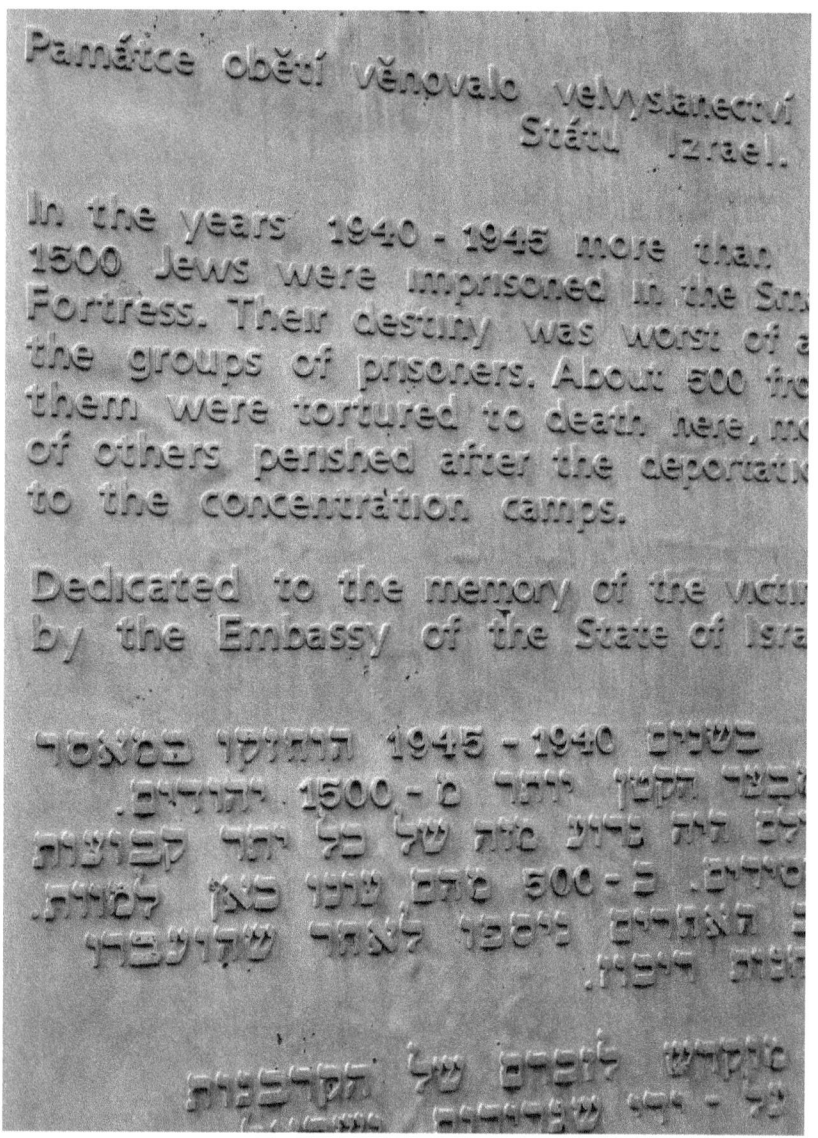

*Terezin Concentration Camp Memorial*

All of it seemed well-scrubbed and dusted but probably unchanged, worn from heavy use during the war. The other tourists around us talked as little as we did, just looking and trying to take it all in, similar to visiting a library, museum, or mausoleum. Big, empty rooms were once stacked four high with rough, timber-framed beds, storage shelves of lives soon to be moved on, and the spaces refilled from an almost endless supply.

*Terezin Fortress and Concentration camp*

We eventually finished the internal room viewings and wandered out into the air again, the infamous sign "Arbeit Macht Frei" or "Work Makes You Free", a monstrous lie, painted on the opposite wall. We wondered how many tens of thousands of prisoners – men, women, and children, old and young, rich and poor – walked under that sign knowing that there was no escape from the industrialised efficiency of the Nazi system. It looked like some of the external concrete-covered walls had been painted since the war, in a faded yellow with brickwork showing through in places and around doorways.

*Wall Plaque in Terezin about the treatment of Jewish children in WWII*

The end of the walk back to the parked buses passed long rows of small, white concrete block monuments to individuals who died from disease, the adverse conditions, or were murdered there rather than the multitudes sent out on trains to the many death camps in the east. Each monument sat beside a small, flowering, red rose bush. One grave area had a large Jewish star mounted on a steel base rising out of a worn, grey, rock pile. Another area had a Christian cross. Death hadn't discriminated between religions and welcomed all.

My mind felt bruised trying to take it all in. My radar had been on alert for the ghosts of the past, but they seemed long gone. Perhaps even the ghosts of the dead could not bear to be in that place. The atmosphere seemed surreal. The indoor display of horror photos and documents mixed with simple drawings coloured by slaughtered children showed a period of only a few years, another world away from the relative tranquillity of modern life.

Again, the bus trip through the summer countryside back to Prague was quiet. No offering amongst couples or families of sweets, biscuits, drinks, or sandwiches. We were all occupied in our own way with what we had seen. I thought of the Sax family members who had vanished into that place – Judith less than five years old. Grandmother Jana at 67. And the rest of the family. How could those gentle people living their quiet, country lives be any threat to the Nazi regime?

No answers came.

*Terezin Memorial from the President of Israel*

# Chapter 7

# After the War – Rebuild or Relocate. Australia and Israel

While they were still prisoners, the brothers planned that if they were separated when the war finally ended, each would go to a particular, but now unknown, hotel in Prague to leave a message where they could be found. The next brother arriving would read the message and add to it.

One morning, as soon as they were free, Walter arrived at the chosen hotel to be met by Erwin, who was just coming out after leaving the first message. They both went back in and changed the message for Bruno and John.

Home was still over 300 km away, and with buses or trams no longer running, they hitchhiked, mostly with Romanian soldiers going home. The normal four to five-hour trip took them four days.

Homecoming was tragic. They asked people they knew in the town what had happened. Their neighbours told them their sister Ada had been thrown under a train, and two brothers had been killed while escaping. The rest of the family had been taken away and never returned, except for their sister Edith. She had married a non-Jew and spent only two to three months in a concentration camp in Czechoslovakia, probably Terezin.

German records did not include Ada as being sent to a concentration camp, so she may well have actually died under a train. There were no train lines anywhere near their home, so death under a train could only happen elsewhere. She was taken away, probably by truck with other family members. The truck would either have gone to the nearest rail siding for off-loading or to Prague, for those on board to be processed before being taken by train to Terezin. Their brothers, Otto and Ernest, were included in records of those who died in Auschwitz in 1942. The "brothers killed while escaping" comment by the neighbours may have been about other extended family members.

Their mother, all of their sisters except Edith, three nieces, and one nephew (the children of their married sisters Irene and Martha – Kurt and Lilly, Ina and Eva) were all murdered by the Germans in Auschwitz. Most of the large extended Sax family, over 100 members, had also been killed.

The brothers found, when they finally returned to their town, that the family house had half the roof caved in due to the heavy weight of winter snow loads. No one had been allowed by the Germans to clean it off as was normal in winter, or to occupy it. This would have made sense to the Nazis because when they had completed their plans, no Jews would exist to occupy their houses.

**Bruno standing behind the original Sax house in Novy Hrosenkov, on a visit years after the war.**

John had already returned to Novy Hrosenkov and had gone to visit their sister Edith, living about 30 kilometres away. Erwin and Walter arrived there a little later. They would have felt like aliens in a strange land, so few of their friends and family having survived, while the non-Jews had continued with their lives, restricted by the war but still alive. They stayed several days but had to return to their English army unit.

*Sax house, Novy Hrosenkov. Modernised front view.*

The first step was to travel back to Prague and then Pilsen to wait for a flight to France. Once they arrived at Rheims in France, the Americans provided them with food, cigarettes, and all their needs. Eventually, they returned to England, where they were put into a camp for soldiers waiting to return to Palestine. That was where Bruno joined them. He had been in England since the war ended, having been liberated early without first visiting their home town.

Before they were flown back to Palestine, Walter married his girlfriend, Charlotte, in London. John and Walter attended the wedding, but Erwin had already left for Palestine, while the other brothers stayed in northern England for a holiday. After his visit back home to discover the fate of their family, the most important issue for Erwin was to find out the truth about his wife's alleged affair while he was a POW.

Once they were back in Tel Aviv, Erwin met with Gaby, and three days later, he left her and arranged for a divorce. Bruno, John, and Walter remained friends with Gaby, but Erwin was not impressed by their continuing friendship. John and Walter stayed with her on future visits when they returned to Palestine. Walter made a request to the Army Headquarters to go back to England for two more months. This was refused, and Walter, instead, had 70 days of vacation in Palestine. The brothers were still enlisted as soldiers and had to wait six to seven months before they were demobilised.

*Erwin Sax's Army Pay Book*

Finally, they were civilians again. Erwin was discharged in January 1946, after more than five years in the Army, most of that time as a POW. Along with many other Czechs in Palestine, they wanted to return to Czechoslovakia, now the Germans were defeated. After a frustrating, complicated, and time-consuming mixture of inefficiency, higher priorities, lack of available transport, and failed Czech government promises, they found a way to get to Suez in Egypt. For several weeks, through March and April 1946, they had to wait in a United Nations holding camp composed of hundreds of tents at El Shatt in the desert beside the Suez Canal.

3729/PP&TJ/T 11/45     Substitute Form for A.F.B. 108 B

## 13465 APPENDIX TO A.C.I. 318/42
(If this CERTIFICATE is lost no duplicate can be obtained)

Army No. Pal/13321   NAME   SAX. ERVIN

Effective date of Discharge   8. Jan. '46.

Total Service: Years   5   days   57

Rank on Discharge   Pte

Cause of Discharge   Release H & S. group.

Service outside Palestine/Syria.   4 years 175 days.

Medals, etc.   Africa-Star.

Corps for which enlisted.   PNR. CORPS.

Corps from which discharged   PAL. REGT.

Transfers, if any, to other Corps   PNR. CORPS – PAL. REGT.

Previous service in H. M. Forces   Nil

Military Conduct   VERY GOOD

Date 30. Jan. '46    [signature] H. DEARMAN
Officer i/c Palestine Records, M.E.F.

The Palestine Record Office

*Erwin Sax Army Discharge form dated 30.1.1946, Palestine*

*El Shatt, Egypt, 1946. Erwin is with the dog.*

**United Nations refugee camp, El Shatt, Egypt, 1946**

Eventually, they were allowed into Cairo to join a boat trip to Italy, and from there a train arranged by the Czech government took them to Prague. The train also took many others who had been soldiers in the British Army or the Czech Battalion back home.

When Bruno returned to Palestine, he met then married his girlfriend, Chagit. Back in Czechoslovakia, John, initially joined by

Walter, worked in a sawmill, but Erwin first went back to Novy Hrosenkov. He tried to track down definite information about his mother and daughter Judith who had both been taken by the Germans. Reports existed of them being sent to a concentration camp, but at that time, no confirmation could be found. Erwin searched on his own, and when he had married Martha, they continued their desperate search together, knowing the small chance of finding them alive.

Erwin and Martha married on the 5$^{th}$ April 1947, at Havlickuv Brod, a city of about 23,000 and a hub for regional roads and railways. The city is close to the historical boundary between Moravia and Bohemia, and north of the small town of Polna. The regional centre is Jihlava, a city of around 51,000 and the oldest mining city in the country. They moved to Polna sometime after the wedding, and Erwin worked for Mr Patek in Polna. Photos at that time show him in jackets and office-type clothing, enjoying social outings with Martha and the Patek family, so his timber mill days had changed to a more settled life. Their home in Polna is shown in the background of available photos, a large two-storey, solid building in a semi-rural setting. They were obviously doing well at the time. Jane was born in Jihlava on the 18$^{th}$ of December 1948. The family left Czechoslovakia nine months later.

*Martha and baby Jana/Jane Sax, Polna, Czechoslovakia, 1949*

Bruno, years later, explained to Jane that when he was in Israel, Erwin finally found out, from the Diaspora Museum in Tel Aviv, '*Beit Hatfutsot*', that both his mother and daughter had definitely died in Auschwitz along with the other family members. That is why Walter had written, back in Czechoslovakia, "Erwin sort of disappeared" when he was searching.

Bruno, being able to speak several languages including Hebrew, assisted a Jewish company with the transport of goods to Palestine and eventually decided to stay there. He first undertook study at Charles University in Prague on his interrupted medical qualifications, completing them in October 1947. He then spent time in the new Israeli Army before returning to civilian life as a doctor in Israel.

There are different memories of what the brothers first recorded when they returned to Novy Hrosenkov. Their memoirs were written years after it happened, mixed with confusion and different perceptions. The neighbours had 'borrowed' a lot of the contents of the Sax family home, and a large quantity of hidden silver was missing, never to be found. The still-standing part of the house was occupied by the neighbours, people who had been close friends but now had plundered the house contents, without any rent being paid. When the brothers visited, they even saw the neighbouring family members openly wearing Sax family clothing, with a table decked out with Sax cloths and crockery. No apologies were made or offers given to at least share what had been in the Sax house.

In *Walter's Story* – which covered Walter's life – the four brothers didn't want to live again in the original family house, and the sawmill had been converted into barracks during the war by the Germans. Martha's memories of the time, after marrying Erwin, were that the four brothers had the sawmill working again. However, Walter was not a lumberman, so he and his new wife, Charlotte, moved to Prague, where they were lucky to find a two-bedroom flat on the top floor of an eight-storey building. After several short-term jobs, Walter used a contact to buy carpet cleaning machines from England and entered the carpet cleaning industry. Walter and Charlotte's first son, Paul, was born when they were living in Prague.

From the clues left from the brothers' memoirs, Erwin and John, and possibly Bruno, worked the restored sawmill for a while, soon after they had returned. They probably lived somewhere in the town rather than in the original Sax house, because of the damage and the neighbours' occupation during and after the war. The exact details are unknown.

*Sax family members after the war:
Rear from left-Eva, Alenka, Martha, Evanka.
Front left-Bruno, John, Josef. Alenka, Evanka and Josef are Eva's children.*

The ghosts of that house, with memories in every room from generations past and the loss of nearly all of their relatives due to the German extermination, must have been a huge burden. Their sister Edith/Eva lived nearby but in a different town, so they were alone and had to salvage a future for their new families from the devastation of the war. Jewish life in Czechoslovakia had also almost been wiped out, with the majority being removed to the gas chambers and concentration camps or used as forced labour by the Germans and worked to death. The fact that this occurred to many millions of people with the slaughter being a centre-piece of Nazi policies is beyond all understanding of reasonable minds.

The communist coup of the Czechoslovakian Government in February 1948 changed everything once more. All activities were now controlled, with quotas or production targets being created for all industries, even small, rural sawmills. The government targets for sawn timber production by the Sax sawmill were not possible to be met, and so records were fabricated to keep the inspectors at bay. The brothers began to understand that they could be in trouble in future under the Communist regime, not just from the falsified records for timber production.

Erwin went to Prague and saw large buildings full of records being created by the central management for all industrial production. With luck, for a while, they could be safe, but eventually, their false records would be discovered, once government officials had caught up with their study of the stockpiled details.

The time between when they arrived back after the end of the war and when they left the country once more is confusing when trying to tie the operation of the sawmill at Novy Hrosenkov with available photos and the pieces of information given by the brothers' writings. The communists took control in February 1948. John may well have worked the sawmill right up to the time he left for Australia later in 1948 with Walter and family. Erwin and Martha lived in Polna before and after Jane's birth in Jihlava in December 1948. Bruno completed his medical training at the university in Prague then went to Israel. Walter was not a timber mill man and was cleaning carpets in Prague until he and his family left for Australia.

From that confusion, they decided to leave their home country and move for good – first to escape the Nazis, and now the communists. This time, with so few members of the family left, the brothers didn't want to leave anyone behind. However, their only remaining sister, who had survived the war, Edith, was married to a non-Jew and had a young family. She chose to stay with her family in Czechoslovakia and battle through the tribulations over decades of living in a rigid communist state.

The few travellers who braved the Communist regime to visit Prague, even in the 1980s, believed the country was one of the most depressing places on earth. That eventually changed in the summer of 1989 when 300,000 residents gathered in Wenceslas Square and the Russians went home, finally.

Walter had already arranged false passports for their move out of Czechoslovakia, but Charlotte didn't like the idea of taking the risk of being caught. She was able to arrange an immigration sponsorship from an ex-aircraft navigator from Australia, whom she had met in England during the war. Expensive but legal passports were finally received to allow Walter, Charlotte, and their one-year-old son, Paul, along with John, to go to Genoa, Italy. There they went on board the steamship *Napoli*. The ship arrived in Fremantle, Western Australia, on the 15th of October, 1948. The trip was uneventful, after the dramas they had been through in previous years and they had a first-class cabin. This was paid for by the American Joint Distribution Committee, a Jewish company Walter had worked for soon after the war.

Visas were arranged through the father of Charlotte's contact in Australia. They arrived with very little money or valuables, apart from Charlotte's diamond earrings hidden from the extreme search undertaken by Czechoslovak customs officials on all people leaving the country. They were part of a movement of refugees and displaced persons from Europe to Australia under an International Refugee Organisation Group Resettlement program.

Erwin, Martha and baby Jana sailed later from Genoa, Italy, on 15 September 1949, arriving in Fremantle on 23 October 1949, a year after Walter and John. They were aboard the *Continental* and did not have a pleasant voyage. Genoa was suffering from a port strike, and Erwin, along with other men on the ship, helped load luggage. Unfortunately, in the confusion, he didn't load their own cases, and so they borrowed clothes all the way to Australia. Their bags eventually arrived on a different ship.

The route of these ships from Italy through the Mediterranean Sea and then the Suez Canal to Australia must have brought back memories for Walter, John, and Erwin. They had been kept in the United Nations refugee camp at El Shatt, Egypt, just across from the city of Suez, while waiting for transportation to be arranged to get them home to Czechoslovakia. The extensive tent camp had existed right through the war until a few years after it ended. It had held mostly Yugoslavian refugees who were transported away from their homes to save them from the German invasion of that country – yet another irony from the war.

Erwin and Martha were sick for some time after eating bad seafood on the ship. Italian passengers looked after Jana for that time, nick-naming her "bambina bella".

One final negative impact commented on by Martha was that she had a few small diamonds hidden in her balls of knitting wool, but the diamonds were either lost or stolen. They were never found, and for years she carefully unrolled her wool hoping to find them. The diamonds would have made a huge impact on their start of a new life in Australia if they had been retained. Martha would have remembered the good shoes stolen from her on the ship heading for Palestine in 1939.

The family arrived in Fremantle with only the £5 per person allowed to be taken out of Czechoslovakia.

*Erwin and Martha Sax's Australian Landing Permit, 1949*

# Chapter 8

# Growing Up in Katanning and Perth, Western Australia

When Erwin and his family arrived in Fremantle four years after the war ended, he arrived to a fast-growing population with a great lack of housing. The war effort had almost put any new house building on-hold in Australia. Due to the lack of manpower, transport, and materials, it was calculated that Australia needed at least 300,000 houses built to catch up after the war. That effort would take over five years if given the highest priority. This was similar to other countries affected by the war, even into the 1950s.

In Europe, the need was for the replacement of whole cities destroyed by bombing, fire, and war-shelling. In Australia, apart from the lack of men and materials, the unprecedented influx of immigrants from the UK and other parts of Europe caused the problem.

Western Australia's growth rate at that time was 3.5%, one of the highest in the world, compared to 2.6% for the whole of Australia and 2.3% for Canada.

20,000 houses were built by the State Housing Act, a large effort, but still 30,000 below the target.

A royal commission in 1947 looked into improper practices for granting building permits. Housing Commission employees were even being offered bribes to approve building permits and allocate materials.

But John and Jarmila Sax had already found a house to rent, having arrived one year earlier, as had Walter and Charlotte.

Erwin, Martha and baby Jane first stayed with John and Jarmila, in Victoria Park, in a house amongst pine tree plantations.

Erwin's background as a forester and an operator of sawmills initially did not make it easy to get a job. Australia's timber industry was not as modern as Europe's, with a higher level of safety issues and risk-taking.

He finally found work in a factory at Tuart Hill, an area dominated by chicken farms.

Again, they moved, to stay with Walter and Charlotte, with the formal address listed on the 23 October 1949, as 128 Hubert Street, Victoria Park.

Erwin was still on the lookout for a better job and eventually moved to the rural town of Gnowangerup to work as a labourer on a farm called *Clear Hills* and later to *Hollywood Farm* at Cherry Tree Pool as the farm manager. John and Jarka joined them there, and they started a sawmill to supply cut-timber to build and expand public buildings in the town. Cherry Tree Pool was midway between the rural towns of Kojonup and Katanning.

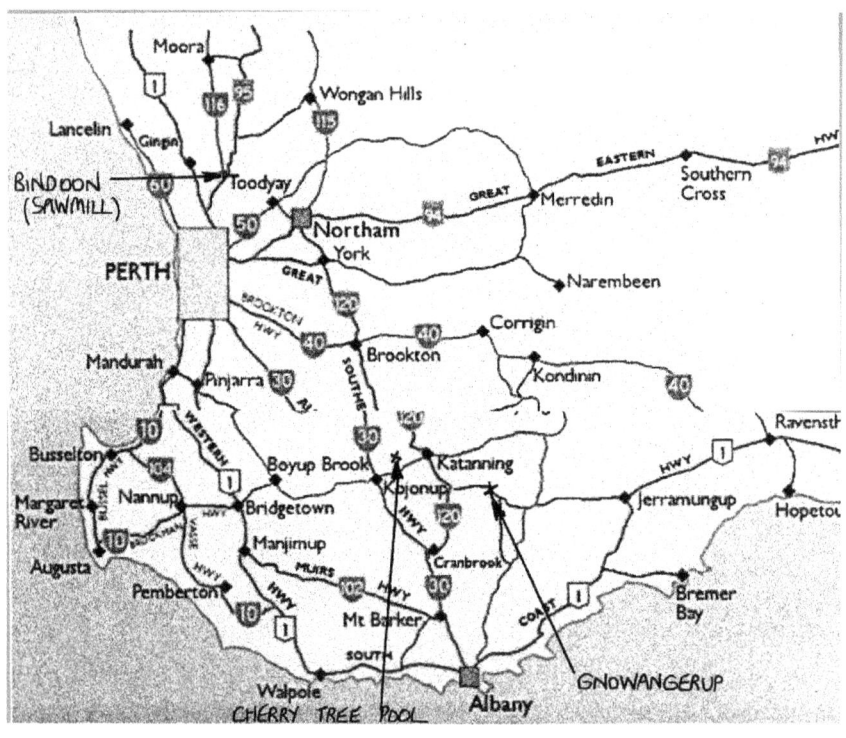

*Map 6, showing the southern part of Western Australia and the locations of Gnowangerup and Cherry Tree Pool where Erwin worked on farms.*

One job in the 1950s on rural properties around Australia was the fighting of a war – this time against rabbits. They had overpopulated to become a plague and had spread to every corner of the country. At times it would look like the land was actually moving with the massive number of these vermin per square mile. Farmers would lay out baits in the morning, often in a shallow trench, and run a line of poisoned seed or chopped apple pieces in the trench. At the end of the day, the dead rabbits would have to be collected by the truckload, every day over many months. The bodies would be stockpiled and burnt. Until new methods were introduced to control this pest, such as new poisons and viruses that spread across the rabbit population, most green living things were eaten or dug up. Tree saplings were destroyed, and crops ruined. Gradually the numbers were brought under control. Erwin and John would have been caught up in this battle when they worked on farms at Gnowangerup and Cherry tree Pool.

*John, Jane and Sol, with a truck load of dead rabbits, Katanning*

When Walter and John first arrived in Fremantle and Perth, they quickly gained work, probably due to their sawmilling background, at a sawmill about forty miles north of Perth.

The work was very hard and hot, with the milling experience

cutting the hardwood Jarrah timber being completely different from the softwood pine milling of home. After two or three months, John found a better milling job further south.

Walter went back to Perth and got a general farmhand job at a mixed-use farm outside Perth, but still twenty-seven miles away from any shops.

After a year as Australian residents, Walter and Charlotte became Australian citizens, which allowed them to work anywhere. They moved to Perth, and Walter became a furniture store salesman.

From there, he lived and worked on a chicken farm, eventually owning the farm and working to produce and sell eggs, while also becoming the manager of a small, army surplus store. They worked both jobs for three years, without a break or a holiday. In the end, they struggled to get ahead even with the extremely hard work.

With this experience, they decided to immigrate to Canada for a change and, hopefully, a better life, to swap the heat of Australia for the cold of Canada. At least the environment there would be familiar to their winter experience growing up in Czechoslovakia. They sold up and were on a boat to England after twenty-eight days, then to America. They arrived in England in November 1952, and after a short break, boarded the *Queen Mary* for its last voyage to New York.

*Martha, Jane and Jarka/Jarmila, Katanning*

John, Jarka, and baby Solly stayed in Western Australia, working and living on the farm at Cherry Tree Pool, but a short while after Walter and Charlotte left for Canada, John left on his own to meet up with them and stay in Canada. As soon as he got a job there, he sent word back to Western Australia, and Jarka with Sol travelled to be with him.

John had decided to investigate Canada soon after Erwin contracted bad asthma while working at the Cherry Tree Pool farm. This came from the dust on the farm, sawdust from working at the sawmill, and also breathing rat poison and breaking up hard bags of superphosphate fertiliser at the Gnowangerup farm.

Several times he had to be taken to Kojonup Hospital for treatment. Because of this, the decision was finally made to find a permanent town-based job in Katanning and live there. One benefit, amongst many, was that Erwin could join the local chess club there, to take up the hobby or pastime he had enjoyed so much in the past.

*Erwin Sax playing chess in Katanning.*

From here this chapter is composed of stories written by Jane Trigg, nee Sax. They are her original memories and her own composition:

## *Photos and Fragments*

I was in my mid-teens before I knew that, according to Jewish law, I was Jewish.

It was not that prior to my teenage years people were celebrating Bar Mitzvahs and fiddling on the roof around me, and I was too dim-witted to notice. On the contrary, nothing overtly Jewish was happening around me. My family celebrated Christmas and ate pork. We didn't look Jewish, I thought. We wore no funny clothes.

There was my ski-jump nose, of course, but I had too-narrow an experience of ethnic groups to recognise my features as Semitic. There were other clues, too, fragments I can piece together now I know how to look for them.

At the time, I didn't realise I was Jewish because neither of my parents or anyone else around me mentioned it. My father maintained a conspiracy of silence which lasted until his death at the age of 88.

### The story begins:

Outside it is freezing. The wind slices the sky, bangs against the back door of the old house, and seeks out the cracks in the timbered walls. Inside, a fire blazes in the old 'Metters' stove. A pot of chicken soup simmers on one edge. My mother stands at the stove, turning the potato latkes which are my favourite food. She calls them potato pancakes. I watch the latkes sizzle in the hot fat and slowly turn brown. Surreptitiously, I nibble the crisp edges of one which has just been cooked and which my mother has placed on a warming plate near the pot of soup.

"Jana, don't be so impatient. It is nearly lunchtime." She smiles at me and I sprinkle the pancake with salt and begin to eat. I'm eight years old and at school but now it is school holidays. Lunchtimes on holidays are special.

The phone rings, causing us to start. It has not been installed for very long, this magical device which sits so imposingly on the wall.

"Watch the pancakes for me," says my mother, moving the pan to the side and going to the phone. She listens quietly, then looks puzzled.

"Yes," I hear her say. "This is the home of Mr Sax." There is a pause.

"His first name? It is Irwin." Another pause.

"Ervin? Yes, that is his name in Czechoslovakia. Why do you want to know?"

The pause is longer this time.

"I see. A letter. From Israel. You think Ervin should come in to see you. I think this afternoon it could be arranged. 2 o'clock at the Road Board Office. I will tell him. Thank you."

I do not know what Israel is and have only a vague idea about the Road Board but they sound important. I make excuses not to play with my best friend who lives next door. All afternoon I help my mother in the small shop which is at the front of the house, waiting for my father to come home.

When he returns, my father is silent. The only evidence of his appointment is an envelope.

"It's a letter from Bruno," he tells my mother. He tells me nothing.

At night I lie awake in my small bedroom listening to the sound of their voices rising and dipping like waves on the beach. They talk in rapid Czech and I cannot make meaning from their words. All I follow is the tone of the conversation. My father's voice is defensive, defiant, and firm. My mother pleads, placates, soothes. I catch a mention of my name and fall asleep.

In the morning there are four black and white photos on the kitchen table. It is years before I recognise that they represent a victory for my mother. I finger them gingerly, reverently. One is of a man in front of a large building. Now, with adult eyes, I can see that it looks like a six-storey office block and is un-finished. A temporary ramp leads to the entrance and scaffolding is still attached to one end of the building. Modern Israel is emerging. Then I ignore the building, focusing on the man in the foreground who wears a white shirt, black pants and what seems to be a white apron.

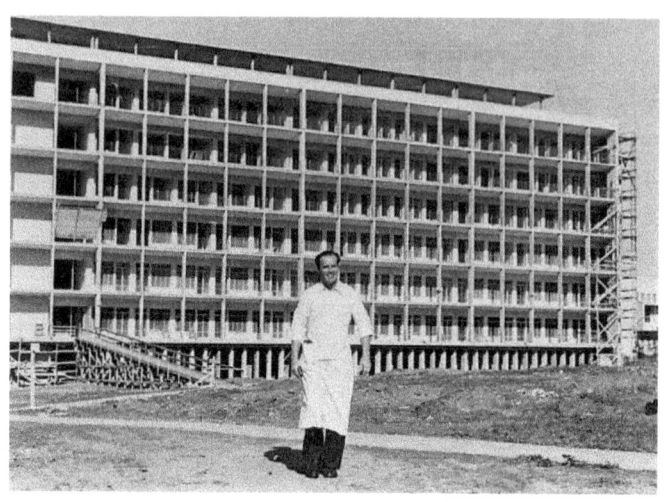

*Dr. Bruno Sax, in front of a new hospital, Israel*

This, my mother tells me, is my uncle Bruno. He is my father's brother and a Doctor. The photo is of his hospital in Tel Aviv in Israel. Another of the photos is of Bruno at his desk. I take in the information. Even then I delight in the sound of the words. Uncle, Tel Aviv. I have a distant memory of the word 'uncle'. Tel Aviv is a new word. So too is 'Bruno'. I try them out. I am too young to notice that there is a phone on Bruno's desk. Bruno has a phone. We have a phone. No one makes a connection.

*Dr. Bruno Sax, at work, Israel*

Another two photographs are of my cousin, Ruti. In one photo, Ruti is a baby, lying on her stomach on a rug. In the other, she is a child of two or three, a pretty child with curly hair and a big smile. She has a lollipop to her lips. I am delighted, captivated.

For the next few years, a smiling child holding a lollipop becomes my concept of 'Israel'.

When I am much older, my mother tells me that for two or three years prior to the arrival of Bruno's letter, his three brothers and sister didn't know where we were. My father never wrote. The last place we were known to have lived was Katanning and finally, in desperation, Bruno wrote to the Katanning Road Board and asked if we still lived in the area or if anyone knew where we had gone.

It is not surprising that I have an unusual concept of terms like 'Israel' and 'family'. Family was the three of us. We did not have Jewish names like Moshe, Golde and Miriam. We were Ervin, Marta and Jana. Not that we got to keep those names in Australia. Anglicised, we became Irwin, Martha and Jane. Apart from the three of us, 'family' arrived in letters and parcels in the mail. The contents of these communications were always cryptic. Occasional letters from Eva. A photo from Jarka and Sol, dressed in warm coats and hats, standing by a bare tree in Toronto. A book of children's verse written in Czech from Viktor in Prague. The prettiest pink nightie I had ever seen and some newspapers from Walter and Shari in Los Angeles.

A family disbursed.

The nightie arrives when I am in high school. I start to become interested in my background, my origins. I resent being an only child, questioning why I have no siblings. My father turns it into a joke.

"We had you and thought that was enough to inflict on the world," he quips.

I am not pacified but know not to question my father further. I fear one of his silent rages and their consequent pressure on my mother. She hints at a miscarriage, reticently, as she is uncomfortable talking about sexual matters. I have teenage children of my own when I meet Bruno, now a gynaecologist, who tells me of my own difficult birth and their concerns for my mother who was 36 when I was born. This is old for a first-time mother in 1948.

My paternal grandmother had probably had 10 of her 13 children by the time she was in her mid-thirties.

I continue to go to the Methodist Church I have been attending for years. My mother originally sent me to Sunday school because that is what Australian families did in the fifties. I attend an active and lively youth group. Most of the group are there because of social contacts; to get a girlfriend or boyfriend. I sense I am different because I enjoy the religious experience. I enjoy seeking. I also enjoy belonging.

"Mum, was I baptised when I was a baby?" I ask.

"Yes, I think so." She is preoccupied, evasive.

"Where are the papers?" I pester. "All my friends have papers. I need to show them at church or I'll have to get baptised again."

"You were baptised at the hospital in Jihlava," my mother replies, "and I don't know if there were any papers. We don't have any. It might be easier if you are baptised here anyway."

My mother often joins me at church services. My father doesn't come. Not yet. Now, as a teenager, I want to be baptised. It is important for me to belong somewhere, to be part of a larger family.

Our photos are not arranged neatly in photo albums, with each photo having a neat inscription as I find in friends' homes. Some are placed haphazardly in old albums, photo corners keeping memories precariously in place. Others are stored loosely in an old box. I flick through them, trying to make sense of them. My mother talks openly now that I am older. I look at a photo of a young girl and a young boy. They are squatting, playing with some ducklings. There is a larger photo, a close-up of the girl. I wear my hair as I did at that age with a customary central bow.

*Judith Sax with ducks and friend, before WWII*

"Look, here are a couple of photos of me. Who am I playing with?"

I continue to rummage.

"Here's another one." A different dress but the same bow.

I peer at the photo.

"Where was this taken?" The buildings are old and wooden and there appears to be a bath outside on some cement blocks. "And who is the woman?"

My mother is silent. For a while she says nothing. Then she speaks, she does so quietly.

"That is Grandma Sax, your grandmother."

"But she died before I was born," I say. My tone is accusing, angry. Something is wrong. I have been told that my four grandparents died before I was born. Now it seems I have a grandmother after all, or did have and no one has told me. My mother is silent again. I look at her face and my rage dies. Whatever she has to tell me is difficult. I encourage her to talk; and for once I keep quiet and listen. And so I hear the story of Judith, my half-sister and for the first time, some of the story of my family.

I hear how both sets of grandparents lived in villages in Czechoslovakia; my mothers' family near Brno and my fathers' family on the border of Slovakia. Both families were Jewish and my parents were bought up as practising Jews, a practice they later gave up. In their twenties, my mother and father married. My mother married a young lawyer named Karel and my father married Gaby. Judith, the girl in the photo, the girl I thought was me, was their daughter.

My mother tells me that just prior to World War II, because of anti-Semitic feeling, anyone who could leave the country was encouraged to do so. An escape route was planned through to Palestine. My mother went with Karel. My father and Gaby wanted to go, too, but agonised over Judith. The boat trip they were about to undertake was illicit and dangerous and people were advised not to take children. The old and the young would surely be safe in Czechoslovakia. Judith was left with Grandma Sax.

After the war and without Gaby, whom he had divorced, my father returned to Novy Hrosenkov. Of the 11 children, their spouses and children who had been living before the war, only Eva and her family and my father and his three brothers remained.

Judith and Grandma Sax were no longer in the village. There were reports of them being sent away to a concentration camp. Nothing was confirmed. They searched, my mother said. Firstly, my father and then when they were married, my mother helped. They only left for Australia after they had exhausted all leads and all possibilities.

"Why doesn't he ever speak about it?" I ask.

My mother shrugs her shoulders. "He feels badly about it," is all she says.

I must feel bad about it, too. I don't ever mention my Jewish background to anyone until I am 19 and can't talk about it openly until much later.

It is again Bruno who fills in some of the gaps when he visits us in Perth. He tells me, as my parents did not, how my father found the names of Johanna and Judith Sax on the list of those killed in the concentration camps when he and his brother visited Beit Hatfutsot, the Diaspora Museum in Tel Aviv. I realise as he speaks that I have been harbouring the hope that I have a sister alive, somewhere. The feeble hope sputters and dies. As it must have died with my father.

After my mother dies aged 77, my father is depressed. I try to cheer him up on the phone, telling him of all the good things he has done and how wonderful his grandchildren are. He refuses to be encouraged.

"Jana, I have done some things I regret," he says.

I take a risk.

"I know about Judith," I tell him.

"How long have you known?"

"For a long time."

He is quiet on the other end of the phone.

"You made a decision based on what information you had," I say. Now he is more Jewish than I realise.

Now that he has mentioned it, I wanted to talk more, to finally bring it out in the open.

"You wouldn't know how it would turn out. What you did is nothing you should be ashamed of."

"It is nothing to be proud of," he says sadly and hangs up. He never refers to it again.

Forgiveness. Guilt. I believe in one, my father in the other. Maybe he is more Jewish than I realise.

"The Lord is slow to anger, and abounding in steadfast love, forgiving iniquity and transgression, but he will by no means clear the guilty, visiting the iniquity of fathers upon children, upon the third and fourth generation."

I am only the first generation; or the second depending on how I count. It feels like the third or fourth. Maybe I am more Jewish than I realise.

On her return from Israel, my middle child is ecstatic. She has had a wonderful time with Bruno and Chagit, their children, all the grandchildren and Chagit's extended family.

"Do you know," she says excitedly, "that I could live in Israel and become an Israeli citizen. I had a Jewish grandmother."

"Yes Kathe, I know. Do you want to go and live there?"

"No. But it is nice knowing I can. Come," she says, "and catch up on the family. Come and have a look at my photos."

## *Memories on the West Australian Farm*

Jana was the first to see the car coming.

"Mummy, Daddy," she called. "Pan Williams is here."

"Mr Williams," Marta corrected Jana's lapse into Czech automatically, her mind preoccupied with the importance of what she was saying.

It was Friday, farmers shopping day and Marta and Erwin were almost ready to get into the truck and go to town. The pantry was almost empty. Erwin had worked hard for days on end and needed the rest and they had promised that day to Jana. She loved the monthly visits to town and had been marking off days on the calendar since their last shopping day. Marta had promised her some new shoes and some material for a frock. And now the owner and his wife had arrived on one of their surprise visits.

While Marta waited for the William's old Holden to bump its way down the track and pull up at the front gate, she quietly explained to Jana that they'd have to wait until the next week to go to town. "And live on mutton and rabbit again," she thought bitterly.

She was surprised at the calmness with which Jana accepted the decision and realised she was excited at the prospect of visitors. It brought home to her once again her isolation. For Jana to be excited by a visit from Joe and Ethel Williams was a sad indication of their lack of social contact.

*Martha and young Jane, in a Western Australian wheat field*

Marta was pleased now that Erwin had worked so hard recently. At least everything was in order and ready even for one of Joe's inspections. The stock was in good shape now there had been a bit of early rain and the grass had begun to grow. The fences were as good as hard work and second-rate material could make them. There was even almost enough superphosphate for seeding. Joe had bought the super before the war because he could get a large amount cheaply. It had sat where it had been dumped and moisture had set it rock hard. It might still be sitting there had Joe not taken advantage of Erwin's willingness to work. He didn't know and wouldn't have been bothered if he had, that Erwin jumped out of bed during his nightmares after a day crushing super.

Joe's inspection of the property would have begun as soon as he'd come to its boundaries. He would have already noticed its tidy, prosperous appearance and Marta hoped for Erwin's sake that there might be a word or two of praise this time.

"Hello Joe, Ethel, it is nice to see you," said Erwin.

"...Lo Erwin, Lo Mrs Sax," Joe replied in his timeless voice as he climbed out of the car. "It was such a fine morning that Ethel and I thought we'd go for a drive and we just happened to end up here."

Marta laughed to herself. It was 60 miles from the home farm where they lived and Joe would never go anywhere just for a drive. Sightseeing was a waste of time in his opinion. He would never admit he'd come to inspect the farm, however, and there was always an elaborate charade played out around Joe 'happening to be driving past'.

"See the home dam is looking dry. Could do with some more rain here too."

"Oh well," thought Marta, at least it wasn't criticism and after polite greetings all around they moved into the house.

Once inside, the first task was to stoke the fire and put on the kettle for the inevitable cup of tea. Marta felt uncomfortable and unhappy about the morning tea. Normally she had a good stock of home-made cakes or biscuits, especially some Czech specialities which Erwin and Jana loved, but this time the cupboard was almost bare.

"Like Old Mother Hubbard's," she thought with a laugh, recalling Jana's nursery rhyme book which was helping her learn English.

They made do with what food there was. Except that Marta always provided a large spread whenever they came, the Williams would probably not have noticed the lack of home baked food. Despite their three prosperous properties, their usual morning tea was a cup of tea and Granita biscuits. Small wonder they were as lean as greyhounds.

Marta was quiet during the morning tea. Her command of spoken English was still less than perfect. Erwin kept telling her it would never improve unless she practised but she didn't feel like practising on Joe and Ethel. Erwin was talking to them both on farming matters. Jana sat on Erwin's knees, pleased to be a part of adult conversation and delighted when Mrs Williams praised her good manners.

If Marta's tongue was still, her thoughts were busy. At first, they had centred on the morning tea and then in a panic about what she would serve for lunch. Once that passed, she thought about the house. After the tiny dwelling they'd occupied on the home property when they had first started working for the Williams, the recent house seemed enormous. The home property house had been filthy before they had moved in and this one had been as bad, probably worse. It had been unoccupied for a while and there were damp patches where neglected cracks had let the rain in. Erwin had a bad attack of asthma during the winter mainly due to the damp and they'd had to fight old Joe to even get the worst of the cracks repaired. Worse than the dirt and the cracks, though, had been the rats. They'd been everywhere. On the unlined enclosed back veranda which also served as the wash house, Marta could see their tails hanging over the rafters. They'd made such a din at night. She shuddered at the thought.

Erwin had worked hard outside and they had both worked hard inside. Now the house was clean, warm, comfortably if sparsely furnished and rat free. If only Ethel could see it and realise it didn't take money to make a home. Marta doubted it would even register. If it did, she would be more likely to suggest a drop in salary because they seemed to be managing so well. Marta wondered if she was being perhaps a little uncharitable.

It was decided that she would stay at the house and prepare the lunch while the others went around the farm.

"Might as well see the place while we're here," Joe had said.

It was an arrangement which suited everyone, especially Jana who delighted in going around the farm with her father. While Ethel found the bathroom, Erwin helped Marta stack the dishes. As they worked, they made a private bet that as soon as Ethel saw the vegetable garden she would say, "Oh, what lovely tomatoes. Aren't they dear in the shops?" Marta even put a paper bag aside, having long since learnt that Mrs Williams would never buy what she could be given.

She remained true to character. As they went through the garden she made polite noises about the display of flowers but it was the vegetable garden which sparked the only real interest she'd shown so far.

"Oh, what lovely beans. And look at those tomatoes. Joe, just look at the tomatoes. Aren't they expensive in the shops now, dear?"

The last remark was addressed to Marta, who said she get her a few to take home.

Marta made good use of the time they were away. Erwin had killed a sheep midweek so she still had plenty of meat. She chose a number of chops and put them in the oven to cook. She put a few potatoes in a saucepan and boiled them to make a potato salad. She picked the tomatoes for Mrs Williams and a few more for lunch. There was still one lettuce and the last of the cucumbers. She decided she could always add a few hard-boiled eggs if she needed to. The hens had been laying quite well lately. She decided to make a cake for dessert and just put it in the oven with the chops when she heard the car coming too quickly down the track. As it neared the gate, the horn tooted.

Waiting outside, Marta saw Erwin lifting Jana from the car. He was holding a cloth to her face and even from a distance Marta could tell it was bloodied. Her eye! She had lost an eye! Couldn't they even be trusted to take a child for a drive around the farm? The doctor. They must get her to the doctor. The nearest was miles away. Jana would be blind for life.

Marta took in only a small part of Mrs Williams' chatter, designed she knew to calm her down. Ethel had been a nurse prior to her marriage and Marta realised afterwards that she had been subjected to Ethel's 'soothe an anxious mother technique'. It did penetrate her anxious mind that Jana had not lost an eye. However her talk of 'only a small scratch, …the men looking at the sheep, …one of the dogs out, …Jana at the car window,… other dog trying to get through the window … didn't mean any harm' grated on Marta's nerves. Her concern was for Jana. Blame could be apportioned later.

Jana lay very quietly in Erwin's arms while Marta washed her face. Marta wasn't sure if Jana was in shock or whether there really was little pain. Ethel had been right. The eye was untouched. The blood had come from a deep gash on one side of the eye and a few smaller scratches on her cheek.

Although the damage was much less than Marta's imaginings, she still wanted to take Jana to the doctor. The gash could need stitching and she wanted her to have a tetanus injection. As soon as she voiced this intention both Joe and Ethel spoke at once.

"I don't really think we need to go to the doctor, dear."

"Unnecessary. Waste of time."

"We'll put some Solyptol on those scratches."

"Ethel here's a nurse. She knows what to do."

"She's young and healthy and will heal quickly."

"Besides, I wanted to shift some sheep this afternoon with Irwin and check the machinery for seeding. Can't come all this way for nothing."

At Joe's last words, Marta saw red and spoke out to say if he hadn't come on one of his unannounced, unwelcome visits, they would have been in town and none of this would have happened. Either he trusted them to run the farm or he didn't. And if he did trust them and thought they were doing a fair job, why did he pay Irwin such low wages? And miss their one day in the month off. Weren't they are entitled to even one day a month off?

Marta continued in the same vein, mustering all the good English she knew and lapsing into broken English or Czech if that proved insufficient. She didn't know who looked the more surprised, Irwin or the Williams. Joe and Ethel probably didn't think she knew so many English words. Marta hoped her language reflected more of Old Mother Hubbard than the shearers they'd had on the property a while ago. She blushed at the recollection of some of the shearers' language.

Joe and Ethel seemed to take her red face for anger or embarrassment and during the confusion, Marta went to check on lunch. She left Irwin with Jana and the Williams. While she was in the kitchen, she could hear voices. She'd done it now, she thought. Joe would be asking Irwin to leave. Where would he find another job? At 40 years of age it wasn't easy to start again in a new country, especially without a reference. Although she found the Williams trying, Marta loved the farm. She looked around at the old, comfortable kitchen. It would be hard to leave. Then her mind caught sight of the bloodied cloth at Jana's face when Irwin took her out of the car. No one would stand between her child and medical aid. The Williams could take their job and go…

She turned with a start as Joe came into the kitchen. He couldn't meet her eyes and stumbled over his words in uncharacteristic fashion while he told her that he and Ethel thought she and Irwin should go on a holiday.

"Get away for a bit, Mrs Sax. You and Irwin have been working so hard. The coast is very nice. You haven't been there yet, have you? Jana would enjoy the beach. I'll give Irwin a small bonus, so you'll have some money to spend. And I think I'll increase his salary a bit when you get back. Just a bit, to show we appreciate what you're doing here."

Jana still had her sight; Irwin still had a job; they were going on a holiday, their first in Australia and maybe there would be a rise in pay. Marta smiled, then burst into tears. Joe looked away and went back into the other room.

"Bloody foreigners. All the same. All temperamental. All temperamental."

Marta could imagine him saying it to Ethel all the way back home. But she didn't care. She didn't care.

*Jarka, John, Sol, Jane and Martha, on holiday, Albany, WA*

*Jane Sax – on display!*

# A family of shopkeepers:

Outside it is freezing. The wind slices the sky and bangs against the side door of the shop. Inside it is little better. The shop is large and the floor is cement. To please Mum, Dad has bought black rubber matting to run along the counter but it hardly warms the floor at seven in the morning. We move quickly to try to keep warm, blowing on our hands as we go. When she comes in later in the morning, Val, who is a partner in the business, will be wearing mittens, the fingers like deep pink sausages in black skins. I disdain the mittens, obstinately clinging to chilblains instead.

"I'll do the fridge," says Mum, in typical fashion, taking on all the worst jobs. It is not just that the fridge is cold but all the shelves have to be wiped down and any meat which even looks suspect has to be sorted out. I am just emerging from a 'polony only' phase and moist Polish sausage and the wrinkly skin of kabanos is more than I want to tackle at this hour in the morning.

I leave her to it and begin to clean the long counter in front of the fruit and vegetable shelves. I scrub down the wood, my task made easier because I didn't realise the benefits laminex or melamine surfaces would bring to the job. I clean under the scales and then, because Mum has cleaned the fridge, I tackle the meat slicer, carefully taking it apart, boiling the kettle to get some warm water to wash it all down. It's the only way to get the hands warm and I suffer the sausage meat effect of hundreds of slicings of polony, silverside or ham for a few moments of warmth.

A truck reverses up to the door. It will be Cyril, the courier. Cyril the Squirrel as I've called him since I was young and learned the power of language and of rhyme. I hear low voices. Dad has come to give Cyril a hand to unload the fruit and vegetables which came three times a week from the markets in Perth.

When we first started the little shop, Dad used to get the produce himself. He'd go off early in the morning in the little Morris Minor utility with its canvas-covered back and bring it all home. As I grew older, that was one of my delights, to go to the station with him. It was like a treasure hunt, finding the boxes marked "I.E.Sax & Co" after the station staff had dumped the goods for all the shops on the station platform and then mostly left the work of finding our own cases up to us. The business has now prospered to the stage where we can afford to pay Cyril to locate and deliver the produce.

*First Sax residence and little shop, Katanning*

Outside, wooden cases slide along the metal tray of the truck, are heaved down and stacked against the wall at the back door. Cyril relays the town gossip, amicably chatting as he unloads. Dad's voice is deep and his accent still strong despite his years in Australia. The door opens.

"Marta, the vegetables are here."

"Coming, Ervin."

Mum moves quickly to give Dad a hand.

For some time, we are all involved in handling fresh produce. Fruit and vegetables which are to be stored go into the cool room; produce to be sold goes from the cool room onto the shelves. We carry, unwrap, unpack, arrange. I stay near the shelves. In summer I might offer to work in the cool room, more eager, then, to escape the searing heat of an inland town. Today it holds no attraction. It is only later that I find it ironic that someone who was born in Europe in the middle of a winter snowstorm should so dislike the cold.

I was born, so I am told and so the records state, in Jihlava, which is a town in the centre of Czechoslovakia. I arrived at night on the evening of December 18$^{th}$; winter in Europe and it was snowing. Typical of the time, my father was not present at my birth. He was not even pacing the corridor outside the Labour ward, ready to hand out cigars – or whatever is the Czech equivalent. He was at our home in the small village of Polna, about 20 kilometres away, having taken my mother to the hospital some time previously. The hospital phoned him after my birth and I know, because he told me when I was quite young, that he was pleased that the baby was a girl. Some years later, having learnt more about European males, I wondered why he had not wanted a son to carry on the family name.

A screech of brakes, a door slamming and the creak of double doors opening, indicates that the baker has arrived. The smell of warm bread and buns reaches us and our stomachs rumble. I arrange the bread on the open shelves under the fruit and vegetables, removing some sticky buns for us to have for morning tea. Mum opens the shop doors and a few minutes later, on cue, Mrs Anderson shuffles into the shop.

"Good morning Jane," she says.

"Good morning Mrs Anderson," I replied, sighing inwardly. Mum is sweeping the veranda at the front of the shop, greeting early customers and waving to people as they go to work. Dad has a sixth sense about Mrs Anderson's arrival and is nowhere to be seen.

"How are you this morning?" I enquire.

I listen absent-mindedly to a general rundown on her health and how her arthritis is bothering her.

"What would you like today?" I ask, once the medical report is complete.

"A pound of potatoes, a small piece of pumpkin…"

"… and is the bread fresh?" I complete the sentence in my mind before she has uttered it. The smell of newly baked bread still lingers in the air and if you look hard, you can still see the steam rising from the bottom shelf. Perhaps Mrs Anderson can neither see nor smell. I hold my tongue, not an easy task for me at any time and definitely not as a 12-year-old.

"… and is the bread fresh?"

"Yes Mrs Anderson, the baker has just been." I hope my grimace through clenched teeth will pass for a smile.

"Then I'll have half a loaf of white, dear."

I attend to her purchases, completing the ritual. She fusses over her purse, thanks me and shuffles out. Mum has come in, tidying and arranging along the biscuit aisle as she comes behind the counter. I envy her ease with customers, her ability to chat and seemingly give them her full attention while still getting the work done. Perhaps the fact that she was born into it has helped:

"Marta, quickly, your father is looking for you. He's very cross. You should be helping your mother in the shop, not playing with the boys. Viktor, you should know better. Jezis marja, we will never make Marta into a lady if you bring her outside and play tomboy games. And does anyone know where Isidore is? Sigmund wants him to help kill the geese. Quickly children."

Reluctantly, Marta followed Rosa, going inside to wash her hands and help her mother in the shop. She felt a moment's frustration with Rosa, even anger. Then she sighed. It was not the servant's fault that she had to come inside, she thought. Her mother must be busy and need her to help. Sigmund wouldn't give it. The shop was women's work. Marta sighed again. Holidays were so precious; a time to see the boys. It was good to play again with Viktor, though since she had been away at school in Brno he had grown and was starting to take a pride in how he looked. He was not nearly so keen to play childish games and get dirty as they used to do. She wondered how long he would be content to stay in Boretice. Handsome Otto was already attracting the girls and working hard on the farm. Quiet Isidore was nearly a man now, different to the other two, with his dark hair and black eyes. He irritated his father and bore the brunt of his infamous temper. Marta knew Sigmund Weinstein was a hard man. The busy store and prosperous farm attested to his skill as a provider but he had little patience with the children. He was not patient with anyone really, except Marta sometimes, especially when she was little.

"Father," said Marta, her nose pressed to the window out at the rain. "I want to go and play with Alenka, but I'll get wet going to her house."

"Not if you run between the drops, Marti," he replied earnestly.

"Oh, thank you, Father."

Marta was out the door, zigzagging to avoid the falling rain.

Surely even Sigmund smiled to see her run.

For much of my life, the location of Boretice (pronounced with guttural sounds and much scraping of the back of the mouth) was a mystery to me. For a long time, I assumed it was near the village of Novy Hrozenkov, on the border of the Czech and Slovak sections of the country where my father was born and grew up.

When I was a child, I can remember asking my mother, "Did you know Dad when you were young?"

"I didn't know him, but I knew the family, some of his brothers and knew something about them, as you do in country villages."

The answer was vague, full of implications rather than information. The villages were nearby; the families knew of each other; there was some contact.

Some years later, I am sitting at the kitchen table at the new house. With its black Laminex-edged with corrugated chrome, it is the height of fashion. The chairs are also chrome with yellow vinyl padding trimmed in black. I am doing my German homework.

"Mum, is this right?" I'm struggling with the order of a difficult sentence.

"No," she says. "That doesn't sound right. It should be…" and corrects my sentence.

"Why do you say it that way?" I argue. "It doesn't say to do that in my book."

"Maybe not, but that's how the Germans say it."

"How do you know that's how they say it?"

"When I was eight, my parents sent me away to a German-speaking school. They wanted me to get a better education than I could get in the village and they thought it would be good for me if I learnt another language."

"Did you like the school?" I am much more interested in these revelations than in my homework.

"It was a long way from home and I was home-sick and lonely. All of the lessons were in German and for a while it was very hard." She pauses, reflectively.

"Who did you live with?" I ask, fascinated, wanting to know more.

She emerges from her reverie. "Do you need any more help with your sentences," she says. "I have to finish getting tea for your father."

I know better than to ask any more. My mother was sent away to school in Germany.

Implications, evasions, gaps which will never be filled, jigsaw puzzle pieces which do not fit together. Boretice is miles from Novy Hrozenkov. The school my mother attended was in Brno, the nearest large town to Boretice and a long way from Germany. I have no idea where she stayed. Piecing together my parent's lives is like putting together a complex jigsaw puzzle with the help of only a faded, out-of-focus photograph taken from far away on a misty day.

The shop. In all of my early memories, the shop is the centre, the focus. First the little shop, then the bigger building on the corner, *Sax's Corner*. Their shadows still hover over me all these years later.

The little shop was a single timber room, originally connected to and forming the front of the house, the only house which my parents could rent at the time in Katanning. In my memory, the page showing the building intact, shop and house together, is hazy. I can remember the house well. Like the shop, it is timber, not only in its frame and outside walls but inside as well. There are three main rooms. A long narrow kitchen runs along the back of the house. It has a Metters wood stove and a tap, not far from the floor, which runs from the rainwater tank outside. To get hot water, Mum has to boil water on the stove. Dishes are washed in a basin on the bench under the window. We not only eat here but spend most of our time in the room, especially in winter.

The kitchen leads into a lounge room whose walls and even the ceiling are wood panelling and its interior is dark and gloomy. Deep brown blinds covered small windows. The first argument I can remember my parents having was over this room. Czech friends, Maria and Frank Rempta, offered to help Mum fix up the room by papering over the walls. Dad was furious. Usually he spoke English, insisting we did too. "When in Rome, do what the Romans do," I can hear him saying. In his tirade, he rants in Czech.

"Why are you wasting money making the place look nice, woman? Do we have so much money we can throw it away? Are we not lucky to have a roof over our heads? When Jana is hungry, will you give her wallpaper to eat?"

We eat as usual; wallpaper lightens the walls. My father doesn't speak to my mother for days.

*Erwin and Martha's store, Katanning. "Sax's Corner".*

My parents didn't intend to be shopkeepers. Especially not my father. He had been a forester with European qualifications, the equivalent of a technical college diploma. His family had owned a saw-mill and Ervin was involved in the business at managerial level. In the months before his death in Busselton, Western Australia, family details about a saw-mill bothered him.

"Have you heard from David's wife?" he asks, eyes half-closed.

"David who, Dad?"

"David Sax, my uncle," he says impatiently as if I am deliberately being dim-witted.

Sigmund's brother, previously hinted at, alluded to in discussions; now named.

"No, I haven't heard from David's wife." I don't tell him that David has probably been dead for at least 40 or 50 years.

"She wants me to take over the saw-mill."

"Does she?" I pause. "Why don't you?"

"Because." Evasions as usual. It is his turn to pause. "Besides, I don't like her daughters."

"Why, what did they do?"

"They were not very nice."

"When was this, Dad?" I haven't heard about the daughters

before and I want to keep this conversation going.

"In 1964," he says definitely. His eyes open. The past fades. "Ah, Jane," he says, "There was something I wanted to ask you. What was it?"

This conversation, with minor variations, is repeated for a number of weeks and then is no longer mentioned.

When we arrived in Western Australia in 1949, it was to the timber industry that Dad turned for employment. As his European qualifications were not recognised in post-World War II Australia, he ended up as a labourer in a mill in Perth. He felt the work was hard and it probably was. It was not helped by the fact that dad was no longer a young man and he had not been used to labouring work in mills in Czechoslovakia. He was also concerned about poor safety conditions in the mill.

As if the typical work conditions were not enough, there were also problems on the domestic front. When we arrived, we lived first of all in Victoria Park with Dad's brother, Walter, his wife Shari and Paul and Robert, their two young sons who had all arrived in Western Australia some time previously. While the brothers were pleased to be together, my mother maintained that Shari was difficult to live with and the boys destroyed my toys. I have no memory of the boys, and none of the toys either. Their loss may not have been at all significant in another family but we had arrived in the country with only £15 between the three of us and any possessions were precious. To make matters worse, there was a post-war housing shortage and landlords were very reluctant to take a family with a child. We lived for a while at Tuart Hill on the outskirts of the city, surrounded by chicken farms but it was not long before Dad looked for another job.

## Farming:

The job he took was as a farm labourer, working for Mr N P Davis, one of the early settlers and an influential farmer in Gnowangerup, 350 kilometres from Perth. At the time, this was about 12 hours from Perth by train, as well as one million kilometres and a century away from my mother's life in Europe.

N P Davis was the owner of a large property called *Clear Hills*, a former captain in the air force, a breeder of fat lambs for export, a director of the Gnowangerup District Cooperative and was involved with the Gnowangerup Brass Band. My parents saw none of this, except for the fat lambs.

From what I can gather, Dad was later appointed manager of *Hollywood Farm* at Cherry Tree Pool between Katanning and Kojonup in the Great Southern region of Western Australia. A younger brother, who I always knew as John, joined him there and together they started a saw-mill. Years later when I met Walter and Bruno, the other brothers, they referred to him as Jan (pronounced in European fashion as Yan). And the father I had always known as Irwin Erwin was really Ervin. When he had applied for Australian citizenship he had been 'encouraged' to take a more suitable Australian name and as there was an "Irwin Street" in the middle of Perth, decided on that. Similarly, Marta became Martha and Jana later became Jane. Much more sensible to be Jane than "J" (as in J), Jarna.

I was Jana for three or four years and of those I can remember probably only one. One year of connection to a Czechoslovakian background and heritage. It is very little and yet it has to be enough. It is fortunate then that although the shop is the focus of my memories, events at the farm are my earliest remembrances.

It is nearly Christmas. I know nothing of Christ in the manger, of angels, shepherds and Wise Men. I only know that Mikulmas comes to good girls and boys on Christmas Eve and may come to me. He will fill my shoes with small presents if I have been good and vegetable peelings if I have been naughty.

"Matka, Matka, where are my rubber boots?" I demand, urgently.

"Why, little Kachna?" says my mother, using her pet name for me. When I was first walking my parents thought I walked like a duck and the name stuck. "Why do you need your rubber boots?"

"I want to put them out for Mikulmas, so he will bring me lots of presents," I tell her. "My shoes are only little. My boots are much bigger." I am very serious.

My mother hides a smile and helps me find my rubber boots.

On Christmas morning, I wake in my cot in the little room next to my parents' room. It is still dark. When I can see, I creep out of bed and go to the fireplace where I have put my boots. I put my hands inside, feeling for presents. I go running into my parents' room, boot in hand.

"Mikulmas has come," I tell them excitedly. "See, he has bought me presents. I have been a good girl."

My parents examine the small gifts, sharing my excitement.

Later that day, my father goes looking for the other boot, the one filled with vegetable peelings and finds it in the wardrobe where I have hidden it.

In the autumn, after the first rains have come, Mum and I go mushrooming in the home paddock of the farm. We pick carefully and my mother shows me the difference between mushrooms and toadstools, the brown underbelly of the mushroom and its distinctive smell. In the Czech woods, my mother tells me, there are many types of mushrooms and toadstools. You can find blue ones, yellow ones. Some of them are edible. She shows me pictures. The prettiest ones, I think, are the red and white ones, the ones my mother calls muchomurka. There are no muchomurka in the paddocks at 'Hollywood', although I always look out for them.

## I Hate Chooks

I hate chooks (chickens). I've hated them since I was about 10 and our chooks got chickenpox. Very few people know chooks could have chickenpox. Any other father would have put the chooks out of their misery by quietly wringing their necks, but not my dad. He got some instructions from the Department of Agriculture then some solution and off we went. Every afternoon after school, I had to help dad catch the wretched things and he'd string them up by the legs. I would then have to dab their heads and necks with the solution. So there I'd be, ankle-deep in chicken manure, painting chooks. It was a long while before I felt the same about eating a chicken dinner again.

## Stories of the Past – Busselton

We always go the same way to see him. Along the cycle path by the bay, turning our bikes sharply left to take the track to the Village.

"That looks Hebrew," he once said, sitting in his wheelchair at the turn.

"What? The pine?" I asked, wondering if he was thinking of Israel. And why Israel and not Czechoslovakia?

"No, those words," he mumbled, looking at the sign.

"Ray Village, Home for the Elderly", the sign says. In English.

We brush past more pines, their sharp fragrance lingering on our clothes, then cut across the lawn, weaving between the trees and the frangipani. We breathe in their scent too, before we park our bikes and enter Corridor P.

Corridor P. No matter how many times staff clean, the corridor always smells the same; the astringent smell of night bottles and near misses at the bowl overriding all.

He lies on the bed, as he always does, legs straight, hands folded across the chest as if waiting for his last breath and pennies on the eyes. I gently shake him awake. He opens his eyes and without acknowledging me or speaking to me, struggles to his feet.

"Where are you going?" I ask.

"To morning tea. I have been invited."

"That's nice, but it's half-past four," I tell him. "Nearly time for dinner."

An invitation lies on his desk. It's for next week.

"Why have I been invited?" he asks.

"They've invited all the residents," I tell him.

He struggles with the information, fails to make sense of it and brushes his hair. It is something he can do. Brush his hair, delight in being invited; and leave me free to remember the past without incurring his wrath, free to tell a story.

## Memories in the Town

I was watching "Sesame Street" with our young son.

Super Grover, a spoof Sesame Street style of superman came flying in to solve yet another problem. His solution to the difficulty: to run around screaming "wooba wooba".

And I was transported back in an instant to my father's first technique when confronted with some unexpected problem – make a lot of noise. In his case it was almost always linked with attributing blame; never to himself and most often to my hapless mother. His alternative or sometimes second technique was stony silence.

A classic case was the time when the gutter leaked.

My parents had moved to Perth after years of living in the country town of Katanning and I was joining them after three years independence. The home they had bought was about five years old, a small but lovely home set in a gorgeous garden. We moved in March and about a month later the first real rain fell after summer. While walking around barefoot on the carpet, as was my habit, I felt a wet patch on the corner of the room and hesitantly mentioned it to my parents.

And the sky fell in.

My father's Achilles heel was money. He had been through two wars and the communist takeover of his country, and had started again from scratch, aged 40. The experiences had made their mark, especially in his ability to cope with problems to which money was a solution. And now we had moved to a new home which had stretched his resources while he waited for the sale of a home and business to be completed in Katanning.

This time I bore the most of his wrath. It was my bedroom that had the problem, therefore the problem was clearly my fault. Dad also said that the people who had sold us the house must have known of the problem. They had put the home on the market in summer when the problem could go undetected. Now we would have to wait until summer and do the same. My mother and I listen to that and more. My father then took refuge in a silence as real and as strong as the walls of our new home and refused to deal with the problem or talk with us.

It was my distraught mother who found the solution this time, quite by accident.

## Hobbies:

Most people have a hobby. Some play tennis or golf and some collect stamps. A number of my friends enter competitions and win prizes on a regular basis. After years living in retirement in Perth, my mother put her name down on the waiting list of old peoples' units.

My father's opposition, aided by the neighbours who didn't want the neighbourhood changed, was the idea that he would die first. Mum could then go to the oldies home, get new furniture and travel.

At times when we were visiting from the country, we would take them to quality retirement or senior citizens homes in the area where they lived to get an idea on what was available.

Eventually her hobby paid off – tranquil gardens, birds, a nicely furnished room, new drapes – at the hospice for the few days before she died.

My father then finally decided the house was too big for him to look after and so he moved, with help from the family, into a retirement unit at St Ives. The furniture from the old house did not look good in the new unit and so he bought new furniture. He then decided he wanted to meet up with his brothers at least one last time and so it was arranged that he would go with Kathe for a family gathering in Singapore.

All of these things are what my mother had pushed my father for them to do in the years before her death.

## A Story about John working on a farm in the West Australian wheat region

John was driving to town slowly, with a tractor on the back of a truck. The tractor needed repairs. Dust swirled behind him from the unsealed gravel road and he had to slow down often for potholes. He also had to slow down further for two cars, parked beside the road. The drivers were chatting and waved as he drove on. The road seemed busier than usual.

Near the town boundary he noticed a car and caravan with a man in the caravan. He continued on, arrived at the garage, and unloaded the tractor on the ramp. He explained the problem about the tractor to Len the mechanic who asked him if he had much to do. He said he only had a bit of shopping for Jarka. He was asked if he would give a vehicle a test run. He was told to go out on the road he'd come in on. He wondered why not use the highway which was bitumen.

Len told him there were suspension problems and the belt needed testing on gravel. He was told to go out about 5 miles and he did as was requested. The caravan was still there. So were lots of cars. It surprised John that quite a lot of cars were parked on the side of the road. Dust to the right indicated the cars were turning off there and dust ahead indicated even more cars.

He slowed down at the collection of cars and pulled in. He was asked if he wanted to smoke. How goes it on the farm? How is old man Williams going?

John could not make it out and asked what was happening. There was a bank manager out to see a client. A mechanic had called in to a breakdown. A farmer whose header was broken down and in for a part was parked there as well. An insurance agent was out selling insurance. There were smiles all around. Someone noticed John's blank look.

*From LHS: Young Jane, John, Jarka and Erwin Sax, on the farm, Western Australia*

That someone took him aside and said, "You see that caravan? That chap is from the Main Roads Department and he is doing a traffic count, to see if we need the road sealed. All hush, hush. No one is supposed to know what he's doing there. Do you understand?"

John understood. In fact, he saw several times, as he test-drove different vehicles for Len, twice going back the same way after a decent interval, and twice turning right to go back to town that way by a different track.

Work started on the new road as soon as the winter rains had finished. From the traffic count the volume of traffic warranted a sealed road.

# The driving test.

Erwin arrived at the farm in late December, just as harvest was beginning. Fields of golden wheat and barley stretched as far as the eye could see. In one of the paddocks, Erwin could see the harvester slowly cutting a swathe through the crop. A truck was parked in one corner of the paddock, ready to receive the harvested grain. He had observed similar scenes, repeated many times, on the drive from the station to the farm. Erwin could start in the morning, his new Boss explained, as he drove the family to the farmhouse. All hands were needed if they were to beat harvesting bans, machinery breakdowns, morning dews and even rain. Probably, because it was a bumper crop, they might get a deluge, even hail, to destroy what was standing. Still, they'd made a good start.

"Always look on the bright side," Joe said.

Erwin was at work early next morning. The air about him was cool and there was a light dew on the ground. Above, the sky was blue and cloudless, the promise he was beginning to learn, of another hot day. They would have to wait until the crop dried out again, Erwin was told. While they waited, he met Stan who was the other farmhand, was shown the machinery and was filled in on the details of the job.

Could he drive the harvester, Joe wanted to know? Erwin supposed he could, though he'd never tried. In his job as a forestry man in Europe, he'd had a lot to do with machinery but they didn't use harvesters. Joe looked at him sharply. Was Erwin trying to be funny or was it just his use of the language? You never could tell with foreigners.

"You can drive the truck then," said Joe. "We go from the paddocks into the silo in town. I'll go with you the first time and show you the ropes, then you're on your own. Think you can manage that?"

Erwin supposed he could. He was good with ropes on the mill. He didn't have an Australian driver's licence though. He'd told them that in the city when he'd been interviewed for the job. Joe looked at him again, this time with suspicion.

"But you can drive a truck, can't you?"

Of course, he could drive a truck. He'd driven cars and trucks in Europe and had a European licence. He driven all types of vehicles in the army. There was no problem with the driving, just with the license. He'd been through all this before with the man in the employment office. Joe should have been told.

"Keep your shirt on, Erwin," Joe said quickly, confusing Erwin who had no intention of removing any of his clothes. "As long as you can drive a truck, you're right. We'll see about a licence after harvest."

Harvest seemed to Erwin to go on forever. The first few days he counted his trips into town and calculated how much grain was in each load. At the end of the first week he knew exactly how much grain he had taken to the silo. By the end of the second week, he knew roughly how much grain he'd carted and had learnt a number of distinctively Australian swear words. That week the harvester had broken down and they had to wait for spare parts to come from the city. When the third week was finished, Erwin heaved a sigh of relief that seemed to shake their small weatherboard house.

It had been a week of hot weather equal to that in North Africa where he had fought in the British Army, without the cooler nights that at least encouraged sleep. Harvesting bans had been broadcast and no harvester was allowed to operate because of the fire risk. Joe had fumed. He had been hoping to catch up on the previous week's lost time. Erwin had no idea how much grain had been carted that third week.

Joe's floods and hail did not eventuate, however, and finally harvest was finished. At the little church in the town the congregation was singing "All is safely gathered in." Neither Joe nor Erwin heard the singing but they both echoed the thought, especially Joe whose bank balance would soon be bulging like the silos in town.

Erwin did not think he would ever regret that the harvest was finished, but after the activity of harvest, life seemed very humdrum on the farm. Joe made sure he was kept busy but it was work which occupied only his hands and left his mind free to do its own thinking. More and more, Erwin's mind became concerned with the matter of a driver's licence. He talked to Stan who told him he would have to pass a driving test and answer questions to get a licence.

Stan thought there was a book about it but he didn't have one. Erwin asked Joe. Normally, Joe would have snapped that Erwin could get such information from the police station. Now he was mellowed by the successful harvest and mumbled that he thought there was a book around somewhere. He was so mellowed in fact that he found the book and Erwin began to learn.

In Australia, cars drive on the left-hand side of the road. Erwin knew that. It was confusing at first but he was getting used to it. Give way to the right. That made sense. It all did, until he got down to the one-way streets. The one-way streets in the city are Hay Street, which runs east to west from Barrack Street to William Street, Murray Street which... It meant nothing. Erwin had been in the city as a pedestrian and the names of streets had meant little to him. His interview was in a building in St George's Terrace and that wasn't mentioned in the list.

Erwin would have given it up except for the knowledge that his job and the family's freedom of movement depended on the use of the farm vehicles. The use of the farm vehicles depended on a licence. The licence depended on the driving test and answering the questions. The one-way streets in the city are Hay Street which runs...

Erwin would have postponed going for the test but for Joe who announced one day that he was going into town the following morning. Erwin might as well go in with him and get his licence. Joe made it sound so easy... and Murray Street which runs from west to east from...

The next morning, Joe left Erwin and the truck outside the police station. Joe went off to attend to his business. Erwin slowly went into the police station. The town's only policeman, who was working at his desk, came to the counter as Erwin entered. Erwin explained that he had come to get a driver's licence, please, if he could. The policeman was tall and solidly built, with broad shoulders and a large protruding stomach. His voice was deep and gruff. Erwin was later to learn that many of the country policeman were of the same construction. He never worked out whether they were chosen for the job because of their qualities or whether their qualities were shaped by the job. He felt dwarfed by the man as the policeman took out a form and began to record the necessary particulars.

Name. Date of birth. Place of birth. He stumbled over Novy Hrosenkov, Czechoslovakia.

"Just as well we don't get too many of those names, mate," the policeman commented. "By the time I've written that on all the forms I need to send to the city, I won't have time to do anything else today. It will give the typists at head office some fun, too." He chuckled at the thought.

Finally, all the particulars were filled in. Now for the test, thought Erwin.

"That will be 10 shillings, Mr Sax."

Erwin handed over the money and watched the policeman complete the form, keep his two copies and give him a piece of paper. It was headed "Driver's Licence."

"I had better attend to this lot straightaway," said the policeman, indicating the two copies he'd kept, "while I can still remember what I've written."

He turned to go back to his desk.

Erwin stood, undecided, not knowing whether to speak out about the test or take the licence and run. Before he could move or speak, the policeman noticed his indecision.

"Anything else, Mr Sax?"

"The test," Erwin stuttered. "I thought there has to be a test."

"Is that all that's worrying you?"

The policeman laughed. "Yeh, there usually is a test. But I've seen you driving Joe's truck in and out of town every day since harvest began. Your driving's as good as any of the other mugs who use the roads in this town. Consider your driving test passed."

## Do you remember Jim?

"Every now and then, usually when the weather is mellow and the meal has been good, we played a prolonged game of "Do you remember?" Almost invariably someone asks, "Do you remember Jim?"

And we all laugh.

I remember Jim well. I can't remember how old he was, what clothes he wore or even what he looked like. I do remember what he did; but then my memory has been helped by countless repetition of his deeds until I'm no longer sure that the memories are all my own.

The events I remember most vividly occurred during the school holidays for I was home all the time then and worked with the men. It was not that I had to. Dad was employed on the farm (along with Jim and Stan) so I was not working on the family property. Nor was my help needed to keep the farm going. I didn't even get paid for it. Old man Williams paid his workers because the law said he had to but the law said nothing about me. I worked because I enjoyed working alongside Dad and the other men and because there was always something happening, especially when Jim was around.

On one occasion, the tractor needed to be towed. Actually, the tractor needed to be towed on many occasions. It was old and on most farms it would have been replaced. The Williams' farm was not most farms and a man often towed the tractor and one of them always managed to repair it. This particular occasion was different because Jim helped. It was different, too, because for once the tractor had not broken down miles from the farmhouses or was bogged to its axles. It broke down at the gate of one paddock which gave a straight run to the machinery shed. Dad drove the truck, Jim drove the tractor and I sat in the cabin of the truck, watching Jim and providing a commentary on progress. Progress was good. It was the easiest tow on record, until Dad slowed down as he approached the dip to the now dry creek bed. The truck slowed down. The tractor did not.

"He's going to hit," I yelled. "He's going to…"

The rest of my words were drowned by the thud of the tractor against the tray of the truck and we lurched forward under the impact. Jim was unharmed and the truck and tractor suffered only minor damage which was surprising, considering that Jim had the tractor in third gear while under tow.

Old man Williams only grumbled when he saw the damage. That was surprising, too. He had more than grumbled over Jim's early attempt at butchering.

Each week one of the men would kill a sheep which was cut up and the meat distributed among the three families on the farm. Jim was unmarried and boarded with Stan and his wife. This meat formed the basis of the families' weekly meat supply. The sheep was always one of the wethers, usually one whose wool was too rough to be worth shearing. Mr Williams would pick them out while inspecting the flocks or when handling them at crutching or dipping and would mark each with a red circle using branding paint. It was then an easy matter for the man doing the week's butchering to round up a branded sheep.

This system, along with the rest of his possible work, was explained to Jim when he first came to work on the farm. Eventually, it was his turn to kill the wether. When it was Dad's turn to kill, I helped if I was at home. I used to have the bucket ready to place under the sheep's neck when the blood started to flow after Dad cut its throat. I helped skin the sheep, too, but my butchering ability at that time was confined to collecting the fat for Mum to render and feeding scraps to the dogs. Dad wouldn't let me help Jim with the kill. He said the last thing that Jim needed would be a half-grown kid telling him what to do. I probably would have offered advice. I was good at doing that, especially at saying "If my Dad was doing that…"

I'm sure the men (Dad especially) became selectively deaf while I was around.

I didn't help Jim, but while I fed the dogs that day, I did inspect the calico bag around the sheep to make sure it was tied on properly. If it wasn't, flies would get onto the sheep while the meat was hanging. The calico covering was secure and I told Dad so, adding, "Jim passed that test O.K."

Dad boxed my ears for trying to be smart.

It wasn't until the next day that the eruption occurred. Dad, Mr Williams and I went down to the paddock to check on the rams. Mr Williams had spent an uncharacteristic amount of money to purchase four rams at a recent ram sale. He planned to use them as the basis for a stock improvement scheme. We drove around the paddock where the rams and a flock of wethers were pastured and found the rams… one… two… three. Dad and I got out of the ute and went amongst them on foot. One…two…three… Dad was the first to realise what had happened. To distinguish the new rams from the others, Mr Williams had branded them with red branding paint. Jim had come to this paddock the day before to choose his sheep for killing. He'd been looking for a sheep marked with red branding paint.

I can't remember how Dad broke the news to Mr Williams. Perhaps Mr Williams even realised it for himself. But his reaction was wonderful. I'd learned at school about volcanoes, how they rumbled and spluttered for a while and then erupted. Old man

Williams became a volcano. He spluttered over his words, finally got control over them and they gushed out in rapid succession. There was much about fools who couldn't tell a wether from a prize ram and lots of words which I gathered to my memory for future use on school friends and enemies. I listened with a growing conviction that Jim was to be lynched or at least flung off the property with his belongings thrown after him. I was disappointed, therefore, with the final outcome. Having got rid of his hot air, Mr Williams subsided into relative quietness. Jim got a long lecture on how to tell the difference between a ram, a wether and a ewe. We were all told to eat the meat slowly and savour every mouthful. In fact, it was a stringiest, toughest meat I had ever tasted and Mum had to boil it for ages to make it worth eating.

If old man Williams got over the incident quickly, then Jim seemed not to have been affected by it at all. He remained cheerful at work and managed an air of "I've done nothing wrong", in the midst of his worst blunders. His favourite expressions were "She'll be right" and "It's the old man's money" (the latter said out of the hearing of the boss.) It was certainly his attitude over the petrol.

The men were seeding at the time and Dad and Jim were sharing a 24-hour shift. Jim was working the night shift from six in the night to six in the morning. At 5:30, he'd stop seeding and drive the tractor a few miles from the paddock to the farm. Dad would start at six and return home twelve hours later. It was a long day and a long night. It was not holiday time this time. Usually much of the seeding was done during the May holidays but this year the rains had been late and I was back at school. I was usually up in the morning when Dad left but I always went to meet him at night. Most nights, I'd meet him on his way home and ride in style to the farm paddock. I made the most of it.

Every few nights Dad would bring home an empty fuel drum and he and Jim would place a full one on the tractor. The 30-gallon drum would be left in the paddock so the tractor could be refuelled when necessary. One night, Jim went off with a full drum. Next morning Dad left at six as usual. After seven, I heard the tractor coming back. I was supposed to be getting ready for school but I stepped out while Mum was busy in the kitchen. It was Dad right enough, with a drum on the tractor. It was empty. The refuelling system in the paddock was dependent on gravity feed as the drum was placed on a small platform and was higher than the tractor's fuel tank. Jim had "forgotten" that the gravity feed would operate even if the tractor wasn't there and had left the hose in the drum hanging over the edge. Consequently, 30 gallons of fuel had run out during the night and Dad had to spend two hours going out and in and out again with a new drum.

Jim laughed when told.

"Musta forgot the hose," he said. "She's apples. It's the old man's money."

The only time I remember Jim's composure being upset was at the end of the harvest, at the beginning of the new year. He'd been sent to burn the stubble and, from the next paddock, Dad and I could see the tractor and combine moving around the paddock and smell the smoke. Dad and I had been working for some time repairing a fence, when he heard a yell.

"Fire! Fire! Erwin, Erwin, come quickly. Fire! Fire!"

We turned to the sound of the voice and saw Jim waving and yelling in an agitated fashion. Dad straddled the fence and ran across the paddock towards the tractor and combine. Jim went with him. By the time I caught up with Jim, I could hardly see anything for smoke. It was dark and dense and smelt like rubber burning. The tractor moved forward and I could just make out Dad driving it. Jim was waving a branch at the combine in a mildly hysterical way. I was about to yell out as I was sure the tractor was on fire and would explode. Then I realised the tractor and Dad were all right.

The combine wasn't.

Jim had decided the burning was going too slowly and was taking too long. Instead of using the combine to rake the stubble into heaps and burning from one heap to the next, he decided to take some burning stubble, drag it along with the combine and set fire to the stubble that way. It had worked well for a few yards and then the wooden seedbox on the combine had caught fire and Jim had left the tractor and combine to "run for his life." At least that is the way he saw it.

"Panicked, stupid fool" was Dad's verdict.

It was left to dad, when he arrived on the scene, to unhitch the combine from the tractor and drive the tractor away to prevent both being burnt. The combine had both tyres and the seedbox burnt out and its paintwork was never the same. Mr Williams bought new tyres and a new seedbox and reckoned "she was as good as new."

I thought differently. I liked shiny new machinery.

Jim decide to leave soon afterwards. He said he had had enough of farm work. He told me he'd been too long in the game and worked too hard. He wanted to go where the work was easier, the pay higher and where a person of his abilities had some future. We moved to another of Mr Williams farms not long after Jim left and we heard of him only occasionally. We often wondered what happened to him. Dad thinks he stayed with farm work as that was all he knew. Mum hoped he married a nice girl and settled down. When I look around at the state of the country and particularly when I deal with government departments, I think I know what happened to Jim. I think he joined the public service. I can hear him now saying, "She's right. It's the boss's money."

## Katanning – by Geoff Trigg

I know Katanning well. I have been there in all seasons, as an engineer working for the WA State Railways, as a tourist and while visiting the Czech friends of Jane's family, after the Sax family moved to Perth and before I married Jane. These friends of the Sax family were Fred and Val Blazek, with daughter Denise. Before Denise was born, Jane used to spend a lot of her holiday time with the Blazeks. In the early days, after the war, Fred worked as a contractor for the Main Roads Department and they travelled to various road or bridge construction projects in the region. Jane stayed with them in their large caravan wherever they camped for a few weeks, including at Albany on the south coast. This allowed her parents to work and be assured Jane was enjoying her holidays away from the shop.

I visited Katanning in the heat, cold, rain and drought, when dust was blowing and with no wind, the sky so big and blue. It's a typical West Australian wheat-belt town, originally small but growing around a railway siding, on the rail line and highway connecting Albany on the south coast to Perth, (the State capital). The same railway brought produce from Perth to the Sax's Corner shop.

Wheat and sheep are the main industries, or were when the family lived there. Erwin worked at the garage fixing tyres, some of those tyres for huge tractors and trucks. Erwin also worked at one time for the Blazeks when they ran a local fuel agency, driving their large fuel tanker that delivered fuel to the big farms. He would fill up their farm storage tanks, which in turn kept the tractors and harvesters running while putting in the crops or harvesting.

Farms in the area grew progressively larger, as more land was needed to support a growing family, some farms growing to well over 5,000 acres. 10,000 sheep or more were often owned and maintained, with only the family members on the farm or minimal extra hired workers.

Sheep meat was always needed by WA butchers and supermarkets, as well as being chilled for overseas exports, with some money coming from animal hides. The main money from sheep was through wool production and its sale, with Australian merino sheep being well known internationally for the highest quality wool. A good year with high wool prices would make up for several bad seasons.

Wheat and general grain production were the other main pursuits. The West Australian wheat belt has always been highly productive, including the years when Erwin and Martha lived there. All wheat farmers waited for late autumn rains, enough to fully commit to the high cost of seed purchase, fertiliser and long days of ploughing and sowing a new crop, to be harvested in summer before Christmas. If the rains were poor, or fell at the wrong time, or storms, hail, and high winds damaged the crop then farmers would have to battle along for another year, hoping for a good season next year to save them.

Bit by bit, machines got progressively larger, complex and more expensive, but they got the job done faster and more efficiently than longer hours on small machines. During the Sax's time there, they would still have seen surplus World War II trucks, bulldozers and even the odd stripped-down army tank working on farms, bought at clearance sales as the Army reduced its scale from the war years and dumped equipment that had no further use in peacetime.

The typical main street view hasn't changed much over the years. Dirty farm utilities, 4 wheel-drives, and trucks still show the strong connection between retailers and farming families. Farm and contractor trucks cart sheep to and from the local stock sales yards as well as one-way trips to the large export abattoirs. Large, brand new tractors, ploughs, grain harvesters and chemical spray rigs are displayed in several machine-sales yards, along with rusty, tired-looking second-hand machinery outlets. During grain harvest season, in the olden days, bagged grain would have been carted to the rail siding, to be replaced now with huge road-trains carting 120 tons in one load to the bulk storage bins beside the rail yards, or south on the highway to the port of Albany.

In the 1950s and 1960s, the views would have been similar, but vehicles would have been smaller, lack the high-tech of modern machines, and be older vintage. Things were simpler in those days.

## *Sax Family residential addresses in Western Australia:*

The following residential addresses for the Sax family were mostly listed in the regular government census reports covering all Australian residents:

| | |
|---|---|
| 23/10/1949 | When Erwin, Martha and baby Jane arrived in Western Australia, they first stayed with Walter at 128 Hubert Street, Victoria Park |
| 1953 Census | Cherry Tree Pool farm |
| 1954 Census | 60 Tayler St, Katanning. |
| | Erwin classed as labourer |
| 1958 Census | 36 Amherst St, Katanning. |
| | Erwin classed as shopkeeper |
| 1968 Census | 9 Annie St, Katanning. Shopkeeper |
| | (The Sax Corner Store was on the corner of Amherst Street and Annie Street, Katanning) |
| 1970 Census | 9 Neil St, Rossmoyne (suburb of Perth). Retired |
| 1977 Census | 9 Neil St, Rossmoyne |

*A visit to Israel, 1977 – All together again: Top LHS: John, Chagit, Walter, Zohar, Ruti, Martha. Bottom LHS: Erwin, Bruno, Yifat*

# Chapter 9

# Martha Sax nee Weinstein

## Violets for Martha

*School assignment by Rachel Trigg.*
In February 1990, my grandmother, Martha Sax, died. Before her death, my mother had taken notes about her mothers' life and family. When I was asked to write a biography for my English class, I thought it would be a good opportunity to use those notes on what I already knew about my grandmother and write her story. This was something my mum had been wanting to do for some time, so she was quite pleased to let me do it.

When I wrote the first draft, I used the name by which I knew my grandmother: Oma. *Oma* is the German word for 'grandmother' and my sister and I had called her this when little because we couldn't pronounce *babka*, the Czech word for grandmother.

The name of this biography, *Violets for Martha* is only a small significance to the story, but Oma and I shared a love of violets. They are a flower which I will always associate with her and the name seemed suitable to me.

> **Note:** Short sections of the assignment have been not included because they have already been covered elsewhere in this book.

My grandmother, Marta Weinstein, was born on the 16th April 1912, in a small Czechoslovakian town named Boritice near the Czech-German border. Her parents were Katherine, nee Viegel, and Siegmund Weinstein. Three boys – Ernest, Otto and Viktor – were born before Marta. She was the baby and only girl of the family. Viktor, the youngest boy, and Marta were very close and remained so all of their lives.

*Viktor, Katherine, and Siegmund Weinstein*

The Weinsteins lived on a small farm and Marta's parents ran a general store. They were a middle-class family and had some wealthy relations. Marta's mother had a maid named Rosa to help with cooking and household chores. This was not unusual and most middle to upper-class families had someone to help around the home.

As a result of having three older brothers, Martha (as she was later called) was a tomboy. She much preferred to play with her brothers than help in the kitchen as was expected of a girl at that time. Helping around the house was something that had to be done, however, and Martha also helped in the shop and in the garden. She was very fond of flowers, especially violets.

The Weinstein family was Jewish, although they didn't practice the religion strongly. Many families in the area Martha lived were Catholic, as were most of the Weinstein's neighbours. Martha had many Christian friends and learnt a strong tolerance for all faiths and religions. Siegmund Weinstein was a very good provider for the family, but like many eastern European men had little patience. He preferred to look after the farm while his wife ran the store. Like Martha in later years, Martha's mother loved talking to and dealing with people. She was also a great cook, making strudel, dumplings, potato latkes and many other Czech delicacies.

Martha often talked about the great times the family had making eiderdowns and quilts. The family kept geese on the farm, which they used for eggs and meat. After being killed, the geese were plucked of their feathers and this eider was made into bedding. Because the feathers were so light, people trying to coax them into pillows or quilt covers often ended up covered in feathers, while the material remained empty.

*Martha Weinstein 1922*

After finishing her schooling, Martha was sent to Prague (Czechoslovakia's capital city) to live with and work for her father's brother and his wife Irma. Auntie Irma was a very strict, orthodox Jew. She often interfered in the lives of her relations and was very strict with her family.

It was Martha's job to help her Uncle in a large department store he owned and sometimes mind Auntie Irma's children. While working in the department store, Martha met Walter Sax, a flirtatious young man who was employed by her Uncle. Walter introduced her to John, Erwin, and Bruno Sax – three of Walter's brothers. Martha was to have strong ties with the four brothers all of her life.

Shortly before World War II, Martha's older brother, Otto, announced he was engaged to a Roman Catholic girl. Auntie Irma was outraged. She was against mixed marriages and told Otto he must marry a Jew. Under strong pressure from Auntie Irma and other narrow-minded members of the family, Otto broke off his engagement. Sadly, this decision probably cost Otto his life. During the war and Hitler's genocide program, most Jews were rounded up and placed in concentration camps. Jews married to Christians were usually spared. If Otto had married his fiance as planned, he probably would not have been killed by the Germans and might still be alive today.

According to a Czech proverb, "such is life."

In 1930, several years before Adolf Hitler came to power and a second World War was even considered, Martha went to Italy on holidays. At eighteen, Martha was a pretty young woman, a hard worker, and still a tomboy. It was during her Italian tour that Martha met Karel Werner, one of the five men and four other women holidaying with her. Karel was a wealthy Jew who had inherited money from relations. He was not used to hard work, but was a promising musician.

Karel and Martha married sometime in the early 30s and for the first two months of their marriage they toured Italy and Yugoslavia in a Studebaker. They planned to be in Italy for a month but stayed for two. Italian Fascists were in control of the country then. Martha added Italian to the languages that she could speak and understand. The marriage was thought of as a "good" marriage by Martha's relations, but unfortunately, it wasn't entirely happy. They had no children.

Some years later, when it looked imminent that Czechoslovakia was to be invaded by an anti-semitic Germany, Martha and Karel decided to leave their homeland and head for what was then Palestine. The Zionest movement had sent out an invitation for all Jews to come to Palestine, but the British – who were controlling the area – had other ideas. Martha and Karel set off on a long journey that was to take them through several European countries on the verge of war. They first travelled to Vienna, Austria, by land, arriving on the 13th of April 1939. In Vienna, they boarded a ship named *Kraliza Maria*, which sailed on the River Danube.

From Vienna, Martha and Karel sailed through Hungary, then on to Yugoslavia, passing through Belgrade and along the border between Bulgaria and Romania. The *Kraliza Maria*, still following the Danube, finally cut across the eastern edge of Romania, ending up at Sulina, a town which fronted onto the Black Sea. At Sulina, Martha and Karel left the *Kraliza Maria* and boarded another ship called the *Frossula*. On this ship, Martha re-met the four Sax brothers who were also headed for Israel. Erwin was married, and his wife Gaby was with him. The couple had a baby girl named Judith whom they had left in Czechoslovakia with his paternal grandmother, believing her safe.

They had no idea how long the journey was to take and conditions were rough during the journey. Men were separated from the women, and there was a shortage of fresh water. Buckets had to be lowered down to the sea to collect saltwater if you wanted a bath or needed to clean clothes. This harsh treatment wrecked clothes and shoes and made it difficult to keep clean. What clothing the sea did not destroy was prey for thieves and pilferers. Crime was high, and guards placed in charge of food and water were often bribed for extra rations.

When the boat did finally arrive in Tel Aviv, after passing through the Black Sea, Aegean Sea and the Mediterranean Sea, the British authorities denied them entry. They then fired upon the ship when it tried to enter the port, with two people killed and a two-year-old boy injured. The *Frossula* returned to the sea and after a short rest, Martha, Karel and the others on board the ship were transferred to an Italian craft. This boat made a run for Palestine and beached itself, a common practice among refugee ships. All on board the ship were arrested by the British and then given a meal.

The Sax brothers received similar treatment to Martha and her husband. When they were finally released and allowed to start life in the Jewish homeland, Martha started a launderette. It was very hard work and Karel was little help, but they got by reasonably well. Martha washed and ironed the clothes, while Karel picked up and delivered them. The Sax brothers lived nearby and opened a successful cobbler. Martha thought this was quite amusing as none of the brothers had much patience, and making shoes was fiddly work.

During this time Martha developed a lump on her neck. She was told it was just a fatty lump and that removing it could paralyse her.

Meanwhile, the Nazis had overcome Czechoslovakia, and on September 1st, 1939, Germany invaded Poland and World War II began. Soon the four Sax brothers decided that they would join the army, as many other Czech men were doing. They fought for the British Army in a Czech division, but were captured by the Germans and placed in a concentration camp. It was some time around then that Martha learnt that her brothers, Otto and Ernest, had been killed, along with many other Czech Jews. Luckily Victor survived, probably because he married a Roman Catholic. Irwin and Gabby Sax's daughter Judith was also among the dead.

On the positive side, Martha and Karel were getting along well financially, though their marriage was failing. Martha had a friend who designed clothes, and she was asked to model for her. She accepted happily and was soon a well-known face around Tel Aviv. Her picture often appeared in the Jerusalem paper. Because Palestine was not directly involved in the war, it was a fashion centre of sorts. France was in ruins at that time and the idea of having a designer dress made in Paris was stupid, to say the least.

1945 brought the end of World War II and also the end of Martha being Mrs Werner. She and Karel divorced, and Martha returned to a ruined Europe. Many of her relations had been cremated in concentration camps, but some still remained. Victor, to whom Martha had always been close, was alive and well with his wife, Boshenka. They went on to have two children – Helena and Marketka.

The four Sax brothers had survived the war and were released from the Prisoner of War camp where they were being held. Sadly, Erwin and Gaby's marriage did not last, and they divorced soon after Erwin was released. Erwin, John, and Walter returned to Czechoslovakia, where they met up with Martha again. With Erwin and Martha both single again and having known each other for some time, it was no surprise they fell in love. They were married in a simple ceremony on 5 April 1947.

They both wanted children and on the 13$^{th}$ of December 1948, 18 months after becoming Mrs Sax, Martha gave birth to a girl. Erwin had been hoping for a daughter and was delighted. He called the baby Jana (after his mother) Ada (after his favourite sister). Martha would have preferred Jana Katherine (after her mother) but didn't mind too much.

After giving birth, it was customary for middle and upper-class women to stay in bed and not get up for about a week. It was also usual for the father not to be present. To us now, this is no longer the practice, and when new mothers finally were allowed up, it took them another week to recover from spending a week in bed for no reason.

Things seemed pretty good for the first time in a while. Walter had married and he and his wife, Shari, also had a child, a son they named Paul. John Sax had married a woman named Jarka and the remaining brother in the Sax four, Bruno, was single and studying to be a doctor. In 1948, part of Palestine had been declared a national Jewish state and was christened Israel. Bruno later went to this new country where he completed his medical degree. He and his sabra wife Chagit and their family still live there today.

But the situation in Czechoslovakia was not to last. Communist Russians soon arrived and the four Sax brothers realised they would not have freedom if they remained. The brothers were again working the sawmill but the centralised communist system required them to achieve an output of cut timber that was not possible to achieve so the records had been falsified. Erwin went to Prague and saw the buildings full of records on outputs from a large number of businesses. He knew that eventually their saw-mill records would be inspected and the false numbers discovered.

The brothers realised they would not have freedom if they remained, particularly when the false saw-mill records were discovered. Martha and Erwin decided to follow John and Jarka and immigrated to Australia. They arranged legal passports and left their birthplace for a second time, this time for good. They were each allowed to take only five British pounds out of Czechoslovakia, but were much luckier than others who later tried to leave and were made to stay.

Taking Jana with them, Martha and Erwin travelled to Italy. There was a strike at the port, so Erwin helped load luggage onto the ship. Unfortunately, in the confusion, Erwin forgot to load their own luggage and they sailed without it. It was sent to them at a later date, but during the trip they had to make do with a limited amount of clothes. Martha had to borrow clothes from fellow passengers for baby Jana.

The trip would not have been too bad, but Martha and Erwin both ate seafood which had gone off and developed food poisoning. Jana was looked after by some Italians on the ship and was often called bambino bella. They had hidden some diamonds in balls of wool, but somewhere along the line the diamonds had been stolen or lost. For many years afterwards, Martha unravelled and searched through her wool, trying to find them.

Martha and Erwin had been sponsored out from Czechoslovakia

by a former Australian soldier Erwin had met in the war. However, they did not want to rely on them for food or money. At first, the family stayed with John and Jarka, who had already been in Australia for several months. The house was in Victoria Park, near a pine plantation. Erwin found it hard to get a job. He had been a forester in Czechoslovakia, but as the Australian timber industry was years behind that of Europe's, jobs were scarce. Erwin finally found work in a factory, and the family moved to Tuart Hill which was mainly chicken farms at the time. It was late in 1949 and accommodation was also becoming scarce. Martha, Jana, and Erwin moved in with Walter and his family who had also migrated to Western Australia. Later, the family moved to a farm in Gnowangerup, then Cherry Tree Pool near Katanning, where Erwin had a job managing a farm. Walter, Shari, and their son Paul left Australia for Canada. They were later to move to Los Angeles, America, where they settled down.

Erwin, Martha, Jana, John, and his wife Jarka moved to Cherry Tree Pool and happily started managing the farm. Martha got on very well with John, but less well with Jarka. However, this wasn't much of a problem. Late in 1951, Jarka and John had a son whom they named Solly Erwin. John and Erwin soon put their forestry skills to use and started a small sawmill. Timber produced from the Sax Brothers Mill was used in the Katanning Town Hall, the RSL Hall and many other buildings around the district.

The two families grew their own vegetables and kept their own poultry. One Christmas, Martha and Jarka wanted to cook one of their own geese for Christmas dinner. Erwin and John had promised to kill the bird but were very busy on the mill. As Christmas Day drew near and the goose had still not been killed, Martha got impatient and decided to kill the bird herself. She caught the goose, chopped its neck, and left it to die. A little while later, John came into the farmhouse kitchen.

"Why is there a goose running around the yard with its head on one side"?" he asked.

Everyone rushed outside to see Martha's goose with its neck only partially cut. This became a family joke, and Martha was ragged about it for years.

Cherry Tree Pool was a friendly community and had its own tennis and cricket clubs. Erwin and Martha often joined their neighbours for a friendly game. Unfortunately, Erwin suddenly contracted bad asthma. While in Gnowangerup, he had crushed superphosphate and had inhaled rat poison. These combined to make it extremely hard to breathe, and several times Erwin had to be rushed to the Kojonup Hospital, close to death. Martha could not drive and her English ability was limited. The only times she could get in to visit Erwin was when John drove her. It must have been very lonely on the farm, although all the neighbours were very nice. Because of the isolation and Erwin's asthma, Martha, Erwin and Jana moved into Katanning. John, Jarka and Sol left the farm and Australia. They sailed to Canada to join Walter but remained in Canada when Walter, Shari and Paul moved again.

Meanwhile, the Australian Saxes temporarily lived with the Wakes, a Katanning family. Erwin got a dirty job in a garage putting on tractor tyres, and Martha and Erwin began searching for a house. The only one available had a small shop attached to it, but they took it anyway. The house was made mostly out of Jarrah timber and was very dark. It had a small kitchen at the back with an old metal stove, a lounge room and a main bedroom. A veranda at the front was partially enclosed to provide a small bedroom for Jana and there was an outside toilet under an old pepper tree. The laundry was located at the back and there was no running water, so if anyone wanted a bath, water had to be lugged from the back of the house to the bath at the front.

Martha decided that during the day she would open a small shop attached to the house for something to do. She still understood little English, but as Erwin helped her and made her read for herself, she was learning steadily. She also learnt about Australian ways. One of Martha's first customers was Mrs Betty Sugars who came in for a tin of baked beans. Martha had heard of green beans and French beans but baked beans in tins was something new. She ordered the baked beans and also tinned spaghetti which was unknown in Czechoslovakia.

The shop was a great success as Martha was very good with people. It started to become a social outing to go down to Sax's Corner for everyday items. Children were often sent to the shop first thing in the morning to buy the newly delivered and still warm bread. It was not unusual for only the crusts to be left. Erwin soon started delivering groceries on a trolley after he finished work in the afternoon, because not everyone owned cars. This eventually led to him quitting his job in the garage to run the shop and deliver groceries full time. Martha and Erwin bought a Morris Minor utility in which to deliver groceries, because it was becoming impossible to finish the rounds on foot. Erwin placed a wooden plank between the two front seats for Jana, who was now about six, to sit on, and the family would drive around together, delivering food to other families.

Sax's shop grew and prospered. Martha decided to teach herself to read English when Jana started school and brought home Year One reading books. She did this largely by herself, but had some help from Erwin and other friends. Erwin and Martha met two other Czech families. Val and Fred Blazek and Maria and Frank Rempta had also left Czechoslovakia after the war and became good friends of Erwin and Martha.

During this time, Erwin began buying Martha many different electrical gadgets to use around the kitchen. On one occasion, Erwin brought home a pressure cooker and then refused to eat anything cooked in it because "it all tasted the same." Martha, who was not very adept at using electrical equipment, soon solved the problem of what to do with the cooker by accidentally blowing the top off it one day.

Soon the little shop which Martha had started had more business than it could handle. Erwin designed a new house to be built next door for the family. After it had been completed, Martha and Erwin built some new, larger shops on the corner. The house with the little shop attached to it became the storerooms for the new shops.

Soon after moving into the new house, Martha decided to plant some daffodil bulbs to brighten up the yard. One morning she went out to check on the plants which were just starting to unfold their buds. She was surprised and delighted when she found that the buds had fully opened overnight and that each daffodil had a perfect flower. Martha called all her neighbours around to see her beautiful garden and even offered to pick them a flower each. She carefully started to cut the first stem, but stood up in dismay when she realised that the flower which had come away so easily in her hand was actually plastic! The night before, Erwin had bought some fake daffodils and had arranged them in the garden to surprise his wife.

Violets were not the only flowers for Martha.

This was the end of Rachel Trigg's assignment.

Martha's brother, Victor, was in the Czech overseas army in World War II, serving in the Middle East and England and returned to Czechoslovakia in 1945. He and Bozenka stayed during the Communist government era, which only ended with the 'Velvet Revolution' in 1989.

By 1992, Victor had died and Bozenka had bad health. Bozenka's brother Vasa wrote a letter to Jane Trigg which gave a sense of the hardship living under the communists:

*"Since your visit a lot of things have happened here. From 1/1/93 our state won't be Czechoslovakia but the Czech Republic. The Slovaks wanted it. They believed that their interests were not respected by the Czechs. In reality it was the other way around, as they will soon find out. In contrast to Yugoslavia, this separation we hope will be peaceful. Two years before, democratic states very willingly stopped conflict in splitting 1000s of kms but they are unable to stop dividing countries in Europe.*

*A year ago, Uncle Viktor and I, by a Declaration of a Minister of Defence, were rehabilitated and got a paper because during the whole time of the communist regime we were like members of the army and hence were discriminated against and persecuted. Uncle Victor and I and a lot of others could only work manually as labourers. Bozenka couldn't attend the celebrations so I stood in for her. Viktor was promoted to lieutenant in memorium and I, as a professional officer, to colonel. It was too late for most of our friends.*

*I must tell you that, healthwise, Bozenka is a lot worse. After Viktor's death, she learnt to live with it. Later on, her physical condition worsened. She lost a lot of weight and she started growing big sclerosis (hardening of the blood vessels?) Marketka* was too sick to take her because my sister wasn't capable of looking after herself. (Bozenka was living with Marketka). It is sad and I feel sorry for her because she has had a very hard life. For three years during the war she was imprisoned by the Germans as a revenge for not being able to jail Viktor (Viktor was in Palestine in the British Army).

I hope that your family is healthy and that you enjoy beautiful summertime weather. For us it started an unpleasant winter. This year we had an exceptionally hot and very dry summer. The best in some 200 years...

Regards,

Vasa and family"

# Chapter 10

# Walter's Story by Mary Hunt

In 1999, an American woman by the name of Mary Hunt wrote down the results of an extensive audio recording of Walter's memories about his life. At that time, Walter was her Aunt's accountant, and he would drive from Los Angeles to the Aunt's trailer park which sat on a tributary of the Colorado River. He would often fish in the river, sitting on a rickety, old pier on the river edge, during long, hot days.

Mary believed Walter had held in the pain of his war experiences for so long many of the stories had faded beyond recognition. Much prying and patience were applied to bring the stories to the surface. His sons, Walter and Paul, also urged their father to remember details about his life.

Approval was generously given by Walter's family for the compilation, *Walter's Story*, to be included in this book.

I'm sure we are all very grateful to his family and Mary Hunt for the details that might otherwise be lost, being made available to add to the complete story of the four brothers.

**Mary's story begins:**

Jana, originally Yohanna in German, and Zigmund Sax lived in Novy Hrozenkov, Czechoslovakia. Like most families of this time, the Saxes had many children. Walter was born right in the middle, on July 15, 1910. All totalled there were six boys and five girls. The oldest was Irene, then came Martha, Otto, Ernst, Edith, Erwin, Walter, John, Ada, Ruth, and finally Bruno. Somewhere in between two other children, who each survived less than two days, were also born.

The village of 7,000 or so citizens was situated in the Beskid

Mountains between two ranges, going up to 5000 feet high. The distances between the tree-top heights varied from only a few miles in some places and 20 or 30 miles in others. Roughly 5 miles from Novy Hrozenkov, the ranges met. The main street went through the middle of the village with roads going to left and the right into the valleys. Novy Hrozenkov was a popular summer vacation spot in the mountains especially suited for skiing and drew a fair share of big city tourists. After climbing some 4000 feet up into those mountains, you could ski down in about two hours and literally be in Walter's back yard.

*Typical ski slope near Novy Hrosenkov*

There was very little industry, two or three sawmills and a glass factory. Agriculture existed as a means for farmers to feed their families with very little sold. The greatest industry was forestry, and from that, timber. Walter's family owned one of the three sawmills. Originally called Sax Brothers, the mill was run by Zigmund and his brother, David. So, with a bit of farmland for family food, forest land, and the sawmill, the family lived and grew.

*Sax's Bridge, crossing the river very near to the Sax Sawmill. It has since been replaced with a modern concrete structure.*

For entertainment, the family, along with neighbours, teachers and foresters would ski in the winter, arrange dancing lessons and play card games. In the summer they would enjoy volleyball or soccer and go fishing. It was a life with the family at its centre and dependent on family, neighbours and friends for everything.

Walter remembers his childhood being normal for that time. When the children turned 13 or 14 years-old, they were sent to relatives, usually their mother's relatives, in a big city. There each teen was educated in their desired subject, and because they would normally have attended German schools, they also learned the German language. The only difference was Erwin and John, who attended a special forestry and sawmill school and became experts in timber and running sawmills.

Walter was sent to a German-speaking town and attended a

German commercial school where he learned bookkeeping, accounting, and German. He didn't know where the other siblings went to school, except for Ernst, who studied in Vienna at a high commercial school and could have become a professor or doctor of commerce. Unfortunately, in 1925, Walter's father died of a heart attack, and Ernst had to come back and help manage the sawmill. His father's death changed the composition of Walter's family quite a bit. The eldest brother Otto, also an expert in sawmills and timber, became the business manager, aided by Ernst and Jana, with the mill being renamed *The Jana Sax Sawmill*. In 1939, when the world began its descent into World War II, Jana, her children and their families were all healthy and blissfully ignorant of the times to come.

Czechoslovakia was part of the Austrian/Hungarian Empire, created after the First World War. During that war, only the men had to serve, and the economy was affected. Otherwise the civilians lived and worked reasonably normally. But this time word was going around that Jews were being sent to camps. They didn't know specifically about concentration camps or what happened in them, just that they went to camps. Many Jews were employed at German or Austrian businesses or had personal connections in Germany and Austria. Since 1933, when Hitler came to power, Jewish properties were taken away from them. Those who could arrange it left Europe for America and other countries. One of Walter's cousins came from Vienna after the occupation of Austria and lived very close to Walter. He told stories of how the Austrians and the German-Austrians behaved toward the Jews and how they beat them. The Jews had to wear yellow stars to be differentiated from the general population. The Jewish people were frightened of what would happen. It was all new to Walter and his family.

At the time Walter and his brothers were still in Prague, the Germans didn't try to arrest Jewish people or send them away. When Hitler, in March 1939, marched his army into and occupied Prague, people became understandably upset. By then, most people knew Jews were persecuted in Germany, then in Austria, and feared the same would happen in Czechoslovakia. This caused a big panic to begin. It wasn't until after the war that Walter and his brothers found out the extent of what happened to the Jewish population and their own family.

# Leaving Home

*Walter Sax, Accountant in Prague, 1938*

Walter had been in Prague for six years working as an accountant in the division of a large company. Bruno lived with Walter and was attending medical school. In late March or early April 1939, Erwin and John went up to Prague. The brothers knew they had to do something. After many long discussions, it was decided they should immigrate. Erwin was more interested in politics than the others and he had an idea of what was happening. So they started looking for a way to get out. Their mother didn't want to immigrate. She believed that even if she lost the sawmill on the property, she could survive during the war with the help of neighbours and friends she had acquired during her life.

At the time, many organisations of various sizes and capacities had sprung up, among them one called *Black Rose*. *Black Rose* arranged the transport of Jews from Prague to Palestine. Most voyages started in Vienna, then to Romania and from there across the Mediterranean to Palestine. It was an expensive journey, having to secure not only the train seats but also the transfer from the train to the boat and the boat hire itself. The Saxes planned to take that trip. On the last day of April, Erwin and his wife Gabriella, John, Bruno, and Walter boarded a train in Prague. (Thinking the trip unsafe, Erwin and Gaby left their daughter Judith in Czechoslovakia where she eventually perished.) Early the next morning they were in Vienna. There they transferred to a boat, and, under the watchful eyes of German soldiers, they left Vienna on the Danube. They felt free. Walter remembered passing through Budapest because it reminded him of Prague. On the right side of the river was the government buildings and castle, and on the left side, the commercial and manufacturing part. Each mile of the journey bought them one mile closer to freedom and safety, or so they thought.

Several days later they arrived in a small harbour on the Black Sea in Romania. At the town called Sulina, a ship was to be waiting to take them to Palestine, but it wasn't there. It took three or four weeks before the ship finally arrived. The ship was a former cattle transport, converted with hundreds of bunks approximately two feet wide by two feet high, where some two to three hundred passengers were literally stored. The food and conditions were very poor, but within five days they saw the Palestine border. However, three miles before Palestine, a British gunboat asked the ship's captain by radio to state what he was carrying and where was he going. Instead of complying, the captain turned the ship around and with full power steamed out into a neutral space. The British shot at the fleeing ship and a father running to catch his little girl was shot and killed. He was the only casualty. The ship headed towards Turkey but soon they ran out of sweet water (drinking water) and were forced to head back towards Palestine.

The ship made it as far as Beirut where they were taken in. The passengers were put into an internee camp where they waited for something to happen. The Palestinian Jews arranged to pay another ship that was transporting other immigrants to Palestine to pick them up. The ship left Beirut and during the day met on the Mediterranean Sea with the second ship. They transferred from one ship to another and continued on to Palestine. As they closed in on Palestine a little boat came and signalled the ship to hurry forward. The ship literally ran onto the beach of Tel Aviv. The younger people, the original passengers of the ship, who were far younger than Walter and the others, jumped into the water and were picked up by the British Army. Then they came to Walter and the others, unloaded them, and put them in an internee camp.

## Palestine

Because their internment was just before the Jewish holy day of Rosh Hashanah, the Jewish New Year, they were only held for fourteen days instead of two to six months. When they were released, they were granted Palestinian residency. From then on they were on their own. They did not celebrate Rosh Hashanah because having just been released from the internee camp, they were like lost sheep in this foreign country.

The Jewish people of Palestine, who were in the minority to Arabs, knew about Hitler's march through Europe, but like Walter and his brothers, they did not know or comprehend the extent of the concentration camps or the genocide. When they were released, a cousin with whom Walter had worked in Prague met them. He gave them one British pound, with which they bought salami, bread, and tomatoes and spent the evening dining in a park. The Labour organisation contacted them and helped organise them in a camp along the same vein as a Kibbutz. (A Kibbutz is a place where people live together, work together and from the earnings of their combined labour they buy life's necessities.) They were put in a field with tents. Given beds and blankets, they started life in what is called a Chavora. A Chavora, unlike a Kibbutz, is not meant to be permanent.

Not everyone from the boat joined this Chavora. Those who had relatives already in Palestine went to stay with them. There were maybe one hundred people in the camp. A separation of duties was organised. Walter was minister of the kitchen (a little hut) and Erwin was minister of labour. Erwin would go around to see what work needed to be done and who was hiring. If a road was being built, they would dig ditches. There was a total of five ministers who ran the camp. Erwin started to hustle for labour and everybody, ministers or not, had to work. Very often, the four brothers worked together digging ditches for roads or highways, breaking stones, or whatever was necessary. In the late fall, when the rainy season came, the field they lived on became very muddy. So they were given permission to move out under the condition that they would find work and accommodation. There were each given a few pounds to start.

The four brothers and Gaby rented a house with a little garden to grow vegetables and started their new life. If one of them could find work, the rest would live off the earnings. Everybody had a trade. Erwin and John were carpenters, and Walter was in the lock and mechanical business. They were able to find quite a lot of work. Erwin and John even laid the foundation for a safe in a police station. The supervisor told them that they wouldn't make much money if they put too much concrete in it and that they should put big stones in it to take up space.

Because money was so tight, the brothers started making wooden sandals for Gaby to wear. John cut wooden soles, Erwin finished the wood, polishing and smoothing them, and Bruno and Walter put the leather straps on. While she was walking on Tel Aviv Beach, many people, especially other women, asked her where she got the sandals. They were interested in getting some for themselves. Out of that, a new business started. The sandals came in different sizes. They found that if string was wrapped around a balled-up fist, that measurement would equal the length of strap needed. For a bigger strap, just loosen the fist. Within a few months, they had two or three helpers and two then three agents, selling the sandals, not only in Tel Aviv but also in Haifa. They were doing quite well.

Eventually, something happened on the war front that convinced Erwin that they could no longer sit by. Erwin, being the oldest, discussed it with other Czechs and it was decided that the brothers should join the Army.

## British Soldiers

They contacted the Czech Command in Jerusalem but the quota was full. They were told to join the British Army. So sometime in late 1940 or the beginning of 1941, the four brothers became British soldiers. The recruiting officer, after first signing up Erwin, then John, said to Walter, "Don't tell me, you are a Sax too." Walter said, "Yes." Bruno got asked the same question. The flabbergasted officer probably questioned the man behind Bruno, also.

After their training, the brothers were sent to Egypt and from there to Tobruk, in the desert. They were not a fighting unit, more like a service unit. They handled mostly non-perishable goods, transporting them to the larger camps for storage. Cigarettes and processed meat, fruit, and similar items. From there, others distributed it to the British units in the area. Many German bombers flew over them because they were very near to the harbour. The bombers nearly hit their barracks, but it didn't last long because command decided they were needed in Greece.

They went by boat to Greece. Because they were not a fighting unit, they didn't have many weapons. On guard duty, they had to borrow the weapon from the guard they were replacing. They had maybe eight rifles to fifty or eighty men. Once in Greece, the Germans continued to close in on their site so they evacuated further south. At one point they were to have taken a boat to Crete, but in daylight it was impossible. So, during the day they hid in the hills, sleeping or just staying quiet and still. A few soldiers left for Crete the first night, but most of them remained in Greece.

The second night when they were lying in a line an officer told Walter, "You, Corporal, are in charge of this line. At daybreak board the ship and go to Crete." When Walter woke up at 4 or 5 o'clock in the morning, he was alone. They had all gone. So it was every man for himself. Walter got up and started walking and eventually met up with his brothers. Several of them took a lorry or truck and headed south on their own. Around 5 o'clock in the evening, they arrived at a village. They sent two men to arrange for a private boat to Crete. But before nightfall, the Germans parachuted down and Walter and his brothers were captured.

## Prisoners of War

From then on they were on the move from one small camp to another, then on a train to Austria. They spent almost three days on a cattle train with about 40 or 50 men in each railway car and were given only one day's rations of bread. In Austria, they were sent as a working party to Tryol but after three weeks they moved to their permanent camp, Stalag VIII in Upper Silos, Poland, in a town called Lamsdorf.

When Walter and the other prisoners arrived at Lamsdorf they could hardly walk. They were unable to march but instead were like old men putting one foot in front of the other slowly. They were surprised to see, when they entered the camp, an amputee playing soccer, with one wooden leg running and kicking the ball around. They couldn't believe it. At that moment they couldn't imagine where they got their strength.

They soon found out that they were getting food parcels from the Red Cross. A parcel contained maybe five or six pounds of foodstuffs. They were all different, some from New Zealand, Canada, Australia, Scotland and America, too. They usually contained Klim (a brand of canned milk), powdered milk, biscuits, butter, cocoa, chocolate, jam, Spam or some other meat and Marmalade. It was all very good, according to Walter. Groups of six men would split one parcel a day and that would add to the German soup. Food in camp was very bad. They managed very well and continued to grow stronger.

Red Cross packages came every week to both the camp and the working parties. Some prisoners didn't eat all of the goods that came in the Red Cross packages, so they started little stores. They would set up tables under a barracks window and sell their leftover items. What was the prison's currency? Cigarettes. For a certain number of cigarettes, say five, you could buy a can of jam. Chocolate was a little bit higher. Even from the German civilians you could buy things with cigarettes. Walter bought a silver Schafhusen, the best German watch, and he paid only three packs of cigarettes for it. The prisoners would even buy radios from the civilians. Practically every barracks ended up having a radio. Just about everything could be bought with cigarettes or chocolate.

Chocolate was also a popular form of currency with the civilians. In Germany, Poland and other places, for a bar of chocolate you could have a prostitute for maybe two nights. You could see a dentist and have a tooth pulled, anything you wanted for cigarettes or chocolate.

Walter had a girlfriend, Charlotte, from before the war. She was not so much a romantic girl, more like a friend who was a girl.

Charlotte was born in the eastern part of Czechoslovakia at the far end of Slovakia. The town had about 40,000 people. Walter had met Charlotte's father in Prague. Then, Walter went on a trip through Charlotte's part of the country. Around six months later the whole family came to Prague. Charlotte had gone to England as a supervisor for a group of children being transported out of Czechoslovakia to safety in England.

While in England she joined the English Women's Auxiliary Air Force (WAAFs). There the cook, who was also a Czech, asked Charlotte if she knew any POWs. The cook wanted to start a correspondence. Charlotte didn't know any POWs except Walter, so she gave her his name. The first parcel Walter got from the cook included 1000 cigarettes. And every month or so she would send 500 more. Since cigarettes equalled money, Walter was rich! He never had any problems getting the parcels, either. Someone from the Red Cross came every month to make sure the prisoners received their packages. If something went wrong it quickly got straightened out.

When the prisoners first arrived, the guards were strict. The barracks were inspected every day. A headcount was taken every morning and discipline was very tough. As the war went on and the Allies position was strengthened, the guards softened and near the middle and end of the war, the POWs were basically running the camp.

The British and American soldiers were treated better than the Russian soldiers. During World War I, the Germans were treated well by the British prisons, so it was reciprocated. Even though the guards knew that Walter, his brothers and the others were Jewish, they treated them like any other British soldiers. They respected the uniform. The Russians they treated like dogs, in retribution for the way Russians had treated the German soldiers during World War I.

Towards the beginning of their imprisonment, somebody in camp made a map showing the location of the Russian and German armies. The Germans would pull down the map whenever they saw it. So somebody came up with the idea to paint a big map right on a barrack wall and to use a red string for the eastern front and blue string for the western front. They would mark it every day according to the radio announcements they heard. The Germans were often surprised at the information that showed. When the map depicted fighting going on in a certain area, the guards would say "we are not there" or "that is not true" and the prisoners would reply "sure you are, you will hear about it on the radio in a few days." Even the German commander would come by, from time to time, to check the fronts' progress.

The camp was run quite similar to the television show "Hogan's Heroes". Every second board of the barracks beds was given to build underground tunnels that were hidden under pot-bellied stoves that slid to the side. In the camp, they had a big field set aside to play different sports, a theatre and a school that taught almost any subject the prisoners wanted. Walter returned from work parties several times and attended school. He took English, both elementary and advanced, diesel engine repair, hotel management and French. Later on Walter found a Canadian from Québec, a French-speaking little soldier, and he became Walter's teacher.

Once a year or so, a Bridge Tournament would be arranged and one year the brothers participated in that tournament. There were 120 pairs which meant 120 games you had to go through to get to the semi-final. Three of the four Sax brothers and a friend of theirs made it to the semi-finals.

One winter the Germans were afraid the prisoners would get cholera, so they were forced to sleep with the windows open, but each prisoner only had two very thin blankets. It was very cold so what the prisoners did was to put in between the blankets newspapers or, if they were lucky, crêpe paper and put it all together making a sort of sleeping bag. The paper was warmer than the blanket and kept the cold out and the warmth of their bodies in. It worked quite well. They also would run around to warm themselves up, especially their feet, before going to bed.

One year the Germans dug huge pits, about half the size of a swimming pool at the end of each barrack in order to have water close by in case the barracks ever caught fire. At one such pool, when the ice melted in spring, they found a body. None of the POWs were missing, so it must have been a German. It was not unusual for the guards to plant an English-speaking German in the barracks to find out what the prisoners were up to. This must've been one who got found out.

About two years into their captivity, Erwin got a letter from Palestine. A woman had written that Gaby was having an affair with a friend of theirs who had come from Czechoslovakia on the same boat as Walter and his brothers. She said that Gaby was very happy with him. Erwin didn't know what to do; he walked around like a zombie for a few days, arguing with himself. After a couple of weeks he said, "I forgive her".

Some 18 months before the war ended, a big placard was put up in the camp. It was propaganda used for preparing the prisoners for life after the war. It was a picture of a kitchen, with a big table and under the table was a sergeant with the marking 'POW' on his back. At the front of the table was a strong woman with a wooden spoon in her hand and the caption was "Prepare for the Home Front". It was meant to encourage the prisoners to exercise. So, every morning on the football field the prisoners got together. One or two would lead the group and for an hour they exercised. In the beginning it was very painful, but then their bodies got used to it. The big advantage to exercising was that afterwards they could take a shower. Showers were normally allowed only once a week.

Latrine facilities were set up so that all the different barracks used the same latrine. There would be two rows of back to back holes in the centre of the room, maybe ten or so long, and one row against each wall. Men from different barracks would sit back to back and talk to each other. It was called the "Shit House rumours" which was the fastest means of spreading information about what was happening from one barracks to another.

The prisoners had themselves well organised. They had all kinds of underground services. There was even an escape committee. No one really knew who was in charge of it, but if they found a worthy subject, who knew a little bit of German, they helped him with papers, photographs, German money and information about what cities or towns he could get assistance to further his movements. Once, in the hospital, there was a British pilot who had an appendix operation. The pilot was a Czech boy named Joseph, but they called him Joe. The escape committee approached Bruno to switch places with Joe so he could escape. Bruno was not only a Czech, thus he spoke the same language as Joe, but also he was of the same height and had very similar features, down to the appendix scar, although Bruno's scar was much older. It also meant that Bruno would have to change from the Army to the Air Force.

Erwin generally had the last word when major decisions were to be made and the brothers followed whatever he said. When Bruno wanted to risk his own escape, he asked Erwin if he could and Erwin said no. He told Bruno, "What should I tell our mother if you get killed?" Erwin finally said it was okay and Bruno agreed to help Joe. So, one day he went to the hospital and later that day Joe came out of the hospital as Bruno. Joe, as Bruno, was sent right away to a working party where it had been arranged that he would escape. Bruno, as Joe, was sent to Joe's camp near Berlin. When Bruno arrived a German sergeant said, "You are not Joe. You look like him, but you are not Joe." Bruno said, "Yes, I am Joe." So the sergeant sent him to a German medical officer. They had a long discussion and Bruno confessed that he was Bruno Sax, not Joe. They agreed to keep Bruno one more day then he was sentenced to a week of confinement at their camp to serve the sentence. They never heard any news about Joe.

There was a botched attempt by the Allies to land at the second front before Normandy. The camp guards found out that German soldiers had been tied with chains around their wrist and string tied on one thumb running up their back and around their neck then to their other thumb. Some Germans so restrained had died when the ship they were on sank. So the camp guards retaliated by putting the POWs in the same position. They were put in chains, 18 inches between the arms. But soon they learned how to take them off and leave the barracks. If they were caught they would be chained again. By late afternoon, the Germans had run out of chains and had to resort to Red Cross strings. It was a huge fiasco for them.

## Working Parties

When they first arrived, the four brothers, being NCOs (corporals and above) were not required to go on the working parties. At the beginning, just like in the camp, the Germans were tough on the working parties. They were strict and didn't listen to the prisoners. But again, like camp, it eventually became quite lax.

Eventually an order was issued stating that everyone, including NCOs, had to go on the working parties. Working parties were usually within 100 miles of camp. They lasted as long as a particular job took or as long as the prisoner wanted to stay. If the prisoner got fed up, they just said that they wanted to go back to camp.

Normally you went on a working party if you needed or wanted something that could only be gotten outside the camp.

On one working party, about 40 of the prisoners were sent to a paper factory, where they made cellulose. Wet wood was mashed up and made into a heavy cardboard paper, which was then sent to different factories to make real paper. The conditions there weren't bad, but it was hard work.

One working party was quite close by. It was a forest party where they marched maybe 2 miles to the forest. On the way there, the prisoners noticed there was another camp filled with Jewish civilians. To let them know that they were Jewish too, Walter and the others would sing Hebrew songs as they passed by. The camp occupants applauded as a means of acknowledging that they knew who the prisoners were. A few months later the camp was empty. The Germans had taken them away and the POW prisoners never found out where.

Only a few months later another order came down that NCOs did not have to work anymore. So, Walter and his brothers returned to camp. But Walter started having troubles with his teeth. The camp had a hospital, but the only dental care provided was extractions. If a prisoner needed a filling he would go on a working party in an area where there was a dentist who took cigarettes or chocolate as payment for his services. So off and on the prisoners would switch working parties in order to get their teeth fixed. Walter did that once and got a tooth implant. It was a quality product, too. The dentist stepped on the tooth with army boots to show how strong it was. It cost Walter one cocoa and two packs of cigarettes.

One of the working parties was at a sand quarry. The sand was used to manufacture glass. When the sand was washed it was a very light colour and the grains were like crystal. It was washed properly, loaded on big railway wagons and sent to glass factories. The quarry was located directly opposite a railway station.

The POWs saw every train, which were not many, that passed by. They would wave to the civilians on the train, flirting and having a little fun with them. There the work was comparatively easy. Because of the war, the civilian workers were old men. They could load a wagon in four hours. Two wagons in an eight-hour day. It took the prisoners less than one hour to load a wagon, which meant in less than two hours they could complete their daily task. Sometimes they had to work Saturday or Sunday, as needed. Once, on a Saturday, one of the civilian guards came wearing a SA uniform. The prisoners told the guard they wouldn't work under the SA, only under normal guards or civilians. There was a big argument, but because they needed the prisoners to work, they sent the SA man back and a civilian took over as supervisor.

On that same working party, Walter decided he wanted to go fishing, but he didn't have any hooks. There was a large maintenance shop where two men worked and Walter asked them if they could help him make a hook. They agreed. The manager of the quarry came in and asked Walter what was he doing there. Walter explained what they were doing and the manager helped, too. He even showed Walter how to make a reverse hook so that the fish would stay on. The hooks were made from steel needles. They were heated up and squashed into shape.

The manager asked Walter several times when he was fishing and was always friendly, asking, "Are they biting?" Walter would say, "No, I cannot catch anything." But once he actually had six trout thrown up in the grass behind him. By the end of the day, he had a total of twelve fish. Somebody suggested they should make one for the guards, so Walter asked the guard, "How do you want the trout, on butter or like a wiener schnitzel?" The guard said, "On butter, if I can choose." When Walter brought the fish in, he started to fiddle with the guard's radio and picked up the BBC.

One of the guards on this party was really strict. He didn't allow the prisoners to go fishing, so the prisoners stopped working overtime. They wouldn't load more than two wagons between four of them. When the foreman found out why the prisoners weren't working as hard as they had been, he went to the guard and said that he would sign for the prisoners and be responsible for bringing them back by 5.00 pm. From then he didn't actually sign for the prisoners, he just told them to do their work and be back at five.

Because this was one of the working parties that lasted several months, somebody suggested the prisoners raise rabbits to add variety to their meals, so they asked a guard to buy them one male and three female rabbits. The prisoners made a few cages and put one POW in charge of feeding them and taking care of them. After a few months they had so many rabbits that it was time to start eating them. The first supper they ate the rabbits, the man who was in charge of them cried and didn't want anything to eat. He had gotten very attached to the rabbits. He had named each of them and played with them, putting them on his shoulders and they had become his friends.

On another working party, the cook killed a dog but he didn't tell the prisoners. Then after dinner he started to bark and they asked him why he was doing that. He told them they had eaten a dog. They of course were surprised. He had prepared it quite well, with a lot of onions and even garlic, so the taste was covered up. It tasted like normal meat.

## Escape / Freedom

Walter didn't know what was happening towards the end of war, because for the last few months he and Erwin had been on a working party at a sawmill which was in the Czech territory of Sudetenland. The order came to the camp that they were to evacuate because the Russians were pushing the German army west. So, they loaded up the prisoners (there were around twenty-five) and with the German soldiers they headed west by train. The Germans were very depressed. It reminded Walter of the prisoners when they first arrived in camp. One of the German guards tried to make a deal with Walter. He would give Walter his Lugar pistol when they got close to the American side and Walter could hand the guard over to the Americans. The guard figured he would get treated better that way. Unfortunately for the guard, Erwin and Walter escaped from the train.

One night, when the train was stopped in a Czech village, Erwin and Walter escaped and hid in a pigsty overnight. In the morning, when they were found, it was by a lady who, finding out they were fellow Czechs, took them in. They were taken to the heads of the village and greeted with food and drinks. They stayed there for three or four days. The villagers provided Walter and Erwin with food for their trip to Prague. There was still fighting going on and Erwin and Walter ended up on different trucks and got separated.

Bruno and John were in a different camp at the time of the evacuation. In fact, because Bruno had been in a fight with the German guard, he had been sent back to Sagan to serve his sentence. Because Sagan was near Berlin, Bruno actually got evacuated three weeks before Erwin, John and Walter.

John, still at the camp Bruno was at, was a few days west of Walter and Erwin so he also had a head start on them.

## Home Again / England / Palestine Again

An arrangement had been made between the brothers months before that, that if something happened and they were separated going back to Prague, they would go to a certain hotel, which all of them knew, leave a message and the next one who came would pick the message up and write another one for the others to follow. So, one morning, Walter got to the hotel and Erwin was coming out. Erwin asked Walter if he had read his message. Walter said no, that he had just arrived. So, they went back to the hotel and wrote another note for John and Bruno. They had to find a way to get back home, which was about 200 miles away. Buses and trains were not running so they hitchhiked, mostly with Romanian soldiers who were heading east towards their homes. The trip, which normally took four or five hours, took them four days.

When they came home the greeting was very sad. Their neighbours told them that their sister Ada had been thrown under a train, two brothers were killed escaping and all the others had been taken away and never returned except for one sister, Edith. She was married to a gentile and spent only two or three months in a concentration camp, towards the end of the war, in Czechoslovakia. Her husband was a dentist. They had three children, one boy and two girls. Except for Edith, their entire family had been killed in the camps including their mother, all their sisters, three nieces and one nephew.

When the British and American soldiers went home, they had girlfriends, wives, homes and families to come home to. Huge celebrations and jobs awaited them. Walter and his brothers had nothing. Their family was gone and most of the other families were also gone. Before the war, they had 126 cousins and uncles. If they walked through the main square in Prague they would run into a relative. Now, they had no one but each other.

Seeing their house was indescribably sad for Walter. Their house was half brick and half a wooden addition. One winter there was too much snow on the roof and the Germans didn't allow anyone to clean it or push the snow down, as was normally done. The heavy snow broke through the roof and fell into the rooms below. Nobody was allowed to go in.

John had come home before Walter and Erwin and had left a message with the neighbours that he was going to see their sister Edith who lived about 20 miles away. Walter and Erwin decided to join them there. They stayed there several days until it came time to go back to their unit in England. First they went to Prague. From Prague, they were sent to Pilsen where the aeroplanes left for France.

Every morning they went to the airport and if no plane was available they went back to the city. One day they were picked up and sent to France, near Rheims. There, Americans welcomed them with food, cigarettes and anything they wanted. The same travel problems occurred there. There was not enough transport to England. But within a few days they arrived in England. They were segregated into a camp populated with Palestinian soldiers who were to be shipped back to Palestine. There they were finally joined by Bruno, who had been in England since the end of the war. So again they were all together. Erwin, being the only one married, pressed to go back to his wife. When Erwin arrived in Palestine, something happened and within three days he left Gaby, filed for and was granted a divorce.

Later on, when Walter, John and Bruno visited Palestine, they would stay with Gaby because they were still good friends with her. Erwin was very cross with them, that they still patronised her. But they liked her. She was a good woman and a friend and they got a free roof over their head.

While the brothers were in London, Walter met up with his girlfriend, Charlotte and within two weeks they were married. While Erwin returned to Palestine, Walter, Charlotte, John and Bruno stayed in the northern part of England near the Wedgwood factory. They visited the factory and had a mini vacation and honeymoon before returning to Palestine. When they arrived in Palestine, Walter went to Jerusalem, to the British High Command, asking to be sent to England for two more months. He was told that the British didn't even have enough air space for their boys, so Walter ended up getting another 70 days of vacation. After the vacation, they had to go back to the Army and await their discharge. Discharge went by number according to how long the soldier was in the army. About six or seven months later they were demobilised. Then it was time to look for a way to get back to Czechoslovakia.

In the three big cities, Tel Aviv, Haifa and Jerusalem, there was a big movement for the Czechs to go home. The Czech government promised to send a train to Italy to bring the Czechs back home. So they had to find a way to get to Italy. Organisations formed and they joined one. Several weeks later they left for the Suez Canal but the boat was not waiting for them like it had been arranged. They were put up two or three miles from the city of Suez. There they waited while communicating with the High Command in Cairo, but nothing happened.

It was decided that someone had to go to Cairo to intervene. A Czech official and a translator, who was Walter, went to Cairo. From the Suez Canal, they hitchhiked to Cairo. The Egyptian police helped them to find people who would take them the distance and after visiting and arguing with the High Command, they said they would do the best they could, but the transportation still wasn't ready. So Walter and the Czech official returned and within three weeks they got word that a boat would be ready soon. They packed up, got a train to Suez, boarded the boat and soon arrived in Italy. A few days later, their train, sent from Czechoslovakia especially for them, arrived and a few days after that, they arrived in Prague.

After being together for five years or more, when the brothers arrived in Prague, each one of them went a different way. Bruno didn't want to immigrate to any other country but Palestine. Because he spoke several languages including Hebrew, he assisted with the transport of things to Palestine and he eventually stayed there and married a 'Sabra' – a woman who was born there – Chagit. Bruno also went back to school and became a doctor. As for Walter, Charlotte was waiting for him. She had already rented a room for them. Erwin, John and Bruno went completely different ways. Erwin disappeared and John went to work in a sawmill somewhere.

## Civilians/Home Again

The first Christmas after leaving the war, Charlotte, Walter and his sister, Edith, visited their old home. Again, their next-door neighbours welcomed them. The two families had been close because they had five boys, like the Saxes, and during their childhood the family's boys had paired off, according to age. The girls too, were very friendly. The neighbours invited them for Christmas dinner. A noontime meal, not their family dinner, only for the Saxes, Charlotte asked Walter, "Are they so rich?"

Walter told her to look at the corner of the tablecloth. And there was 'S' for Sax on the linen tablecloths. Looking around, Walter saw more items that they had taken from his house. Then two boys, maybe 17 or 18, came in, both wearing short jackets with fur linings on their collars. The jackets had belonged to Walter's brothers. The neighbours didn't even have the decency to say, "We took it before the Germans could take it. Do you want some of it?"

One of them, who had been Walter's friend, William, took over the Sax's house. He didn't pay rent or even offer to.

In their house, the attic had been made of wooden beams with no top floor. In between the beams the family would keep their valuables hidden under a false floor. In the eight villages in the area, there were about 10 Jewish families. Novy Hrosenkov had only three Jewish families. Because there was no synagogue, the Saxes had two Torahs in the house. When William took over the house, he discovered the false floor and found the Torahs. Because they didn't know what they were, he just threw them in the river.

Walter had an uncle and aunt who had come from the southern part, the German-speaking part of Czechoslovakia, to live with Walter's family. They had an enormous amount of silver that was also hidden in the attic. There were many things never found at the house. But they were only material things. None of the brothers wanted to take back the house and live there. They could have taken it right away, but they didn't want to stay. Walter wasn't a lumberman and the sawmill had been turned into German barracks. It would have taken a lot to get the mill back in running order. Walter and Charlotte returned to Prague. It would be nearly 50 years before Walter would visit Novy Hrozenkov again.

To get an apartment in Prague after the war was very difficult. You had to be a member of the Communist Party to have some pull. Unfortunately, or fortunately, Walter and Charlotte were not communist. They ended up sharing a two-bedroom apartment with an ex-Czech soldier who had married an English woman. The

English woman was very unhappy in Prague and several months later the other couple decided to go back to England. So the newlyweds acquired a nice apartment on the top floor of an eight storey apartment building. They started to look for a job to make money, because they had very little.

Walter's old job was available for him but he would have started at the salary he left, which after six years was not enough. His secretary from when he was working before the war had become the chief accountant for three or four branches of the company. Walter really didn't want to go back to that job. He found a job, then changed to another one after a few months. At the second job he worked for a company that controlled goods being sent abroad, mostly to the American army. For instance, they would have sugar to ship, so Walter had to make sure that each bag had 100 kg of sugar and that there were so many bags on the train. He would go to the factory and check it out. The company needed somebody to handle the timber so Walter asked his boss to hire John and he agreed.

One time when Walter and some of his friends were sitting together, a cousin of one of the men, a Czech lawyer who had been in the French underground, the Marquis, told Walter that he had seen in France a carpet cleaning machine from England. In the hotels in Prague there were big carpets everywhere that had to be cleaned with brushes by hand. The carpet cleaning machine, his friend told Walter, was seven times faster than by hand. He told Walter that he had a cousin in England who was a commercial attache. All Walter had to do was write to him and he would arrange it. So the cousin sent Walter a brochure of the company that made the machines. Walter applied to buy a machine, but he had to have a firm. So Walter started carpet cleaning as an enterprise and since his first son, Paul, had been born by this time, he called it Walter Sax and Son.

After several months, he got two machines. He paid 100 English pounds for each of them. They started first in a hotel. The hotel manager said to Walter that if he ruined the carpet he had to pay for it. The manager also wanted a guarantee that the soap wouldn't harm the wool. Walter had the soap analysed at the University. The professor said that the wool would fall apart. The professor recommended that they use a liquid soap, like pipe fitters used. A company that sold the liquid soap said it wouldn't harm the wool.

Using that soap, they got a contract from a banker to clean his carpets. But first they had to clean a test area. It was a success. So Walter hired an ex-colleague, a legionnaire from the Russian side, also Czech, to clean the carpet. They got seven crowns, around half a dollar at that time, for each square meter. In an afternoon they would make four to five thousand crowns. A big government job would pay ten thousand crowns. They didn't have a car so they went to jobs by taxis. They worked only long enough to get money for passports. John eventually joined them. They made big money with the machines. Walter sold the company to the cousin, tripling his money on the machines alone because they were so hard to get. Walter was the only person in Czechoslovakia to have carpet cleaning machines.

After selling the carpet cleaning company, Walter joined the American Joint Distribution Committee, which helped people emigrate from central Europe to Israel, the United States and other countries. Because he was acquainted with Prague, they put Walter in charge of transportation from Europe. He would charter small planes, thirty to forty seats, from Prague directly to New York. It was cheaper to go by plane than to send the immigrants by boat, because by boat they would first have to go to Sweden, where they normally waited, then travel several days on the boat and everything had to be paid by the American company. Everything went very nicely. Then the Communists started making a lot of problems. They killed the Foreign Minister, John (Honza) Masaryk, son of old President Masaryk, and they wounded the then-current president, Benes, so Charlotte said that they would have to go away.

Walter had already prepared false passports, but Charlotte didn't want to use them. She found in Australia an ex-navigator from England with whom she had been friendly and his father sent them an affidavit stating that he would be their sponsor for immigration. They got their passports, which were expensive. The Czechs had learned from the Germans to charge a runaway tax to people leaving the country. The tax was several thousand dollars each. But they managed to come up with the money and left, via Italy, to Australia. With Walter and Charlotte was their son Paul, who was around one year old and Walter's brother John.

The Czech customs were very severe. They inspected the bigger luggage while it was being packed and checked the smaller one at the border. Charlotte was even stripped down and thoroughly checked. The inspectors thought they were smuggling money and diamonds. But in fact, they didn't have much in the way of money or jewels. Charlotte had diamond earrings, which Walter hid somewhere and the money he got from the American company, two hundred dollars, was officially written in the passport. So everything was all right. A huge bonus for them was that the American company paid for a first-class cabin for them all.

## Australia

The trip was nice and quiet, and for a change, quite uneventful. In Australia, their sponsor, the father of the navigator, who was undersecretary of the water supply, a very high position in the government, secured their visas. The visas were similar to those of displaced persons (DPs), so they were allowed to work only in agriculture, forestry and sawmills. Because John was an expert in sawmills, and Walter at least was acquainted with them, they quickly found work. They worked at a sawmill where mostly eucalyptus was cut. The mill was located about 40 miles north of Perth. The white eucalyptus was called Jarrah. When the boards were dry this particular wood became heavy and hard, like stone. A nail could not even be driven into it. It had to be drilled first. All the processing had to be done while the timber was still wet.

They started work at 7 o'clock in the morning and by 9 o'clock their bodies were covered in a dry white film. All their body salt would come out through their pores and after that not a drop of sweat would come. They didn't drink any water during the day because it would pass through their pores like dew and they would become drenched. As soon as they came home from work, they would start drinking water to hydrate themselves for the next day. Charlotte, at one or two o'clock in the afternoon, would fill up the bathtub with hot water which came not from a hot water heater, but from a hose line that was laid on top of the ground. Straight from the hose the water was nearly boiling hot. If the tub was filled by 2.00pm they could bathe a little after five and not scald themselves.

Food was brought to the sawmill once a week from Perth in an open truck. In the beginning, they would order meat and sugar, flour and so on, but the meat would come spoiled because it was exposed to the sun and very often not properly packed. Flies would have a field day. So they started to live, as far as meat was concerned, on rabbit meat. If they wanted meat for supper they would go behind the paddock about 20 feet or so and shoot a rabbit. The first time it took Walter one and a half hours to skin the rabbit. Then a neighbour showed him another method and after that it didn't take more than two or three minutes. The meat was prepared just as they would chicken or anything else. It was white meat and quite tasty. So they lived like a native, if they wanted to eat meat, they went out and got it.

Two or three months later, John found a much better job at a sawmill in the southern part of Western Australia. The boss was very angry. He told Walter that if his brother goes, Walter goes, too. So they packed up and went to Perth where Walter found a job as a general farmhand. Charlotte called Walter Sir G.F.H. It was a mixed-use farm, with cattle, fruits and grazing land. It was quite large but it was 27 miles from any stores where they could buy cigarettes or anything else.

The first day on the farm, the farmer told Walter to teach a one-day-old calf how to drink. Walter had seen how it was done in the old country, so he put his fingers into the calf's mouth and the calf started to suck his fingers. Walter then pulled the calf's head down into a prepared bucket of milk and after a few tries the calf worked out how to drink out of the bucket himself. The calf became so friendly that Walter gave him a name, "Blacky". Whenever he called, "Blacky, come," the calf would follow. Often Walter would take Blacky home with him for lunch. Paul had a good time with the animal. Even when the calf got older, was castrated and lived in the paddock with the other cattle, if Walter called, Blacky would come running. Walter and Blacky had a good time together.

Once John came to visit. He had been injured at the sawmill and had come to recuperate with Walter and Charlotte for a few weeks.

Occasionally, Walter and John would borrow an old army rifle from their boss and go hunting for kangaroos. It was very exciting. The kangaroos would stand up like a man on his hind feet and look at them. Once, they actually shot one. It was not very heavy, maybe around a hundred pounds, because it was not fully grown. They ate all the meat, but the best part was the tail. The soup it made was fantastic.

On the farm, Walter did everything that a farmhand does. He milked the cows, drove the tractor, picked fruit, made boxes for the fruit and made traps for rabbits. Once, in one of the traps was a young fox. Walter went to the boss and asked what he was supposed to do with it. The boss told Walter to kill the fox and bring him the ears. It hurt Walter more than the fox. The beautiful animal looked at Walter as if it knew what Walter had to do. From then on, Walter was afraid to lay the traps for fear that another fox would be caught.

Some people in Perth that Charlotte had become friendly with owned a used furniture store. Charlotte had sold the owner her earrings so that they would have something to live on. The store owner and his wife had come to visit Walter and Charlotte on the farm. The man informed them that after one year of residency they could become Australian citizens. This was important in that it meant Walter would no longer be limited to the jobs he could work. They applied, became Australian citizens and moved to Perth. Walter got a job as a salesman in the second-hand furniture store.

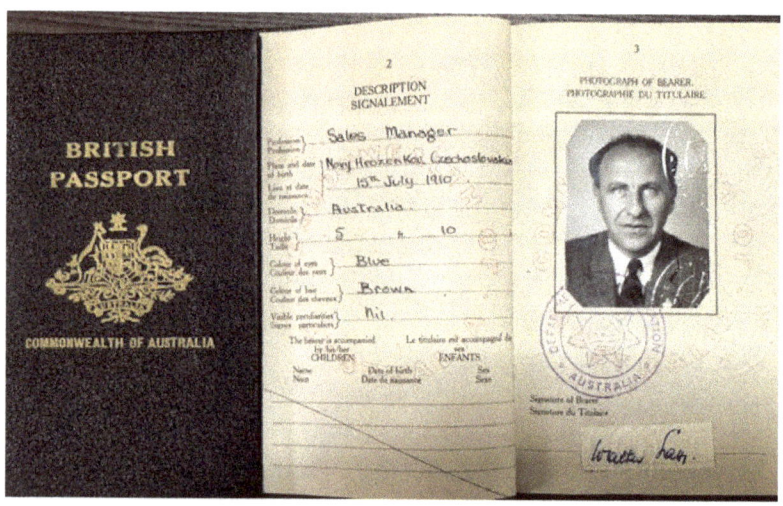

*Walter's Australian Passport, issued August 4, 1952*

Less than a month later, a friend of the store owner's wife committed suicide and left behind him his wife and their two young sons. Charlotte was asked if she and Walter could go to work on the chicken farm that the man had owned. Walter could help the family at the same pay he was receiving at the furniture store. Charlotte would take care of the boys and prepare everyone's meals and they would get free room and board. They agreed to it on a trial basis.

Fate stepped in again and within three weeks the owner of the farm went to visit his sister and in front of her drank a bottle of Lysol and killed himself. The question was what to do with the farm. Representatives of the Jewish community approached Walter and said the only thing was for Walter to buy the livestock, which at that time was reduced to 500 chickens and the remaining farm equipment and supplies, for 300 sterling pounds. That was a lot of money. At the time, the exchange was four or five dollars to the pound. Two Czech friends offered to loan Walter the money interest-free. So Walter and Charlotte became poultry farmers.

Walter didn't know anything about raising chickens. The Australian government was very helpful. They sent Walter an experienced poultry farmer as an instructor and he spent many days with them. They bought 1,500 one day old chickens. The instructor taught Walter how to handle them, how, at 8 to 10 weeks to inoculate them, and soon Walter was raising chickens. In the meantime, two wool buyers needed a manager for a small army surplus store and the rabbi recommended Walter for the job. They came and asked Walter if he would take the job. The pay was very good, but what would he do with the farm? It was a big decision. Walter decided to take the job and keep working the farm. He worked eight hours a day in the store, came home at 6 o'clock and ate dinner. Then he would prepare the food for the chickens until midnight and distribute it to their bins.

He would sleep maybe six or seven hours. In the meantime, during the day, Charlotte would collect the eggs, put them in trays and then put the trays in wooden boxes. When they had a full load, Walter would take them to the egg board. In Australia, especially Western Australia, the egg board was a necessity. The farmers were not allowed to sell the eggs directly to stores or private individuals. Everything went through the egg board. The egg board made sure price gouging didn't take place in the areas of Australia that were not heavily populated. They didn't just have an egg board, they had a potato board, an onion board, etc.

For nearly three years, they worked like slaves. They didn't have a single vacation and didn't have much to show for all their hard work. Charlotte wanted to quit the farm and move to the city. Walter was making enough money as a store manager to afford the rent for an apartment, but apartments were so scarce that landlords were able to charge a premium. In addition to the rent, landlords charged key money, just for the privilege of getting the apartment. One of Walter's bosses had a friend who was a doctor. The doctor told them of a lady who had an apartment, was ill and would die soon. When she died, Walter asked his boss to speak to his friend on their behalf. The boss told them his friend was a miser and that it wouldn't be easy or cheap. The friend agreed to give them the apartment, but he wanted £300 key money. When Walter came home, he told Charlotte the situation.

While discussing the options, Walter suggested they moved to Canada. They had been getting the Los Angeles Sunday newspaper for about six months, so they knew that there were many jobs available in Canada. Because they were citizens of a British Commonwealth country, they didn't need permission to visit Canada or to immigrate. They only needed to have chest x-rays taken. Charlotte, who had been cooking at the woodstove, turned around and told Walter that if they paid all they owed and still had $1000 left, then they could go. Walter figured out that if they sold the chicken stock and supplies, they would get between $1500 and $1800. More than enough!

## England again / America / Canada / America

They registered to immigrate, and within 28 days, they were on the boat to Canada (via England and America). When they left Australia, John (who was now married) stayed behind. Eventually, he went to Canada, too. He lived with Walter and Charlotte for a while, got a job and then sent for his wife to come to Canada. They stayed in Canada and had a son, Sol, who would become a doctor.

They arrived in England in early November 1952 and stayed with one of Charlotte's WAAF friends and her husband, an Irishman. They had a good time in England. They stayed in a suburb of London and were able to go to the theatre. Time passed quickly, and they were anxious to get to Canada. They booked passage on the *Queen Mary*, which was making the last voyage to the United States. Four or five days later, after a stormy voyage, they arrived in New York.

They went through the immigration procedures in New York and got a one-week transit visa. In New York, they met one of Charlotte's cousins. He was a concentration camp survivor. In the camp, he had been caught stealing food and was supposed to be killed. But when someone else lying near him died, Charlotte's cousin disfigured the man's face and switched identities with him. When the week was up, Walter and Charlotte wanted to stay longer. They went to the immigration department and the man reviewing their Visa told them that the 20 on their Visa looked an awful lot like 28 and they could go ahead and stay another week.

Before Christmas, 1952, they arrived in Toronto, Canada. There the immigration was easy. They showed the officials their passports, gave them their chest x-rays and that was it. They were now Canadian residents.

*Walter's Canadian Landed Immigrant Visa, Feb 2, 1953 – issued at Niagara Falls, Ontario.*

They got a small apartment and within a week Walter started work as a book-keeper. Later on he worked for himself, doing bookkeeping work. He made the acquaintance of some Chartered Accountants, the equivalent to CPAs in America. They found Walter a job as an office manager at a wool mill in Meaford, on Lake Ontario. Meaford was a very small town of 3000 people, roughly

120 miles north of Toronto. On one side of town was the lake and on the other, the Blue Ridge Mountains. It was beautiful.

There they lived the quiet, small town life. Within two years the mill went bankrupt. They closed for two weeks around Christmas time then started to work again. Walter's Chartered Accountant friends told him they had another job for him up north in Timmins. Timmins was very far north. The pay was much better, but it was also much colder. Walter accepted the job and was there within a short time and he became controller of the two sawmills. He was very busy and very prosperous. Walter's most senior boss was friendly to Walter and his family. He insisted that his controller live in a nice house, not in an apartment, so he gave them the down payment for a house and they soon found one. The Saxes joined the other 40 Jewish families in the community.

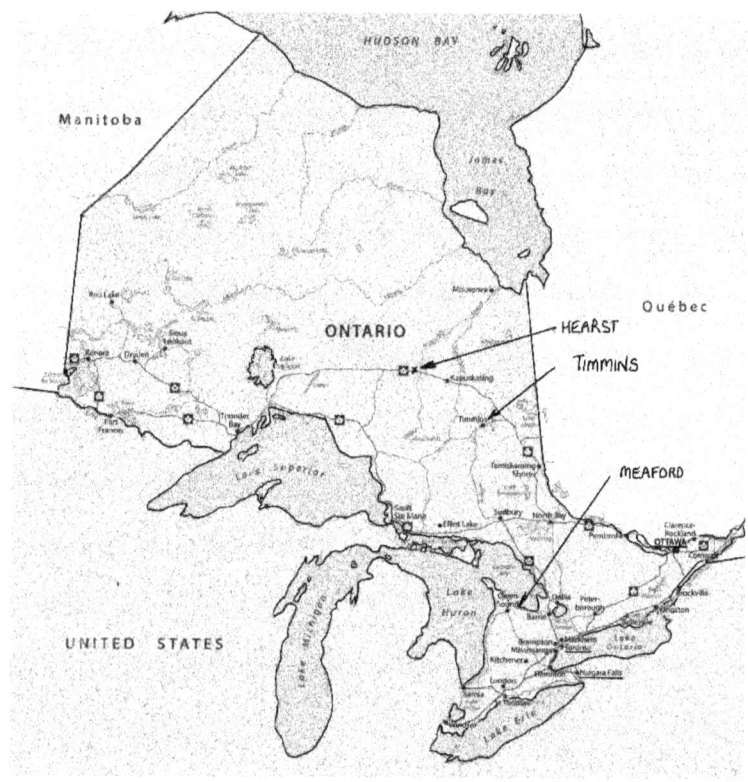

*Map 7a, showing the locations of Meaford, Timmins and Hearst in Ontario Province*

*Map 7b, showing Canada, Ontario Province*

Timmins and the neighbouring town, Shoemaker, were known for their gold mines. Big, prosperous gold mines. At that time a person could buy on the black-market pure gold for $28 an ounce. The control price was $35, but Walter never bought any. It was in Timmins that they received a note from the American Embassy that their Visa had been approved and that they could go to America anytime they wanted. Charlotte was very excited. Walter gave his notice and in October 1956, the family of four arrived in America. Robert had been born in Canada and was just over a year old when they crossed the border.

*Charlotte Sax and baby Robert*

California was like nothing they had known before. After all their travels, especially direct from the cold climate of northern Canada, California was like heaven on earth. They went swimming that October because the weather was similar to the middle of summer for them.

*Walter and Charlotte in California*

In Canada they needed hearty foods to keep warm. They stopped eating their normal diet of fatty foods, such as roast duck. In California, it was the opposite and they had to eat lighter foods. Within a week after arriving in Los Angeles, Walter got a job as a book-keeper in a construction firm. The owners were from Czechoslovakia which was how he got the work. It paid $100 a week. After a few months, Walter asked for a raise and a more responsible position. The chief accountant, who was also from Czechoslovakia, told Walter that the owners didn't want to give him a raise. So Walter found a higher paying job with another construction company. The new boss was crazy. He worked Walter ten hours a day or more. Soon, Walter suffered a heart attack. He was laid off for around two months. After his recuperation, he got a job with a CPA firm.

One day while all four were together, Charlotte, perhaps spurred on by the burgeoning feminist movement, announced that she wanted to move out. She said she couldn't live with Walter and the boys anymore. She wanted to get an apartment and see whether she could live alone or whether she would come back to them. Six or eight months later, Walter received a letter telling him not to discuss anything with his wife. Charlotte was applying for a divorce, and any communication between them had to go through her lawyer. Walter spoke to him several times and in 1976 the divorce was final. Walter had to pay alimony plus Charlotte collected social security. She moved around quite a bit. But Walter and she were still friendly. She moved to Las Vegas and stayed there a few years, then Walter found her a room in Hollywood.

A few years later Charlotte was diagnosed with some form of sclerosis. The progressive disease eventually forced her to live in a convalescent home for the last three or four years of her life. At the end, she was bedridden and looked very bad. Walter visited her often, and up to the end, they were still on good terms.

## Epilogue

Walter only went back once to Czechoslovakia, in the early 90s. He felt people had changed, and not for the better. During the over 40 years of communist occupation, they had learned to move, but not to work. Whether they worked or not they got paid. Everyone

– doctors, engineers and street sweepers – were all state employees. There was no unemployment but work was without initiative. Nobody had ambition for anything except for stealing. In the 30s when the Jews were taken to the concentration camps, people were stealing as much as they could from them. Then it became an honour to steal from the Germans. After the war, when the communists took over everything, and it was nationalised, the people continued to steal. Walter believed that was their life.

Walter and his brothers did not practice Judaism in the camp. In Canada, Walter and Charlotte followed their religion for the sake of the children. They attended Sunday school, Friday Synagogue and kept the Jewish traditions. After Robert had his Bar Mitzvah, he continued to teach Sunday school and was involved until he was 16 or 17. He eventually married a Gentile girl, but she converted and they were married under Jewish tradition in a synagogue. They kept the Sabbath and belonged to a synagogue. Paul, after his Bar Mitzvah, didn't even want to go to the synagogue anymore. But the day Reagan was elected Governor of California, Paul called from Oakland and said it was time for him to go to Vietnam. He got a silver-plated prayer book, a prayer shawl, and a yarmulke and took them with him to Vietnam. Although he wasn't very religious, when he needed it, it was there to cling to.

# Chapter 11

# Bruno Sax: A Gynecologist in Israel

The following information was written by Ruth Harif, daughter of Bruno Sax:

## *Dad – Dr. Dov Bruno Sax*

Dad was an extraordinary man. One of a kind and unique person which once in a generation God sends a man like him to earth to show humanity what good is. Always happy, always sees the beautiful side of everything, willing to help everyone and always with his lot. The most important thing to Dad was his family. For the family, he is willing to do anything. In World War II, Dad joined the British Army along with Erwin, Walter, and Yan. The four of them fell to German captivity for several years. When Dad talked about the captivity, an obviously very, very difficult time, he always remembered to tell us only the "nice" things in the captivity, like the bridge games between them and the Germans, or the chess games, and he never complained about those difficult years. That was a part of his character. To accept what is found and love the existing.

After World War II, Dad decided he wanted to complete his Medical studies in the Czech Republic. When he graduated, he returned to Israel as a doctor and here did the internship. Of course, there was no money. Dad told that he always gave up on lunch and ate a good cake instead. Dad liked cakes very much. This is the love he brought from the Czech Republic. Dad told about the good cakes his mother Yana always made. Dad told that his mother was waking up every morning, sipping a glass of wine to open the day in a good mood and making them a cake or Palacsinta (Czech food

– a thin crepe-like variety of pancake with sweet fillings).

When Dad finished the internship and became a Gynecologist, he worked at Beilinson Hospital in Petah Tikva. All the doctors liked him. He was a great doctor, with a pleasant attitude and a lovely sense of humour. Women who couldn't get pregnant came to him, and his wonderful hands, in most cases, solved the problem. A big part of the treatment was the great faith in him as a person and as a doctor. Dad was always nice and treated all the people around him respectfully – from the department manager to the doctors, to the nurses, and especially to the cleaning staff. There is a well-known story in the family that one day Dad went through Beilinson's Women's department and saw a woman standing on a chair trying to replace a light bulb in a lamp. He immediately helped her off the chair and replaced the bulb himself.

As a father to me, I can only remember good things. We were three kids at home – kids that, as known, sometimes make noise and go wild. Dad never raised his voice or shouted. He was always full of patience with us and solved every problem with a smile.

Dad really liked Mathematics. As a kid, I remember that he always challenged us with Mathematical exercises and problems. When we solved them, immediately a more difficult exercise came, and we just wanted to solve it and move forward.

During the years, Dad made great progress in the profession and he opened a private clinic at home. Mom ran the clinic. Dad worked many hours a day – first at the hospital and then in the clinic. There was never any complaint. Dad always smiled and was satisfied and proud of everything he accomplished – he had a wonderful wife and a lovely mother and three children whom he was very proud of.

During the holidays our house was always filled with wonderful bouquets and cakes that his patients had prepared for him wholeheartedly. Especially, of course, poppy cakes that Dad really loved and he imparted that love to all of us. Until this day, when someone serves me a poppy cake, I can't refuse, and I immediately think of Dad.

Dad loved very much to travel. Every Saturday he was waking us up in the morning and we went to travel. We travelled through all the country. It was very nice, our experience as a very unified family. Initially, there was not much money in the family so Dad bought Dauphine. This is a small and nice car. We were travelling with the Dauphine all over the country. When we got to an ascent, for example the ascents of Jerusalem, Dad was always doing movements with his body as if he was pushing the vehicle, and he urged us to help him and make moves as we push the vehicle too. At the end of the ascent, Dad was satisfied and he was saying: you see – thanks to you we were able to do the ascent. Later, of course, Dad already earned more and the cars were better and didn't need 'help' but we still kept 'pushing'.

Dad was handsome – a tall, good-looking man with blue eyes the colour of the sea. When I was talking to him and watching those beautiful, happy, blue eyes, it always warmed my heart and made me feel good.

I was the eldest, then there was my sister Yifat, and the little one is Zohar. Dad really loved and appreciated the three of us. Dad always gave each one of us the feeling that we, and Mom, are the most important thing to him in the world.

When I was a kid, I learned to play an accordion. I wasn't always persisting with rehearsals. Dad, who loved music so much, told me: "When you grow up, the music will always be with you. When you are sad, it will comfort you, and when you are happy, it will make you happy." That is very true. Every day when I play the piano, I remember it and send Dad the music that will make him happy up there.

Of course, we must talk about the name – Sax. My father was a Gynecologist, so there was always a giggle about the name and the profession: a person who matched his profession to his name. They even wrote about it on the paper several times. They photographed Dad near his sign:

"Dr. Sax Gynecologist."

One day, Dad and Mom sat in a restaurant, and a friend introduced to them a person who palm reads. This stranger, who didn't know my father, took Dad's palm, turned it, observed and studied it and concluded: "You are a wonderful man. There aren't many people like you in the world."

There is no day that I don't think about Dad and remember him. He is always with me.

*Bruno and Chagit Sax*

*Yifat, Zohar and Ruti Sax, children of Bruno and Chagit*

Before moving permanently to Israel from Czechoslovakia in 1947, Bruno completed studies at Charles University Medical Faculty in Prague, with the following translated results:

DEAN'S OFFICE OF MEDICAL FACULTY
CHARLES UNIVERSITY IN PRAGUE
In Prague on October 4th, 1947

## Confirmation

The Dean's Office of the Medical Faculty of Charles University in Prague confirms
that ..................... *Bruno Sax* ............
undertook the following exams of the 1. Medical rigorosum:

| | | | |
|---|---|---|---|
| In General Biology | on May 2nd, 1937 | with Grade D | (Satisfactory) |
| In Physics for Medical Students | on May 10th, 1937 | with Grade A | (Excellent) |
| In Chemistry for Medical Students | on May 4th, 1938 | with Grade D | (Satisfactory) |
| In Anatomy | on October 20th, 1938 | with Grade A | (Excellent) |
| In Histology | on January 14th, 1939 | with Grade A | (Excellent) |
| In Physiology | on March 10th, 1939 | with Grade D | (Satisfactory) |

Dean of Medical Faculty of Charles University in Prague

=signature=   .....................................................

## Letter to Jane Trigg, nee Sax, from Bruno Sax  *October 1966*

"We received your letters and I beg your pardon for answering so late. In May my brother Walter visited us. Because it was difficult for me to visit him, he visited us. Nice of him.

He stayed with us a month. We shall see what will be next year.

Then in August we went to Czechoslovakia, better said, to Moravia. We came to Wien (Vienna), where our friends from the village waited for us in the car. In the village and in the next are some hotels and we visited three of them. We have been in them the last year and felt very good. One can say like in the family. Two of them are situated high in the mountains.

The temperature was between 12 – 22 C. In the beginning it was 10 C at night. They told us that they didn't have a real summer. There were many raining days.

When I came, we had a meeting of the students, who finished the Matura, 61 years ago. Only a few came. Some were sick and many had passed on.

We also met our family; Alenka, Ivanka and Josef. In Vsetin, which is 20 km from where we stayed, my father is buried.

After a month, we returned home and found everything in the same situation as we left. The children are O.K, the grandchildren are growing. Hagit is more or less healthy, and I am feeling well, besides my usual troubles. Doing physiotherapy and walking, and praying it will be better, not worse.

For 3 months we have a new government. They are doing their best, but the Arabs are difficult partners. We hope for the best…

With best regards,

Yours with love,

Hagit and Bruno"

*Bruno Sax and Jarmila, Prague, 1948*

# Chapter 12

# John Sax: A Canadian Citizen

*By Sol Sax*

After leaving Australia and his brother Irwin, wife Martha and their young daughter Jane, John and Jarmila Sax, with two-year-old Sol, arrived in Canada in 1954 after a long sea voyage from Australia via the Suez Canal and Italy. Jarmila complained about Genoa being a very dirty city. They finally landed in New York on 11 August 1954, on the liner *Saturnia*, then crossed into Canada at the Niagara Falls crossing point on 17 August, with little time wasted in America.

They settled in the small but pretty town of Meaford, Ontario, about 150 km north-west of Toronto. Walter, with Charlotte and son Paul, worked as a bookkeeper for the local woollen mill.

*Jarmila and Sol Sax, Canada, 1955*

John had a job in the northern Ontario railway/lumber town of Hearst, Ontario, about 1000 km north of Toronto. John got a job through some Czech acquaintances and ended up grading timber at a large sawmill owned by two Czech entrepreneurs. It was too isolated for Jarmila, and so she and Sol stayed in Meaford with Walter and his family. They would visit maybe once a year and John would come home for his holidays. Hearst was a long train ride from Meaford.

In 1956, they moved to Toronto when the sawmill owners gave John a job as shipper/receiver at their retail lumber yard in Toronto called Weston Road Lumber, where John worked until his retirement in 1983. After a brief stint in an immigrant apartment on Jarvis Street, well known for its 'ladies of the night', they bought a small house in a very multicultural part of the town – mainly Italians, Slavs, Jews, and some white Canadians. John got along with all of them.

In 1958 Jarmila and Sol finally returned to Czechoslovakia to visit her and John's relatives, while John stayed home and worked. While they were away, he bought a small lake-front property in Muskoka, then a three to four-hour drive from Toronto, on a very rocky and uninviting piece of land. It was all he could afford. When Jamila saw this property on her return from Czechoslovakia, she said, "John, what have you done?" But he had vision and convinced her that he could fix it up, landscape, plant some trees, and it would be beautiful ... and he was right.

They spent most weekends and all their summer holidays at their lake-front cottage, which John built himself from the ground up, including the foundations, framing, roofing, interior furnishings, and even the bed frames, dressers and kitchen cabinets. John was very handy with a saw and a hammer and could build almost anything. He was also a very powerful man, with a strong upper body, who could easily lift a large wooden beam, a thick piece of plywood or drywall. Mixing concrete by hand, he poured the foundations, installed all the joists, built the subfloor, all the walls, roof etc. This was all done by hand with the help of a friend called Max also doing what chores he could. Over the course of his 30 years at the cottage, he also built a guest cabin, a storage shed, a dock, and a boathouse.

*John, Jarmila and Sol Sax,
at the cabin John built at Muskoka, Canada*

They lived in the heart of Toronto until 1963 when the lumber yard moved from its central city location to the western suburbs. They then moved into an apartment in a northwest suburb called Downsview until Sol graduated from high school in 1969 and then moved into another much bigger rental apartment closer to work. The space was handy as Jarmila's two sons from her previous marriage (Libor and Bohumil) both immigrated from Czechoslovakia in 1969 and 1970 to live with the Saxes for about a year each, until they got jobs and could get a place of their own. John 'adopted' these young men as if they were his own, helping them whenever he could, babysitting for the kids, and making them an integral part of his family.

Condominiums were just starting to become viable in the 1970s, so they bought one closer to John's work and stayed there for about five years until the building they were in started to go downhill. They finally settled into a much nicer condominium near some parkland where John and Jarmila made some very good friends. They would swim in the pool most nights, and John would often go for long walks in the park.

*John, friend and Jarmila, visiting California, 1983*

John retired at the age of 72 and spent more time traveling with Jarmila, often spending several weeks in Florida for the winter. John was also able to reconnect with his brothers, first in Israel, then in Singapore, and finally, a visit back to Western Australia in 1987 with Sol. Jarmila died in 1986 of suicide following many years of depression and several hospitalisations.

John then reconnected with his childhood sweetheart from his hometown of Novy Hrosenkov, Milada Orsagova, and would spend weeks in the winter there, while she would come to Canada in the summers to the cottage. When Sol married in 1987 and began his family, John, often with Milada, would be the regular babysitter. He loved playing with the kids, and they loved him. He became known as Papa John to almost everyone. He was over to Sol's house so often Sol and his wife Dominique built an extension in the back of their house so that he would have his own apartment. Unfortunately, just as he was starting to move in shortly after his 80$^{th}$ birthday, he died. On June 1, 1992, he went for his afternoon walk in the park and was hit by a young driver while trying to cross a busy road, jaywalking one block away from the crosswalk. He survived the trauma for several hours but eventually succumbed to his injuries.

His funeral was attended by many of his long-time friends and business colleagues, all of whom spoke highly of his intelligence, his humility and his work ethic. He was loved by old and young alike. He was a terrific dad, granddad, and friend."

*Sol, Jarmila and John Sax, Christmas 1980, Canada*

# Chapter 13

# Edith/Eva:
# The Sister who Survived and Stayed

The families of Erwin, Walter, John, and Bruno have all contributed information about the four brothers and their history after leaving for Palestine before World War II, their survival through the war and their relocation to other countries in the years after the war. Unfortunately, similar information has not been available, so far, about their one surviving sister, Edith/Eva. The following history has been pieced together from various sources, including several letters from her family in the early 1990s to Jane Trigg, nee Sax:

*Ruth Sax holding Eva Sax, before WWII*

Edith/Eva Sax was born in 1905, so she was 34 in 1939 when the war started. She had previously married Josef Konarik, a catholic dentist. In 1934, their first daughter, Alenka, was born, followed by a second daughter; Evanka in 1936 and a son, Josef in 1946, after the war.

They lived at Valasske Klobouky, which is south of Vsetin and close to the Slovakian border. Josef had his dental practice there.

Because she had married a non-Jew, she survived the war and only spent two or three months in a detention camp in Czechoslovakia, probably Terezin, otherwise, she would have suffered the same fate as most of the Sax family.

*Eva and son Josef, after the war, about 1947*

When her four brothers left Czechoslovakia in 1947, she stayed behind with her husband and children. While her brothers enjoyed the full freedom of overseas travel and eventual permanent life in four different countries, Eva and her family had to bow down to the communist regime and its rigid control of all aspects of life in Czechoslovakia, if they wanted to work and survive.

*Josef Snr, Eva and baby Josef, in Valasske Klobouky, Czechoslovakia*

*Eva and husband Josef Konarik, in later life.*

Prior to the mid-1980s, all personal written communication out of Czechoslovakia followed a safe but heavily restricted line if the contents were to be allowed to proceed to their destination, whatever the country. No comments were to be made about the government and the economy – definitely no negative comments. No mention about lack of food or variety. No one was to comment on having to wait in queues to buy common goods like soap, medication and basic food items. Nothing could be said suggesting a wish to travel or move permanently out of the perfect Czechoslovakian Communist society.

The 1948 government coup brought down the full nightmare of a Stalinist Communist regime on the lives of all Czech citizens. It dominated all activities, and those not complying with its requirements were dealt with harshly.

The Soviet Union dictated the country's political policies and decisions, with Czechoslovakia firmly concreted into its role within the Eastern bloc, the Warsaw Pact, and Comecon.

The four Sax brothers, with their families, got out just in time, before the Iron Curtain came down. There were many similarities between the "just-in-time" flight from the Nazis before World War II and their escape from communist tyranny.

By 1990, letters from Eva and her family displayed the signs of freedom – comments about industries collapsing, difficulties with finding or keeping employment, doubts on the ability of the government, and thoughts about potential holidays outside of the country.

From the late 1940s to the 1950s, people judged to be not actively supporting socialism could be interrogated, intimidated, put under surveillance, have their homes searched, and all their privacy invaded. Bribes became common. People were reported to the Secret Police for minor disagreements between neighbours or work colleagues. Filing complaints about the system and signing petitions asking for change could mean imprisonment. Companies were headed by tradesmen with no administrative experience, as required by government policies.

From 1949 to 1954, show trials and purges removed Catholics, Jews, former military chiefs, politicians supporting democracy, anyone with pre-war or wartime Western connections, and out of favour high-ranking party members. Such trials were not fair, with defendants being declared guilty before the trial. Judges worked on behalf of the party. At least 200 high ranking people were killed through this process.

Further purges were carried out after the 1968 liberal reforms or "Prague Spring", although there were no executions. After interrogation and intimidation by the Secret Police, the accused were expelled from the party and removed from their employment. Authors who didn't support socialism had their works banned. Government employees and leaders of social activist groups were purged. Stage productions were banned if they did not support the state.

During those years controlled by Stalin, wealthy successful farmers were brought under control of the state. Farms were nationalised and collectivised. 50 ha was the maximum area allowed for privately owned land. Farmers were forced to join the collectives. Those who refused were denied supplies such as fertiliser, seeds, and machine parts. They were also publicly denounced and blackmailed. However, Collectivism was proven to be very inefficient and eventually failed, as it did in other Communist states.

Religion was seen as the major rival to the Party. A religious underground was created by clergy and lay people, as the Party took over church properties. All monasteries and most convents were closed. Many clergy were murdered. Others were jailed or sent to labour camps.

The worker was now the top citizen, often regardless of their minimal management skills. Miners received high wages, pensions and holidays. Workers were paid more than university professors. Low-level employees who were communists received holidays in other socialist states.

Education became centred on the study of Marxism/Leninism. Universities favoured working-class families and the members of communist youth organisations.

The government-controlled media was the voice of the regime, with censorship starting in 1948. TV news was filled with great expectations for agricultural and factory production. After the attempted liberal reforms of 1968, magazines and journals were closed down.

In the 1970s and 80s, many artists were imprisoned or forced to leave the country. Dissidents were shut down by any method available. Discussion or promotion of human rights was banned.

Eva and her family did what the majority of the population did to adapt and survive in these conditions. They spent their weekends improving their houses, retreating to country cottages, growing fruit, vegetables and flowers, and surrounding themselves with nature. They also put time into sport, swimming, skiing, and skating.

Democracy returned to Czechoslovakia with a rush in November 1989, because of the "Velvet Revolution" and 40 years of a Communist nightmare had ended.

There are several letters sent by her family to Jane Trigg, which give some understanding of life in Czechoslovakia during and after the communist government period. They are mostly about the family of Eva's son, Josef, born in 1946, and his family: wife Jana and sons Martin and Petr (Peter).

Eva's choice to remain and live under the extremely harsh communist regime had heavy consequences, with few of the freedoms applying to most western nations. For the short time after the war, when it was possible to leave the country for the west, as her brothers did, it had not become obvious how harsh the government would become in future years, dominated by Stalin-era soviet Russia.

*"Olomouc 10/4/1990* (Translated from Czech)

*Dear Jane and family,*

*Give my regards and best wishes to your parents. I hope they are alright. My mum is alright but she can't see well.*

*She shifted to Valasske Klobouky, her own home, where she stays through the summer. In the winter she is with Evanka in Ostrava, where there is central heating. In Valasske Klobouky, we haven't got it and the heating is by coal. There is a lot of work attached to it and Mum, seeing she is 84 years old, can't manage it…*

*My wife Jana is at the same place of work where she is very* happy. She is the paymaster. She likes sewing where she sews mainly for the boys' trousers and even winter coats, but mainly for herself. Now we can get a German magazine 'Burda' where she finds a lot of inspiration. I have changed my place of work. I am working in the middle of the square in Olomouc where they have got their offices. My job is getting material for the factory. My profession is obtaining materials.

Work here is much more complicated than with you. Merchandise is not here so we have to travel a lot to get the different requirements. I get a work car and I am driving it myself on these trips. Sometimes it is very hard but we hope that it will get better after the revolution.

In November, as you might have heard, the communist reign has finished. Now we are trying to trade a lot with the west, mainly, I think, with USA. It probably will be after the election which we have on the 10$^{th}$ June 1990. We also got a new President. He is an ex author, a very intelligent and clever man. Now we can already travel to the west, but I haven't been anywhere yet. I am going to try to go to Vienna in Austria. For us it is quite expensive, because of the job situation.

John has been here from Canada and Bruno from Israel. In the summer there is going to be a big gathering when John, Bruno and Walter are all coming. For that occasion, I have to have our house painted. Mum is going to be very glad when she sees her brothers. They are coming in August.

Of course, I will go to Valasske Klobouky to greet them.

Once more our sincere regards,

Josef"

"Olomouc 25 Sept. Year?

Hi Jane,

I am sending my best regards to you, Oma, Opa and Geoff…

…Our boys are sending you their best regards. They have 2 months holidays (July and August)…

The weather is very nice and warm. We are going swimming in the pool. We have, of course, no sea here. Maybe we shall go once to Yugoslavia to the sea. Jana likes swimming and warm weather. The second week of holidays we shall have in August. We shall go again to see mum (Eva). We have here holidays one month and the rest we take in winter.

Jane, you asked what we are doing in winter. The boys have half year holidays in February – one week of it. The winter this year was quite good. We hope we shall have a lot of snow. We can go skiing. Before we went more often but lately the winters were not good. On bigger mountains they have cable cars but on the smaller ones where we used to go, we had to climb them on foot. The boys love to go sledding. Till now they don't know any ice skating. In winter they make snow men.

Last winter in January it was exceptionally cold. It was -30C here. It didn't last very long, only about a fortnight, then it got a little warmer. We enjoy very much winter sports. Of course, we have big mountains. About 2,000 metres high and on these mountains there are hotels and chalets. It is possible to travel there and find accommodation. I don't have the courage to go there because it is so expensive.

At last Jana's wish came true. We bought an old house with a little garden. It is about 18 kms from Olomouc. It is about 1,000 squ. metres. The house is very old and it will require a lot of work to repair and install a new roof. Jana has a little garden and we *put in potatoes, vegetables and flowers.*

*We are still beginners but we hope next year it will be better. We planted apricot and peach trees. We will see whether they will be any good because we are quite in the north and these trees require a lot of sun. We travel there on weekends…*

*Once again, my best regards and I wish you and your whole family the best of health and also Oma and Opa.*

*Josef, Jana, Martin and Petr*

**Bruno, Eva, Josef (snr), Jana. In front- sons Martin and Petr, 1989**

*"Olomouc 2.8.90*

*Dear Jane and Family,*

*I received your two letters, which have given me great joy. You write you will visit us. Of course, we will welcome you and are looking forward to meet you both. Do not worry about accommodation in Olomouc, you can stay with us. I and Jana will take holidays in order to be all the time with you. It is not clear to me where you will stay in Prague. Whether you intend to stay in a hotel or at Victors', whether Victor will meet you at the* airport, or whether you want me to come to the airport to meet you there. Please give me these details…Do not be afraid of the winter, because in the last few years there was not much snow. On the way to Olomouc we could stop in Jihlava and Brno…

Now there is bad news and because of it I did not answer your letter promptly. My mother is very bad. In her age we have to expect the worst. After the operation she is in a lot of pain. My sisters and I took weekly turns to look after her. The doctors in the hospital say there is no hope for her.

In August we are expecting the visit of Walter, John and Bruno. They will stay for six weeks. I would like to stay with them a week.

Give our regards to your dad and tell him he will be in our thoughts. I do not know whether my mother will live long enough to see her brothers…

Jana and sons send their best regards,

Joseph, Jana and children."

Letter in Autumn, 1991:

"Dear Jane and family,

I am sorry that I haven't written to you for some time. We have big worries because I was left without work when our business collapsed and was closed down. I am supposed to start at a private business, however nothing is certain. I hope that I will not have to go on unemployment benefits. That is very hard to live on.

It will be still worse in 1992. There is a lot of privatisation *going on here and state enterprises which are still in existence are dilapidated (falling down, crumbling).*

*You asked about the Sax family. I know nothing that you wouldn't know. Nobody has told me anything and now they won't even say. I know that they came from Novy Hrosenkov, in the region of Valasske Klobouky, which is about 60 km away...It is close to the Slovakian border. They are now discussing it in the parliament because the Slovaks want to leave the federation. It would be a disaster.*

*I am writing in sad times. Here it is in autumn weather. The temperature is already on zero and it is raining. Here and probably at your place it is a holiday. At that time, October 28th, 1918, our Czech Republic originated, when the Austro-Hungarian Empire crumbled. On November 2nd is the remembrance of All Saints. I go to Hovezi where both parents are buried. It is close to Novy Hrozenkov...*

*Love and kisses to you all,*

*Josef, Petr, Martin and Jana. (Konarik)"*

Letter in November 1992 (Translated)

*"Sorry for not writing.*

*I have work in my job. We went on a study tour to Hungary – Budapest and Vienna. We went there to have a look how they do the work in our line of employment. I liked it. The firm paid for the trip. Shopping and eating in restaurants is still expensive.*

*Getting ready to split the republic. From 1/1/93 we will be independent (of Slovakia).*

*Winter has begun. For the first time we had a little frost in the morning. It is very unpleasant for me in my job because I go* in the car to clients with offers of steel. The roads are already starting to freeze over and there is more risk of an accident...

Jana has been in hospital with her eyes. One has still from her childhood some small irregularity in her right eye. She is still at home. She is looking forward to going back to work...

I still go home to Valasske Klobouky. We celebrate on 2<sup>nd</sup> November a holiday (Thinking of the departed – that is, All Saints). We all went to the cemetery to see mum and dad's grave.

Love from us all."

*Brother and sister-Bruno with Eva. Late in life.*

# Chapter 14

# Origins

Sax Family history, as recorded by Jane Trigg from her father, Erwin Sax:

The Sax family originally came from Spain, through the Middle East. Because of the Spanish Inquisition, they moved to Austria. They settled down in a village close to the Moravian/Austrian border in Moravia.

Erwin's great grandfather was Jewish. Jews weren't allowed to own land. They were forced into commerce and were treated as unclean so far as society went. Aristocrats (gentlemen) didn't do any trading. As a result of this treatment Jews were looked down on. Aristocrats owned land but said Jews could not own land. Prior to Emperor Joseph II, Jews were only allowed to live in ghettos. Emperor Joseph II did away with ghettos. He was a son of Empress Maria Theresa. She allowed Jews to have property and farms. Before, they had been allowed to have businesses and houses but not farms in the country.

At this time Erwin's great grandfather's three sons came to Novy Hrozenkov and went into business. (Jews went into things like groceries and pubs.)

Erwin's grandfather was Herman Sax. His brother was Baron Adolf von Sax. Adolf began to make commercial honey which was unknown before then. He was made Baron for his work with honey.

Erwin's grandmother was Cecilia. They had heaps of children. One was Sigmund. Also, there was Jakob (in Vsetin) and Karl (in Vienna) – he was killed in World War I on the Western front. Finally, there was Marcus (in Vienna) and Carolina (in Hrozenkov).

Baron Adolf Sax had two sons who ran the honey business. In his old age, the old man had something wrong with his neck.

Without their father knowing, the sons bought cheap, unclean honey and gave it to the bees to purify. The bees died of overwork.

The sons sacrificed the bees. Their Uncle came to have a look at the bees, got so excited and upset that he had a heart attack and died on the spot. His two sons started a lolly factory making lollies from honey but didn't do any good.

Baron Sax had three sons and a daughter. One son was a solicitor in Vienna. When the old man was dead, they started to argue about property. In the end the children didn't get anything. The lawyers got the lot.

Sax is not a common name in Europe. Adolph's marriage was an arranged one. He was shown a photo of his bride-to-be. At the wedding she was veiled. After they were pronounced man and wife, he found out he had married the older sister of the person whose photo he had seen. Adolph made life very hard for his wife. They lived in the next town. Erwin couldn't remember the name of Adolph's wife.

During World War I, Erwin was a child aged seven to eleven years old and not much travelling was done. When he was older, he used to call on Adolph when he went through the next village, a five to six kilometre walk. Adolph told Erwin not to get married. He died when Erwin was about fourteen, and his wife had died previously. Erwin's great grandfather was in commerce, a grocer. By his grandfather's time they were dealing in already-cut wood. Erwin's father started the mill with his brother, David. Erwin's father was 48 when he was called up to fight in World War I. There was no fighting in Czechoslovakia but Czechoslovakia was in the Austrian Empire, so over one million Czech men went to fight on that side. He never recovered from the war, and died in 1922.

One of Jakob's sons, Walter, was in the Czech army in World War I. He spent time in the Czech consulate in Israel. He was sent back to Czechoslovakia then came to Australia a few months before Erwin came out. He went to Melbourne and set up a factory making some sort of timber products. When Erwin moved to Gnowangerup, Walter wrote to Erwin to come to Melbourne. He would give them jobs and had a house ready. Erwin had moved around so much and had just got the job in Gnowangerup so he decided not to go. Erwin wrote to Walter in Melbourne to tell him but heard nothing more.

**Note from Sol Sax, Canada**, about his knowledge of the origins of the Sax family (10 June 1997):

"As for the Sax history, you've noted that Sax is neither Czech nor German. When I asked my father about this, he did mention that "X" is a very common letter in Spanish – a fact you will confirm in any Spanish text. He is aware that his family were "Sephardic", Jews originating from Spain. During the great dispersion of Jews early in the first millennium (known as the Diaspora) many Jews migrated to Spain – likely because of the similar climate and I guess the politics were favourable. There were many great synagogues in Spain – some still exist.

Anyway, most Jews left during the Spanish Inquisition and I assume the Sax's ended up in Central Europe. That's about all I know. Regarding the beekeeper's story ... that's news to me."

**Note from Geoff Trigg**: For added interest in the Spanish origin possibility of the Sax family, on the Spanish Mediterranean coast, south of Valencia, is the coastal city of Alicante. By heading inland, north-west through Novelda, Monovar, Elda and Petrer, you can arrive at the town of **Sax**, which includes a Moorish castle.

History records that in March, 1492, the Spanish Catholic monarchs, having retaken Spain from the Moors, signed a requirement that all Jews were to leave Spain. There was a major exodus of hundreds of thousands of Jews from Spain who went to initially live in the Ottoman Empire. Those Jews became known as Sephardic Jews. Ottoman ships were sent to Spain to pick up these exiled Jews and they were taken to Istanbul to avoid any further mass killing or genocide. Before that exodus, Jews and Moors lived peacefully with Spanish Christians and added to the wealth and prosperity of the country. Many Jews who stayed after 1492 and converted to Catholicism were later subjected to questioning and sometimes death by the Inquisition.

# Table: Sax Family Tree

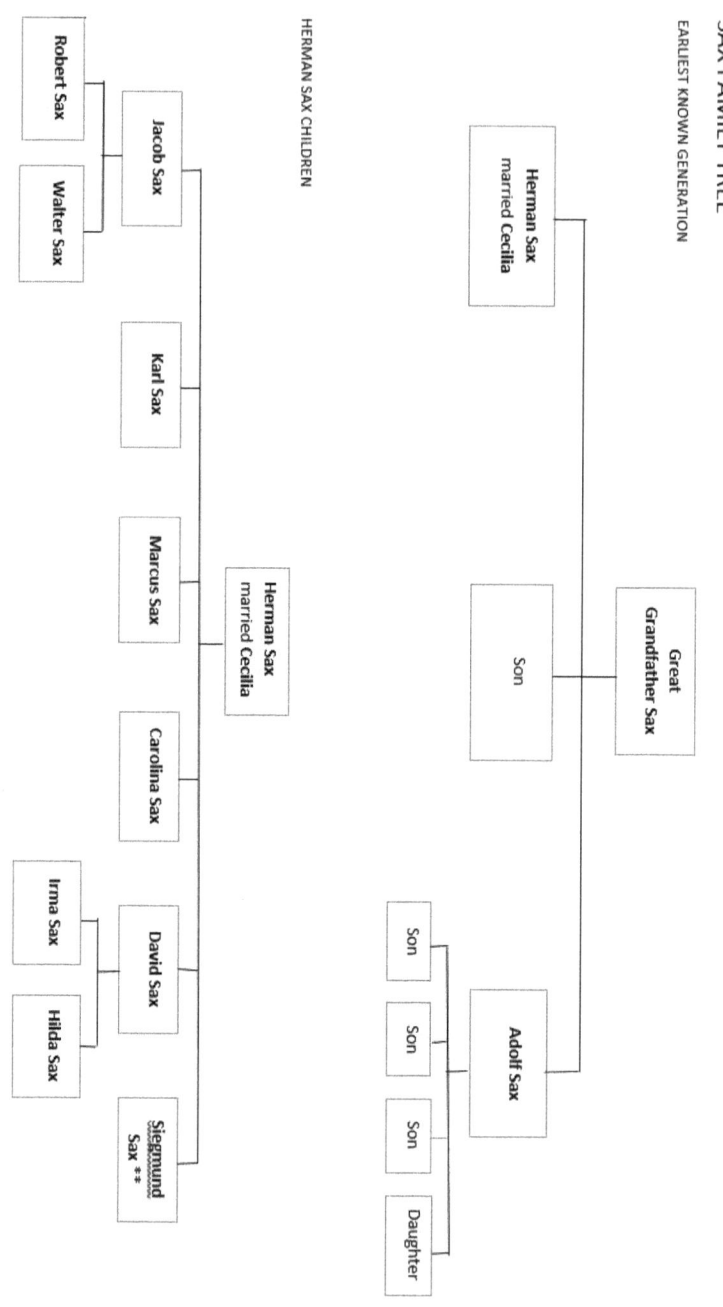

234

# SAX FAMILY TREE

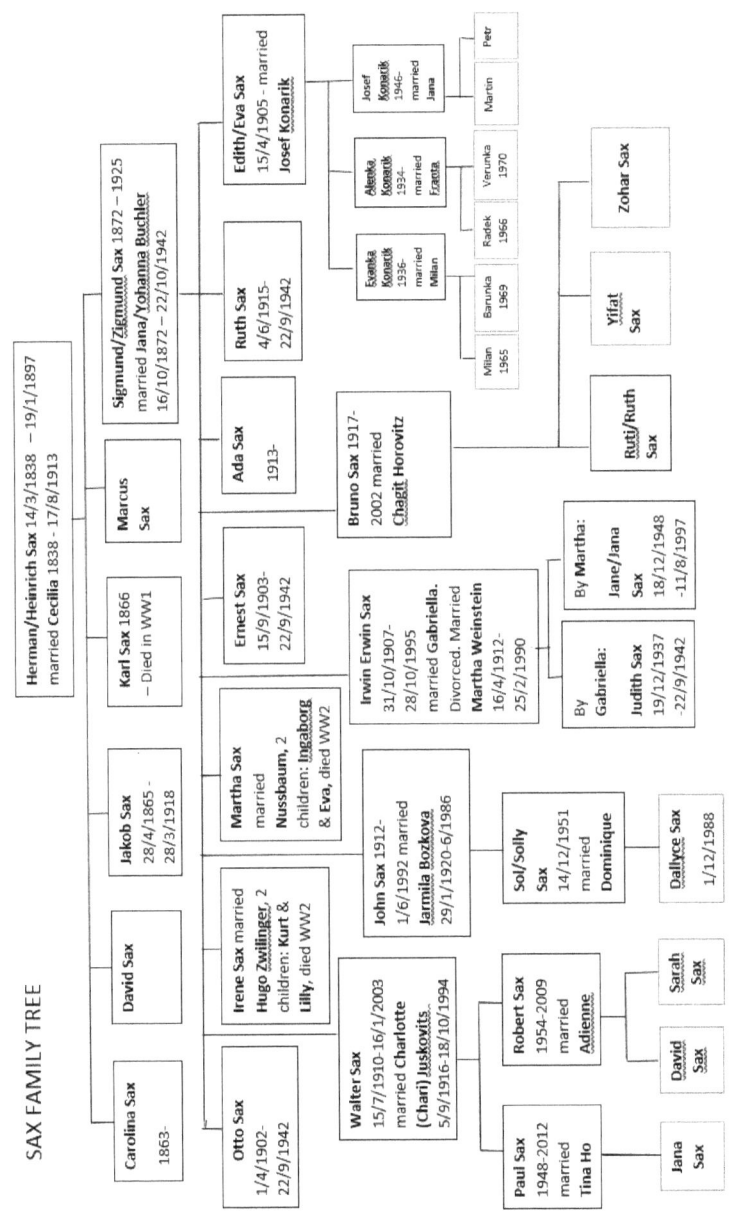

235

# SAX FAMILY TREE
## NEXT GENERATIONS

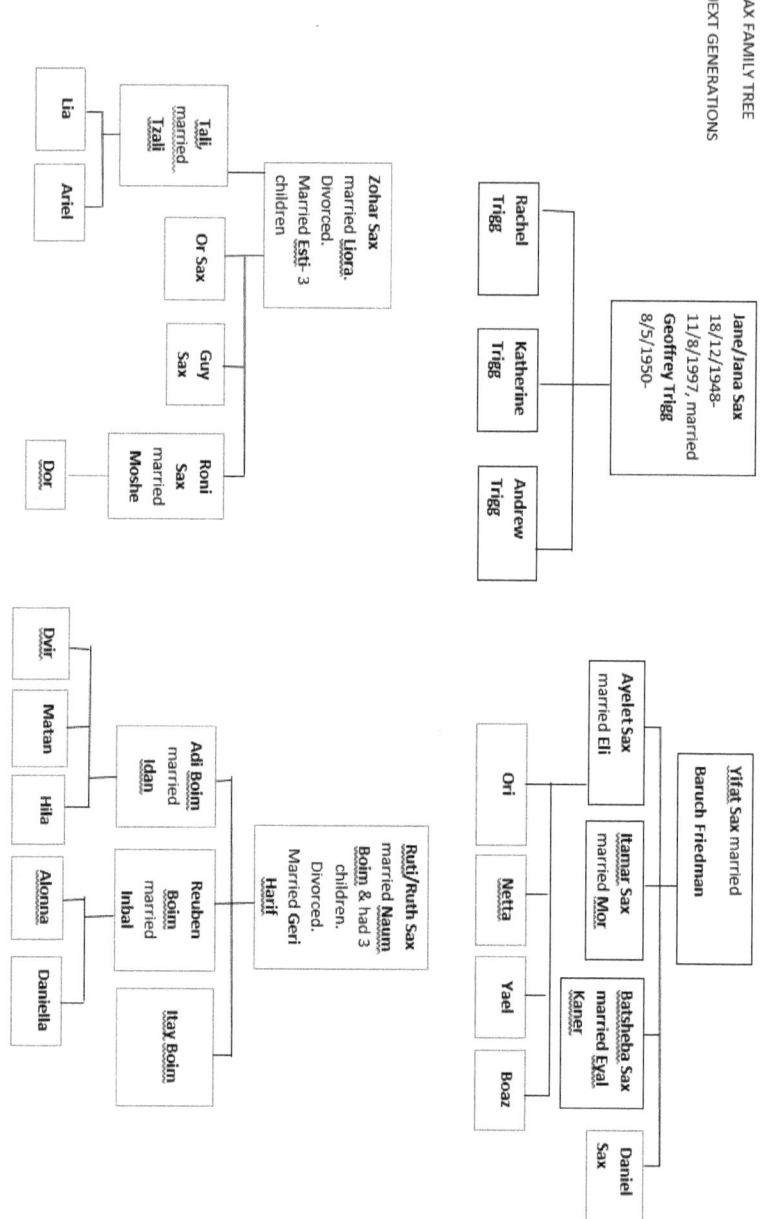

## Family Origins in Czechoslovakia

There are a number of sources of information regarding the earliest known generations of the Sax family in Czechoslovakia.

One tragic list is from the ceiling of the Pinkas Synagogue in the Jewish quarter of Prague. Under the heading for Novy Hrosenkov, the list of Sax family members murdered in Nazi concentration camps is as follows:

|  | Birth date shown on Vsetin memorial |  |  |
| --- | --- | --- | --- |
| Sax, Arnost: | 15/9/1903 | – | 22/9/1942 |
| Sax, Ota: | 1/9/1902 | – | 22/9/1942 |
| Sax, Ruth: | 4/6/1915 | – | 22/9/1942 |
| Sax Judita: | 19/12/1937 | – | 22/9/1942 |
| Sax, Jana: | 16/10/1874 | – | 22/10/1942 |
| Sax, Villm: | 14/3/1870 | – | 22/10/1942 |

In the actual printing, with "NOVY HROSENKOV" in larger red letters, after a number of other family names from that town, the word *SAX* is listed, with the following first names shown with the first letter in red:

| Arnost | 15.IX.1905 – 22.IX.1942 |
| --- | --- |
| Ota | 1.IV.1902 – 22.IV.1942 |
| Ruth | 4.VI.1915 – 22.1V.1942 |
| Judita | 19.XII.1937 – 22.IX.1942 |
| Jana | 16.X.1874 – 22.X.1942 |
| Vllm | 14.III.1870 – 22.IX.1942 |

*Part of the Pinkas Synagogue listing of Jews murdered by the Nazis.*

These names and their birth dates are included on a black stone grave memorial in white letters at the cemetery in Vsetin :

*Headstone of several Sax family members killed by Nazis*

A photo has been provided showing Bruno standing between two Jewish grave monuments, at Vsetin, inscribed:
"Siegmund Sax: 5 January 1925"
"Karoline Kulka GEB Sax 14 December 1924".
Both are probably the dates of their death.

*Bruno visiting cemetery memorials for Siegmund Sax and Karoline Kulka, nee Sax, Vsetin, Czech Republic*

A photo has also been provided showing a grave monument with a Jewish star on the top, inscribed:

"Jakub Sax
28/4/1865 – 28/3/1918"

*Jakub Sax cemetery memorial*

A further photo shows a two-piece grey granite memorial inscribed: "Herman Sax 19 January 1897".

This would be the date of his death.

*Herman Sax memorial*

Another two-piece grey granite memorial is inscribed:
   Cecilie Sax 17 August 1913.
This would be Herman's wife and her date of death.

*Cecile Sax memorial*

Erwin Sax has stated that his (and his sibling's) father, Sigmund, started a timber mill in Novy Hrosenkov with his brother David. He also said that his grandfather, Herman, was already dealing in pre-cut wood, i.e., before the Sax Novy Hrosenkov saw mill started.

On a map, five or six kilometres on the road to the west from Novy Hrozenkov, the town of Hovezi exists. That town name is connected to the Sax family in another document, at an earlier time.

Official archival information exists in regards to the locations of earlier Sax generations, as obtained in Vsetin, on 9.5.1995 and shown below:

## Archive Document from Vsetin, Czech Republic (Translated):

**Government District Archive, Vsetin**
Registered:

Manager,
Ivana Bartuskova
Jedlova 1900
Ostrava – Poruba

Your letter Our No. 390/95 Processed Vsetin on day 9.5.1995
Item: Extract from Census Hovezi and Novy Hrosenkov Districts
Enclosed sending you registered extracts from Census District Hovezi and Novy Hrosenkov from Years 1857 and 1869, from which it is evident that Amalie Sachsova was the Aunt of your Grandfather Zigmunda Sachse.

We recommend for you to get in touch with the archive in Brno (the Capital of Moravia), where they have the District Register of Labuty (which is the birthplace of Amalie Sachsove) and Kyjov District from where the Sachova family comes from.

# EXTRACT

## District Census for Hovezi from Year 1857

| No. 18 | | Birth | Religion | Residence |
|---|---|---|---|---|
| Sachs Salomon | | 1802 | Israelite | Kyjov |
| Sachs Veronika | Wife | 1812 | " | " |
| Sachs Heinrich | Son | 14.3.1838 | " | " |
| Sachs Ignac | Son | 22.9.1840 | " | " |
| Sachs Adolf | Son | 10.10.1844 | " | " |
| Sachs Kristina | Daughter | 1846 | " | " |
| Sachs Amalie | Daughter | 1849 | " | " |

By request, this extract is given to Ivana Bartuskova, resident of Jedlova No. 1900 Ostrava after a 20 Crown payment.

Signature

Vsetin 9.5.1995          PhDr. Ladislav Baletka
Director of Government Archive
Vsetin Archive
(Stamp attached)

# EXTRACT

## District Census for Novy Hrosenkov from Year 1869

| No. 358 | | Birth | Religion | Residence |
|---|---|---|---|---|
| Sax Ignac | | 1840 | Jew | Hovezi |
| Sax Rosalie | Wife | 1847 | " | " |
| Sax Karl | Son | 1866 | " | " |

| No. 439 | | Birth | Religion | Residence |
|---|---|---|---|---|
| Sax Adolf | | 1844 | Jew | Kyjov |
| Sax Terezie | Wife | 1843 | " | " |
| Sax Amalie | Sister | 1851 | " | " |

| No. 466 | | Birth | Religion | Residence |
|---|---|---|---|---|
| Sax Herman | | 1838 | Jew | Hovezi |
| Sax Cecilie | Wife | 1838 | " | " |
| Sax Jakob | Son | 1865 | " | " |
| Sax Karl | Son | 1866 | " | " |
| Sax Zigmund | Son | 1868 | " | " |
| Sax Marie | Daughter | 1862 | " | " |
| Sax Karolina | Daughter | 1863 | " | " |

By request, this extract is given to Ivana Bartuskova, resident of Jedlova No. 1900 Ostrava after a 20 Crown payment.

Signature

Vsetin 9.5.1994 PhDr. Ladislav Baletka
Director of Government District Archive
Vsetin Archive
(Stamp attached)

# Chapter 15

# A Collection of Sax Humour, Facts and Oddities

## From Erwin, Martha and Jane Sax

*From Erwin:* Neighbour with an unfaithful wife. Drunk one night and crying in his beer, "Oh God, Oh God, eight children and none of them mine.
*From Martha:* A well-known help to remove a wine stain on a table cloth is to put lots of salt on it to soak up the spill. When salt was spilled at a restaurant Erwin called for red wine to help remove it.
*From Erwin:* His oldest brother Otto was a dreamer. His second-oldest brother Ernest was more interested in running the saw mill than Otto. The sawmill at Novy Hrosenkov had a steam engine and a room behind it. Otto spent most of his time in that room day dreaming. He willingly helped Ernest but didn't want responsibility and didn't hold a grudge. He was clever and played well at chess and cards. He also bowled, using 9 wooden pins and a wooden ball. "If you can dream and not make dreams your master. Otto made dreams his master".

Everyone helped with the maths at the mill, even the girls. Lengths, widths, volumes, weights, checking costs of items bought and accounts to be sent out.

Bruno was good at languages – French, Czech, German, Latin and Hebrew. He read books in English and did exams in Hebrew.

For some strange reason, electric kettles or jugs, irons and toasters didn't last long with Martha (Erwin's wife) using them. They seemed to fuse out well before time. She could walk down their quiet street in Perth and dogs would run up to their front fence and bark as she went past. She seemed to send out a mental message that she was passing.

Martha made great strudels and cakes, like Black Forest Tortes with seven layers. As she got older the number of layers decreased and the remaining layers got thicker because her eyesight was getting worse. They were still beautiful!

Martha finally had the son she wanted when Jane married me (Geoff). She put a lot of work into Christmas and birthday presents. One time she went into Perth from her suburb on the bus, purchased a heavy crow bar that I had mentioned I was interested in and brought it home by bus. She then gift-wrapped it for Christmas!

She also often asked about what I would like her to make for an evening meal when we were coming to stay for a weekend from the country. That happened a number of times, even when it was a special visit for Jane's birthday. Jane objected but Martha said "Geoff always loves my cooking and tells me that, so I want to cook what he likes".

Gift wrapping was not important for Erwin. Initially gifts we gave him would be wrapped in purpose-bought coloured wrapping paper. We quickly learnt that the paper meant nothing and it was ripped off with no comments. From then on newspaper was the only wrapping for his gifts.

Erwin smoked most of his life – from cigarettes to a pipe and then small cigars. He finally gave up and, to replace the habit, he ate lots of a small tablet lolly or breath mint called "Tic Tacs". His smoking meant his taste buds had almost given up in later years. His eyesight started to fade and when Martha cooked a nice meal, he was often seen covering it with salt, because he couldn't taste or see it, until someone stopped him from adding more.

Slivovitz, a form of plum Brandy they drank in the old days in central Europe, was always kept in a cabinet at the Sax home in Perth. Martha had said that she only drank it when she was ill. When she got the bottle out once to offer us drinks, she found that it was almost empty, so she said, "Have I been that ill?"

Erwin had hobbies, apart from playing cards and chess. He grew strawberries, lots of strawberries. He started with a few pots of plants and then decided to pot the runners from each plant which would then grow even more strawberries. After a few years of potting every runner, he had hundreds of plants. The neighbours knew he always needed new pots and in return they got strawberries and jam back, after Martha had made the jam. Wood turning was another hobby in his later years. That allowed us to buy him good sized pieces of quality wood, to let him create larger bowls, plates or lamp-bases on his wood lathe. He was more interested in finishing the job quickly than taking time to sand and polish the final result. More than once, when given a good-sized piece of quality timber he would take less than a day to convert it to a small tray or bowl, plus a large pile of wood shavings. He was not one for slowly and patiently working to achieve a high-quality product.

His main hobby was gardening – mowing his lawns, pruning his trees and extra watering of anything looking in need of a drink. Their garden always looked lush as did their few fruit trees. Amongst others they had a lemon tree and a grapefruit tree. We were always offered fruit from both trees until we cut open a grapefruit and found the inside moved! It had been infested by an insect called a fruit fly and the eggs turned into small grubs. After destroying the fruit we were given, we told him the problem and he put out baits to kill the insects. With his bad eyesight we often wondered how long he had been eating the fruit, which he loved, grubs and all!

Erwin told the story of why he never liked eating fish in his later years. During World War I, the German & Austro-Hungarian side battled to supply enough food for their armies, so as much food as possible was taken from all parts of those countries and their allies to meet the needs of the troops. Because so many men were in the armies, the country-side lacked the labour to plant and harvest crops. In Novy Hrozenkov the village battled with lack of food. The Sax family had a small lake, pond or dam in which carp fish grew. They were not good eating but were large, easy to catch and fast growing, so many meals included fish. Erwin, in Perth, Western Australia, many years later would often go fishing and loved catching them, and then would give them away. He couldn't stand the taste of fresh fish because of his WWI experiences with carp.

In their retirement years in Perth, Erwin and Martha slept in different bedrooms. Martha didn't need many hours of sleep each night and would often read books in bed late at night. Erwin had a small single bed in his room against the side wall, apart from his main bed in the centre of the room. When we were visiting, Rachel would often have an afternoon sleep on the side bed when she was little. Kathe preferred to use Martha's bed. One wet day, when helping Rachel out of bed, Jane felt that the blanket against the wall was wet. Further inspection showed that the whole side of the bed was wet, as was the carpet.

When shown, Erwin was not impressed but wouldn't talk about it or do anything to fix it. Jane found out about the problem so it was up to Jane to solve the problem – his attitude from the past. After some strong talking, Jane gave up and contacted a brick layer who did maintenance. He came and opened up the brick wall outside the wet area to inspect. He found a lot of brick rubble in the cavity between the two brick thicknesses, which allowed water through to the inner wall. Several buckets of removed rubble later, along with replacement of the bricks for the inspection hole and the problem was solved. Erwin never said a word about the issue again.

Erwin and Martha loved gardening and their garden showed that love. One ongoing problem was the considerable problem of snails being attracted to the lush growth from next door. The neighbours didn't like using snail poison because they thought they were being cruel to the snails. They also thought the problem was being exaggerated next door. The Sax's house number was '9'. The neighbour's was '7'. They started to understand the problem when they found snails with '7' painted on them moving through their garden. Erwin had painted the number on every snail he found coming across the boundary and had returned them home. Snail pellets were soon in use by the neighbours.

Erwin had always loved strong, smelly cheese, like Blue Vein cheese. With the Sax's Shop operation in Katanning, he could use his cheese contacts to make sure he was able to get the type he liked. The smell of the very strong cheese got so bad that he was banned from eating it in the house. When he couldn't be found he would often be in the back shed or garage enjoying cheese and staying out of the way.

Erwin told a story about World War II, when he and his brothers were near a chicken or duck yard, beside a farm house, and probably when they were part of a work party from the POW camp. No-one was watching so one of his brothers quietly walked into the yard, walked around for a short while, in his army greatcoat, then came out. Under the coat he had two chickens or ducks with their necks wrung. They had watched him and had not seen him take the birds. Many skills were needed to survive.

**Two of Erwin's jokes:**
A Jewish man was on his death bed with his family gathered all around. The dying man looks up and says, with his last words, "Who is minding the till?"

Three Jews are christened. First one then the second. The third one asks "What is it like?" He is answered with "Go and find out yourself, you dirty Jew."

**True Story:**
Erwin was the buyer for the Sax Brothers shoe making business in Palestine. He went to buy skins from Polish Jews. He bought and paid for three skins. He took them back and when he unrolled them there were only two. He ran straight back and asked for the missing skin. The Polish Jew said, "Who are you? I haven't seen you before." Erwin said one reason he left Israel was because of the Polish Jews.

At a table laden with food in a Perth restaurant Erwin asked his wife to get him some of "that fish". Martha replied that it wasn't fish, it was pork. Erwin said, "You misheard me. I asked for some of that fish." He knew what it was but a good Jew wouldn't be eating pork.

The brothers' father, Sigmund, was bothered by his young sons playing in the yard nearby so shouted, "Bruno, Walter, John – you over there, whoever you are. Stop playing and being noisy!" He often forgot the names of some of his children.

Sigmund had trouble remembering names. In filling in the forms for a census he knew the name of the man who was in charge of the mill was Adam, so he registered his wife's name as Eve (which it wasn't). After the birth of his youngest son (Bruno) he was found wandering through the town muttering to himself and saw his sister Caroline so he asked her if she knew the name of his recently born child.

Western Australia, in the 1960s and 1970s was exporting massive amounts of iron ore from its north-west region to countries around the world, as it continues to do. A connected attitude of Erwin was that he would never eat pumpkin of any description – roast, made into soup, baked or any other way. He said it was only fit for pigs, which is what was done with it back in Czechoslovakia. Jane had said to him that it tasted great with a roast meal and it had plenty of iron in it. Erwin said if it had so much iron then it should be exported to China or Japan, along with the iron ore.

It came time to move Erwin down to Busselton from Perth, after Martha died, where he would be close to Jane in an aged care facility room with all food cooked and cleaning done. His retirement village unit in Perth had to be emptied and cleaned to be reallocated. Jane and I (Geoff) boxed up his possessions and emptied all drawers. One of us found a lump in a rolled-up pair of socks. Closer inspection revealed several hundred dollars in notes. A number of other rolls of notes were then discovered, after we became more suspicious. We could only speculate that he had experienced several times in his life when he had to leave everything and move to survive without any funds or resources. This was his way of being prepared in case he had to do it all over again. It made us sad just thinking about it.

When Erwin and Martha retired to Perth and purchased a home in the suburb of Rossmoyne, there were street trees planted on each side of the street, one of which was in front of their home. When it was smaller, Erwin would continually prune it back to make the more decorative and colourful young leaves grow out of the pruned branches. Over the years the tree grew higher and pruning became harder. The top branches started to grow around the aerial power cable that connected the house to the closest power pole and the electrical wires along the street. Knowing that I had a chainsaw, he got me to bring it to the city from our country home when we next came up.

The time arrived and I dutifully brought the chainsaw and fuel to Perth. All the gear was assembled on the front lawn while Martha, Jane and the children went for a walk. All the lower branches were easily cut, with only one branch left to remove. It hung over the house electrical connection wire. A rope was tied to the branch and Erwin was given the rope to pull the branch away from the wire with instructions to keep it tight to redirect the falling branch away, while I used the chainsaw. I made the cut. The branch fell – over the wire and ripped it away from the house. Erwin had held the rope without the tension needed to pull it away from the wire. The wives and kids arrived back home to see the electrician reconnecting the power to the house. Erwin got a tongue lashing from Martha but, somehow, he indicated that it was all my fault!

When Jane was young in Katanning she tried hard to learn to speak in the Czech language. She battled along but it is a hard language to learn for a young girl whose first language was English. At one point, with Czech visitors, she tried to impress everyone by speaking in Czech. The result caused amusement and laughter from those listening. Jane got cross and yelled that she was never going to speak in "Double Dutch" again.

While in retirement in Rossmoyne, a suburb of Perth, Erwin took up growing miniature violets as a hobby. He grew them in several large glass containers, placed to get perfect sunlight. He was proud of the beautiful, tiny flowers. He showed his young granddaughters, Rachel and Kathe, how to carefully water them with a small can, and not to get water on the leaves. That was done a couple of times with his guidance. Once, when he was elsewhere, Kathe decided that a small amount of water was good, so a lot of water must be very good. The result was a watering that flooded the containers.

When Erwin saw the result, he didn't get cross with Kathe, but worked hard to try to save his plants. He was sure they were finished. Within a few weeks the plants not only survived but erupted into a huge flowering that he had never seen before, a magnificent display. It left Erwin more than surprised. He had followed exactly what was required in the books to grow violets. Kathe did the reverse and achieved much better results. He could never work out how.

In Siegmund Sax's family bible:

*"On this day my first daughter Irene was born*

*Second daughter etc…*

*On 15th April 1905, my youngest and last child, a daughter, Eva, was born."*

Six more children were born, but none appeared in the bible.

Erwin and Martha demonstrated their Czech-born command of their native language by saying the following tongue-twister "3,000 silver birds (smaller than a quail) flew over 3,333 silver roofs". Apparently, every Czech school child could say it, so it was a good test for anyone who was suspected of being a foreign spy but said they had always lived in Czechoslovakia.

**From Jane Trigg**, November 1989: "We were entertaining an uncle from overseas (from Israel) and were showing him around Perth. As part of the guided tour, we took him to the University of WA with its beautiful buildings and gardens. Wedding parties often have their photographs taken in the gardens and we came across a wedding party posing for the camera. We stopped to look and to admire the lovely bride.

My uncle, known for his gallantry, made admiring comments for a while and then stepped forward. "You may need my services one day," he said and handed her his card. The bride read the card and blushed. My uncle was an obstetrician.

**From Jane Trigg:** It was the busy period early in December and we were all involved in writing our Christmas mail. Our eleven-year-old was adding her contribution by writing letters to put in with the cards. She came in with a letter for her Israeli great-uncle. I read the letter and noticed that she had wished him a Merry Christmas and a happy New Year.

"Kathe," I said, "you can't say that. Uncle Bruno is Jewish. You know that!"

"Oh yes," she said, "but I didn't know he was *that* Jewish!"

# Chapter 16

## Conclusion – Survive and Thrive

This story about the four Sax brothers is based on facts, gained from a range of sources, but a fiction novel including all the situations the brothers survived through would be very hard to believe.

From a quiet life in a small, rural town in Czechoslovakia, where many families were almost self-sufficient, the brothers were plunged into an ever-changing scenario where they had to continually adapt to survive, while others died around them. To do that they travelled to the four corners of the world and finally settled into peaceful lives to marry and have children but rarely mention their adventures, even to their close families.

What were the chances of them all surviving the following situations, to finally die in their beds after having married, had children and grandchildren?

Their first escape was from the Nazis, down the Danube River in 1939. Of the Jews who stayed in Czechoslovakia, over 90% of that population were killed, including most of the Sax family members.

Their escape on the Danube River owed much to Erwin's arrangement to obtain Japanese visas. Such visas were only available through one Japanese man's decision not to obey his government's requirement that no such visas were to be provided through the Japanese Embassy to Jewish refugees.

The *Black Rose* organisation had obtained only 650 Exit permits from the authorities, to allow people to leave the country from Prague, through Vienna, down the Danube to Palestine. Long lines of people waited at their offices to apply for those permits.

Somehow the four brothers, Erwin's wife Gaby, Martha and her then-husband were successful. How did they succeed when so many failed?

On the escape ships, *Frossoula* and *Tiger Hill*, two passengers were killed by British gunfire. The boats could have been sunk, the fate of several similar vessels. The *Frossoula* came close to running out of food, water and medical supplies. They were saved by Arab women from the Red Crescent at Tripoli who arranged for supplies to be made available. The majority of those trying to break through the British sea barricade were caught and spent the war years on Cyprus, in camps behind wire fences.

They created new lives for themselves in Palestine, making shoes and sandals. They were out of danger and comfortable but they still enrolled in the British Army to fight the Germans, a brave act.

While in Palestine, the brothers, Gaby and Martha were not killed or injured with the ongoing unrest between Jewish settlers and Arabs.

Martha fashion-modelled at the King David Hotel in Tel Aviv but had left Palestine before part of it was blown up. That destruction could have happened at any time she was in Palestine, as it did with many other buildings.

They served as soldiers in and around Tobruk, while German aircraft bombed the port area and their barracks, without being injured or killed.

Their unit was sent to Greece to fight the Germans and they could have been killed like many others in the army there as they tried to evade the Germans. All four were captured, alive and uninjured.

They were transported by rail to Lamsdorf POW camp. Many died in the closed-in cattle rail wagons, due to disease, lack of food and water or from extreme, close confinement. This happened after they survived the makeshift compounds and holding yards for prisoners in Greece prior to their long train journey.

They survived their total time through the rest of the war at Lamsdorf POW camp, with a variety of dangers from Nazi SS policies for Jewish extermination, sadistic guards, food shortages, disease and extreme weather conditions.

Erwin was not discovered by the Germans while pushing scrap metal into sawn logs on work parties, to sabotage both the logs and sawmill saws. If discovered he may have been shot along with the rest of the workgroup.

Bruno could easily have been killed for his short-term escape using the help of French prisoners and also during his time in the Sagen penal camp. POWs were sometimes shot for escaping. They also sometimes died in penal camps, particularly when the war was coming to an end.

They escaped Lamsdorf before the Russians arrived and didn't have to join long lines of POWs walking through the worst winter in Germany for years, to escape the Russians. Many of those on that long march died of exhaustion and the cold.

They were together in the same camp for most of the war, four brothers who were not separated or sent to different regions. All survived that experience in relatively good health, regardless of being Jews in a German-controlled POW camp.

At the end of the war, they were transported from Czechoslovakia to France, then to England, Palestine, Egypt, Italy and back to Czechoslovakia. Walter married, Erwin divorced and eventually re-married. Erwin's first daughter had been murdered. With his new wife, Martha, he started a new family, as did the other brothers.

All four brothers were able to return from their experience as POWs to their home town, Novy Hrosenkov, uninjured. There they had the strength and fortitude to cope with the loss of their extended family, their family's sawmill business and possessions and still rebuild, under the oppression of the Czechoslovak Communist regime.

They were not caught by that regime in Czechoslovakia for falsifying timber production records and were able to escape the country before the Iron Curtain came down on Eastern Europe and all escape was closed off.

So much left behind, so many times starting again from nothing, so late in life marrying and having families. They had lived in peaceful valleys, on far shores with conflict possible at any time, being bombed and shot at, behind barbed wire fences for years, in a new nation created out of the ashes of a lost life, in the Australian bush, Canadian ice and snow and the bustling metropolis of Los Angeles.

And still they survived and thrived.

All four brothers dispersed, to wildly different places – Bruno to Palestine/Israel, Erwin to Western Australia, Walter and John first to Western Australia and then to the other side of the world, to USA and Canada. Each of them started with nothing again, to do whatever it took to re-establish and create a family home and a peaceful, abundant life.

If that was a fiction story, considered to be made into a movie, it would be regarded as too unbelievable. It was unbelievable but it was also all true.

*From the left: On their visit to Perth, WA:*
*Bruno and Chagit, with Erwin and Martha.*

# Appendix 1

## Interview with Bruno Sax

Newspaper article: (Translated from Czech by Val Blazak)

**"Holocaust in Valassku – Is Bruno allowed to Remember?"**

A conversation of Dr. Jaromir Krystynek with Bruno Sax

There were three of us, friends since grade 1, when we got together in 1924. We parted in 1936, after graduating to University.

*Question:* I believe you were at the University of Prague?

I studied there, (Doctor of Medicine) to give my mother her wish. Complications came on the 15th of March, 1939, when the University told us that we had to leave because of being Jews. We left the country. Brother Irwin had organised Japanese visas. His wife took his small daughter to Irwin's (and my) mother and we started our trip. Irwin, Walter, Jan (John) and I went by train to Vienna, then by boat on the Danube to Romania. Once there we went to an old ship which was overloaded with passengers. We left Prague on 29 April, 1939, and arrived in Palestine on the 2nd September the same year. We were without money, with our shoes falling apart and because of that it showed us a way out of the misery.

With a piece of wood and strips of car tyre tubes we made our own sandals. Anybody who saw them was interested in where we got them, and everybody wanted some. So we started making them. Because of the big orders we had to employ three local people. We were manufacturing about 70 pairs a day. With the sale we were helped by engineer Schoen, who was already living in Palestine for some time. His wife came from the same place that we did and when she wrote from Palestine to her friends in Hrozenkov we got the reputation at home that we had created a factory in Palestine for making shoes. I hope our mother heard about it and was relieved that we were doing so well. Once again it was Irwin's decision that we live here in peace and with everything we need. But he was thinking about everything that was happening at home, and he felt we should give some contribution to the war so that it will end sooner. We wanted to join the Czech army but at that time they didn't have any interest in us, so we joined the British Army. We had a hard training in the desert and then through Egypt we were transferred to Tobruk.

We had a baptism of fire. My brothers achieved a Corporal ranking and I was a Sergeant. From Tobruk they sent us to Greece. With a good beginning, we had, later on, to pull back because we were outnumbered and overrun by the Germans. We ended up prisoners of war.

From the POW camp we were marched always north and were transported through Austria to the POW camp in Landsdorf, in Silesia. At the beginning the Germans handled us very badly, but after a time, things changed. They started to not just treat us like Jews, but like other British POWs. We could even get parcels from the Red Cross. Had it not been for that, we would not have been able to survive. We were told that Churchill himself had spoken for us. Among the German guards there was one Slovakian who was going home for Christmas and he promised to deliver a letter to our mother. He brought us back an answer from our sister, Ruth. From her answer we found that they were all taken to Terezin (Theresienstadt) Camp.

In February, 1942, we got the news that all, except sister Edit, were taken to Osvetim (Auschwitz). That's where they all finished up, in the gas chambers, even little Irwin's daughter and two small children of sister Ady.

We kept living in our POW camp but when the US front came closer, we were chased from one end to another until the Americans liberated us. But because of the way the Army is, they first transferred us to Belgium, from there to Palestine and only then at the beginning of 1946, they discharged us from the Army.

The homecoming was sad. Of our family home there was only a quarter left. Sister Edit was still in Terezin and the rest of them were dead. We went to Prague. I went back studying and my brothers, including Irwin, were trying to make a living in saw-mills. Then there was a Jewish state born. At the same time in Czechoslovakia the communists were prevalent. That's why we decided to take the world on again.

I joined the Jewish Army and my brothers went to Australia. In the year 1949, I was released from the Jewish Army and was able to continue my studies. I finished my medical studies in 1951. After a year in hospital practice, I went to work in a Kibbutz. I met my wife there, Chagit. She was the third generation living in Palestine. We have two daughters and a son, who presented us with 11 grandchildren.

A small post script now: In Novy Hrozenkov, where the Vranca River flows into Becva, there lived a big Jewish family. There is a bit left of the house and quite a bit of land where there used to be a saw mill. And there is a monument where my old mother and three small children were taken by four soldiers and the other four of us left. There is only a Jewish cemetery in Vsetin with a monument to the name of Sigmund Sax that is left.

# Appendix 2

# Timeline –
# Significant Dates for the Sax Family

| | |
|---|---|
| 14.3.1838 | Herman/Heinrich Sax born, (the four brothers' grandfather). |
| 1838 | Herman Sax's wife Cecilia born. |
| 1843 | Adolf Sax's wife Terezie born. |
| 10.10.1844 | Adolf Sax born, Herman's brother. |
| 1863 | Karolina/Carolina Sax born – Herman's daughter. |
| 28.4.1865 | Jakob Sax born – son of Herman. |
| 1866 | Karl Sax born – son of Herman. Died in WWI. |
| 1872 | Siegmund/Zigmund/Sigmund Sax born in Novy Hrosenkov – son of Herman. |
| 16.10.1874 | Sigmund Sax's wife Jana/Yohanna Buchler born. |
| 1.4.1902 | Otto Sax born in Novy Hrozenkov. |
| 15.9.1903 | Ernest Sax born in Novy Hrozenkov. |
| 1905 | Edith/Eva Sax born in Novy Hrozenkov. |
| 31.10.1907 | Irvin/Erwin/Ervin Sax born in Novy Hrozenkov. |
| 15.7.1910 | Walter Sax born in Novy Hrozenkov. |

| | |
|---|---|
| 30.1.1912 | John/Yan Sax born in Novy Hrozenkov. |
| 16.4.1912 | Erwin Sax's wife Martha Weinstein born in Boritice, Czechoslovakia. |
| 1913 | Ada Sax born in Novy Hrozenkov. |
| 28.6.1914 | Archduke Ferdinand (heir to Austro-Hungarian Empire) assassinated in Serbia. |
| 4.8.1914 | World War I declared. |
| 4.6.1915 | Ruth Sax born in Novy Hrozenkov. |
| 5.9.1916 | Charlotte (Chari) Juszkovic, Walter's wife, born. |
| 15.3.1917 | Bruno Sax born in Novy Hrozenkov. |
| 28.3.1918 | Jakob Sax dies. |
| 28.10.1918 | Country of Czechoslovakia declared in Prague. |
| 11.11.1918 | World War I ends. Armistice signed. |
| 29.1.1920 | Jarmila Bozkova, wife of John Sax, born in Olomouc, Czechoslovakia. |
| 17.4.1924 | Mussolini's Fascists win Italian election. |
| 14.12.1924 | Karolina Sax died. |
| 5.1.1925 | Sigmund Sax died in Vsetin, of a heart attack. |
| 11.10.1927 | Chagit Horovitz (Bruno's wife) born. |
| 15.9.1930 | Hitler's National Socialist (Nazi) Party comes second in German election. |
| 31.7.1932 | National Socialists become largest party in the Reichtag, Germany. |
| 30.1.1933 | Hitler becomes German Chancellor. |
| March 1933 | Jews beaten up by Nazi Storm troopers in Germany. Many Jews planning to leave Germany. |

| | |
|---|---|
| 1.4.1933 | Jewish businesses boycotted in Germany. |
| 10.5.1933 | "Un-German" books burnt in Berlin. |
| 23.6.1933 | All German opposition parties banned. Trade Unions and employer groups dissolved. |
| August 1933 | Jews sent to concentration camps, Dachau the largest. Over 45,000 already held. |
| October 1933 | Arab riots in Palestinian towns against Jewish immigration. |
| 1935 | Germany funds massive rearmament, introduces conscription. |
| 15.8.1935 | Hitler bans German/Jewish marriage. Jews are classed as sub-human. |
| 19.9.1935 | Hitler bans Jews from German public life and removes their citizenship at Nuremburg rally. Jews banned from teaching, farming, radio, theatre, the arts, medicine and journalism. |
| 3.10.1935 | Mussolini's troops invade Abyssinia. |
| 7.3.1936 | Nazis enter Rhineland to reclaim it from France. |
| 25.11.1936 | Germany and Italy sign agreement of mutual support. |
| 1937 | Erwin Sax marries Gabriella (Gaby). |
| 27.4.1937 | German aircraft help Franco in Spain and bomb Spanish cities. |
| 7.7.1937 | UK plans for a state in Palestine as a Jewish homeland, one third for Jews, two thirds for Arabs. |
| 19.12.1937 | Erwin Sax's first daughter Judith born. |
| 14.3.1938 | Germany occupies Austria, with much Austrian support. |

| | |
|---|---|
| 30.9.1938 | Sudetenland in Czechoslovakia signed over to German control in conference between Germany, Italy, France and Britain. Czech government not consulted. |
| 15.3.1939 | Germany occupies the rest of Czechoslovakia by invasion. |
| 15.3.1939 | Bruno Sax forced to leave Prague University, due to Jews being banned. |
| 30.4.1939 | Bruno, John, Walter and Erwin Sax leave home for Palestine, with Erwin's wife Gaby. |
| 1.9.1939 | Germany and Russia invade Poland. |
| 1.9.1939 | Britain and France declare war on Germany. World War II commences. |
| 2.9.1939 | Four brothers and Erwin's wife Gaby arrive in Palestine on illegal ship *Tiger Hill*. |
| 14.11.1940 | Four brothers join British Army in Palestine. |
| 12.12.1940 | Egypt: 30,000 Italian troops captured by Allies. |
| 1940 | Denmark, Norway, Holland, Belgium, France fall to Germany. Dunkirk evacuation. Start of "Battle for Britain" air war. Australia, New Zealand, Canada, India, South Africa and other nations join Allied efforts to defeat Axis armies. |
| 3.1.1941 | Libya: Bardia captured. 25,000 Italian prisoners taken by Australian troops. |
| 7.1.1941 | Australians capture Tobruk from Italians. |
| 12.2.1941 | 400,000 German troops moved to invade Balkans, including Greece. |
| 14.2.1941 | Benghazi in Libya captured by Australian 6$^{th}$ Division. |

| | |
|---|---|
| 15.3.1941 | Rommel leads Afrika Corps attacks in North Africa. |
| 28.3.1941 | Australian 6th Division relocated to Greece along with other Allied units. |
| 25.4.1941 | Allied troops withdraw from Greece to Crete, because of German attacks. |
| April 1941 | Sax brothers captured in Greece and taken to POW camp at Lamsdorf, Poland. |
| 29.5.1941 | Germans control Crete by June 1. |
| 1.6.1941 | 15,000 Australian, New Zealand and British troops evacuated from Crete. Thousands captured by Germans. |
| 1941 | Yugoslavia falls to Germany. Germany invades Russia. Pearl Harbour in Hawaii bombed by Japanese. |
| Nov 1941 | Terezin begins to be used by Nazis as a concentration camp for Czech Jews. Later used to detain Jews from other countries. |
| 8.11.1941 | USA declares war on Japan. On 11.12.1941, USA declares war on Germany and Italy. |
| 1942 | Malaya and Singapore fall to Japanese. Darwin, Australia bombed. |
| Feb, 1942 | Brothers in POW camp receive word that family members, other than Edith/Eva, taken to Auschwitz (Osvetin), including Judith Sax and two children of Ady/Irene Zwilinger/Sax. |
| 7.6.1942 | Nazis slaughter inhabitants of Lidice, Czechoslovakia, in retaliation for the killing of Reinhard Heydrich, German Czech commander. |

| | |
|---|---|
| 19.8.1942 | English commando raid on Dieppe, France, leads to harsh penalties in German POW camps, including Lamsdorf. |
| 22.9.1942 | Judith Sax dies in German concentration camp. |
| 22.9.1942 | Ruth Sax dies in German concentration camp. |
| 22.9.1942 | Otto Sax dies in German concentration camp. |
| 22.9.1942 | Ernest Sax dies in German concentration camp. |
| 22.10.1942 | Jana/Yohanna Sax dies in German concentration camp. |
| 1943 | Sicily landing by Allies. Mussolini deposed. Allies fight back Japanese in Pacific. Italy surrenders. Churchill, Roosevelt and Stalin meet in Tehran, Iran. |
| 1944 | Leningrad freed from German siege. D-Day invasion at Normandy in France by Allies opens Western Front against Germany. Russians reach Warsaw in fighting. Paris liberated. Russian armies reach first German concentration camps and gas chambers. British landing in Greece. |
| 1945 | Russians reach and 'liberate' Auschwitz. Yalta conference between USA, Russia and England to set up new areas of influence in Europe after war ends. Mussolini and his mistress killed by Italian partisans. Hitler commits suicide. United Nations created in San Francisco to replace League of Nations. Atom bombs destroy Hiroshima and Nagasaki in Japan. |

| | |
|---|---|
| 17.3.1945 | Soviet soldiers reach and 'liberate' Lamsdorf POW camp. |
| 8.5.1945 | Germany surrenders to the Allies. World War II in Europe ends. |
| 31.6.1945 | 'Iron Curtin' created. Russia controls eastern Europe including East Germany, Poland and Czechoslovakia. |
| 15.8.1945 | Japan surrenders. War in the Pacific ends. |
| 20.11.1945 | Nuremburg War Trials begin for German war criminals. |
| Late 1945 | Walter Sax marries Charlotte Juszkovic in London, England. |
| Early 1946 | Martha Weinstein and Karel Werner divorce. |
| Feb 1946 | 10 to 15 million people in Europe close to starving. |
| 8.1.1946 | Erwin discharged from British Army in Palestine, after 5 years 57 days in Army. Other brothers also discharged around this time. |
| Mar/Apr 1946 | Brothers wait in U.N. holding camp, at El Shatt, near Suez Canal, Egypt. |
| April 1946 | Boat trip from Cairo to Italy then train trip to Prague, Czechoslovakia . |
| 1946 | Four brothers and Martha Weinstein return to Czechoslovakia. |
| May 1946 | England and USA report on partition of Palestine to create Jewish homeland. Both Jews and Arabs disagree with plans. |
| 16.10.1946 | Ten Nazi war criminals executed in Nuremburg. |
| 22.7.1946 | Southern wing of King David Hotel in Jerusalem, the headquarters of the British |

|  |  |
|---|---|
|  | Administration for Palestine, is blown up by Jewish extremist right wing underground organisation IRGUN. |
| 17.11.1946 | Jewish terrorists kill 8 British soldiers in Jerusalem. |
| March 1947 | Jewish survivors of German concentration camps begin to arrive in Australia. |
| 5.4.1947 | Erwin Sax marries Martha Weinstein at Havlickuv Brod, Czechoslovakia. |
| 1948 | Walter's son Paul born. |
| Jan 1948 | Over 2000 Jews and Arabs die in armed clashes and bombings, because of UN decision to grant a homeland in Palestine for Jews. |
| 27.2.1948 | Communist coup in Czechoslovakia seizes control of government. |
| March 1948 | Ongoing conflict in Palestine between Jews and Arabs. |
| 14.5.1948 | New State of Israel declared. British Mandate removed. British troops begin to leave. Israel opens entry for all Jewish settlers. |
| 18.7.1948 | *Exodus 47* ship incident occurs. Ship with 4,500 immigrants on board, most being holocaust survivors, sailed from France, stopped by British and initially taken to Haifa then passengers returned to France on three different ships. All were eventually taken to Germany until allowed into the new state of Israel. |
| 15.10.1948 | John, Walter, Chari and baby Paul arrive in Fremantle, WA, on *SS Napoli*. |
| 28.10.1948 | John marries Jarmila Bozkova. |

| | |
|---|---|
| 18.12.1948 | Erwin and Martha Sax's daughter, Jana/Jane, born in Jihlava, Czechoslovakia. |
| 1948 | Bruno joins new Israeli Army. |
| 1949 | Bruno released from Israeli Army. |
| 15.9.1949 | Erwin, Martha and Jane Sax embark on *SS Continental* in Genoa, Italy, for Australia. |
| 23.10.1949 | Erwin, Martha and baby Jane Sax arrive in Fremantle, Western Australia 1949. |
| 1949 | Erwin and family first stay with John and Jarmila in Victoria Park due to housing shortages, then with Walter and family. Later move to Gnowangerup, then Cherry Tree Pool farm near Katanning to work on and manage farms. John and Jarmila join them at Cherry Tree Pool. Both Erwin and John work on the farm and set up a sawmill. |
| 1951 | Bruno completes medical training in Israel. |
| 14.12.1951 | Solly Sax born in Katanning, Western Australia. |
| 1952 | Walter, Chari and Paul Sax leave Australia by boat to England, take *Queen Mary* to New York, USA, then move to Canada. |
| Dec 1952 | Walter, Chari and Paul Sax arrive in Toronto, Canada. Walter then worked as a book-keeper. Soon after they became Canadian citizens. |
| 1953 | Bruno Sax and Chagit Horovitz marry. |
| 1954 | Walter's son Robert born. John Sax and family arrive in Canada and settle with Walter and his family in Meadford, Ontario. |

| | |
|---|---|
| Oct 1956 | Walter, Chari, Paul and Robert Sax move from Canada to California, USA. |
| 1976 | Walter Sax and Charlotte divorce. |
| 20.11.1987 | Sol Sax marries Dominique Riccio. |
| 25.2.1990 | Martha Sax died in Perth, Western Australia. |
| 1.6.1992 | John Sax died in Toronto, Canada. |
| 18.10.1994 | Charlotte (Chari) Sax (Walter's wife), died in California, USA. |
| 28.10.1995 | Erwin Sax died in Busselton, Western Australia. |
| 11.8.1997 | Jane Trigg, nee Sax died in Busselton, Western Australia. |
| 16.1.2003 | Walter Sax died in San Diego, California, USA. |
| 11.9.2003 | Bruno Sax died in Tel Aviv, Israel. |
| 2009 | Walter's son Robert died. |
| 2012 | Walter's son Paul died. |

# Appendix 3

## European Political History Impacting the Sax Family

**1938 until the start of World War 2:**

In 1938, on 29 September, the leaders of Britain, France, Germany and Italy met in Munich to sign an agreement that would have great impact on the whole of Europe, particularly Czechoslovakia. Under the Munich agreement the German-speaking border regions of Czechoslovakia were removed from the country and given to Germany. This had an immediate impact on millions of Czechoslovakian citizens who were forced or chose to leave. The start of the movement of the Czechoslovakian population from the ceded regions was underway in May, 1938, but it dramatically increased after October 1st when Nazi army units entered the regions to be occupied as per the Munich agreement.

Initially the refugees fleeing inland were people who feared the Germans because of what they had undertaken prior to the Munich agreement. These included Social Democrats, Communists, Jews and anti-fascist Sudeten Germans. The second wave included government employees, as well as those who did not wish to live in a foreign country and were worried about their future. A Czechoslovak law in February 1939 defined a refugee as anybody who was a Czechoslovak citizen and who had left territory given to Germany, Poland or Hungary after May 20, 1938.

The refugees from the ceded frontier regions filled up towns and villages in the interior of the country and many brought valuable property with them. The Czechoslovakian Red Cross and youth organisations of the region tried to help with this crisis, along with district and municipal offices. By October, 1938, the refugees were living with friends, relatives and even complete strangers. They stayed in schools, guest houses, warehouses and old factory buildings.

The number of refugees continued to rise until, six months after the Munich agreement, in March 1939, Nazi Germany occupied the rest of Czechoslovakia. When Hitler invaded Poland in September, Europe went to war.

## General History from 1918:

The political joining of Czechs and Slovaks after the end of World War I was possible because the two ethnic groups had language, religion and general culture that was closely related. Leaders of the country declared an independent state on October 28, 1918, and this declaration was supported by France and other Allied opponents of Austria. Its western portion made up of Bohemia and Moravia was populated by Czechs and the eastern portion had a population of Slovaks. These two groups constituted two thirds of the population of Czechoslovakia with other nationalities being Germans, Hungarians, Polish people and Ruthenians.

Between 1918 and 1935 the country became a solid Parliamentary democracy and was industrially advanced when compared to most other Eastern European countries. In 1933, when Adolph Hitler rose to power in Germany, the sizable German minority in the Sudetenland became interested in German National Socialism. With the agreement of Britain and France, Hitler took over the German-speaking Sudeten area of the country in 1938. By 1939, all of Bohemia and Moravia were occupied and the two regions became a German protectorate, while Slovakia received autonomy dominated by Germany.

The liberation of Czechoslovakia by Soviet troops towards the end of World War II helped strengthen the Czechoslovakian Communist Party and this reduced the strength of other political parties still recovering from the war. With strong support from the Soviet Union and by the use of clever politics, the communists staged the equivalent of a coup d'état in 1948 and a People's Republic was formed. Under Soviet supervision, the political internal opposition was destroyed, all industry was nationalised and all agriculture collectivized.

The four brothers moved on to their chosen future countries of

Israel, Australia, Canada and the US to raise the next Sax generation in freedom, away from the tyranny of communism.

# Appendix 4

## The Split of Czechoslovakia

### The Split of Czechoslovakia into the Czech and Slovak Republics, as seen in 1993

In 1993, the nation of Czechoslovakia was dismembered to become two separate countries. The border of the split ran very close to the Sax's original village, Novy Hrosenkov. The creation of the new international border created practical problems for property owners whose lands were isolated, split or ended up against the border. The following impacts were considered at the time:

From the 1$^{st}$ of January, small farms along the border, some as small as one hectare, were gathered into the Czech Republic or the Slovak Republic. In most cases, particularly through rural land, no wall or fence was built. Often a small stream would be the border and also the boundary of private land.

A Czech or Slovak farmer could now cross an old timber bridge or go through a farm gate into another country several times a day to find a missing cow or sheep, or to go to work on his potato field, land possibly tended by his family for generations.

In future years, two different governments will adopt or change policies relating to land use, agriculture, health, welfare and a huge range of government requirements that might see old neighbours being directed and controlled with highly varying attitudes and policies.

This occurred in World War II when the two parts of Czechoslovakia were treated very differently by the conquering Germans, with Slovakia becoming more subservient to Nazi requirements, including the treatment of their Jewish population.

The new boundary cuts through the White Carpathian Mountains, which resemble a frozen wonderland in winter. Mixed marriages between Czechs and Slovaks are common and have raised few difficulties in the past. Local dialects have formed over generations by the mixing of the languages from both sides of the new border.

Many have thought of themselves as citizens of Bohemia, Moravia or Slovakia, not in terms of national identities. Bohemians can be more Prague-centric. Moravians think more of and enjoy rural and mountain life.

The new frontier will mean both new countries could head in different directions, moving further apart rather than building on the strengths of both. Membership of the E.U. and the adoption of technology and economic improvements from the west compared to retaining strong relations with Russia and other ex-Soviet countries could further separate their futures.

More Slovaks that Czechs will be impacted on by the split. Some 300,000 Slovaks and 60,000 Czechs will be on the opposite side of the line drawn on the map. They will either seem to be foreigners to their neighbours or will have to consider selling up and buying land back on *their* side of the border.

The Slovak side of the political discussions pushed for and finally won the argument. This made the Slovak leader, Prime Minister Vladimir Meciar, most unpopular, particularly with people living near the border and those with relatives and business dealings across the whole original country of Czechoslovakia.

While unrest on the final decision to split rarely went beyond an argument in the local bar, the more extreme events included grenades thrown into new customs buildings and Czech or Slovak graffiti about what unpleasant things should be done to "Merciar".

The future will determine whether the split was of benefit to one or both new countries but in 1993, many Czechs and Slovaks didn't feel it was necessary, particularly when there was no national vote on this highly important matter.

# Appendix 5

## North Moravia

During the early 1990s, Jane Trigg, nee Sax, collected geographical information on the region her Sax forebears had lived, in North Moravia, Czechoslovakia:

*"Novy Hrosenkov, Vsetin (west of Novy Hrosenkov and slightly north) and Valasske Mezirici (further to the north) are all in the North Moravian district.*

*The northern part of Moravia is more industrialised and polluted than the 'rustic' south – the area around Brno. Rich deposits of iron ore and other minerals are the reason for the industrialisation, originally the centre of the arms industry, but now in decline.*

*Some of the Czech Republic's most fertile lowlands and the gentle Beskydy Hills, including Novy Hrosenkov, are in the area of the Beskydy Protected Landscape Region.*

*Further north is the Jeseniky Mountain range. The Hruby Jesenik has been developed for winter skiing and ski touring. There are plenty of good walks in summer, though at higher elevations the damage to its spruce and larch forests from acid rain, drifting from Ostrava and southern Poland, takes the edge off the experience.*

*Erwin used to go skiing at Javornky, which is a mountain range to the south of Novy Hrosenkov. In the Australian Sax photo album, there is a photo taken in 1992 of Bruno in front of* one of the slopes in this range. Presumably there was no acid rain in this area in the 1920s when Erwin would have been skiing there.

"Dreary" Osrava is the region's administrative centre and largest city. The beautiful, sooty, old university town of Olomouc is its historical capital, as well as the cultural and commercial heart.

The region of western Beskydy is also known as Wallachia/Walachia, or in Czech "Valassko" (Erwin used to use that name.) It's the region of the semi-nomadic sheep-farming people, the Valachs, who moved into the region in the 15$^{th}$ century.

The major towns of Moravian Wallachia are Vsetin and Valasske Mezirici. They were apparently "hotbeds of resistance to Catholicisation in the 17$^{th}$ century". By the 18$^{th}$ century they had inter-married with the locals and had been absorbed into the Hapsburg Empire.

However, they managed to preserve some of their rural way of life, including unique carved timber architecture which can be seen in the Skansen at Roznov pod Radhostem, which is east of Valasske Mezirici.

# Appendix 6

# Australia and a background to its immigration policies

## World War II to 1948

Throughout Australia's post-1788 history, people from many backgrounds had contributed to the growth of the country. Since World War II, the Australian government's planned immigration program continually diversified the structure of Australian society. Millions of people from many ethnic groups were now in Australia. Among them were many from Czechoslovakia who came in several waves or generations for different reasons. Two main waves after the war were the refugees of 1948, known as the February refugees and the refugees of 1968, known as the August refugees. After that, small numbers arrived independently, particularly in the 1970s and early 1980s.

It has been said that apart from the choice of a marriage partner or the selection of a career, the decision to emigrate is probably one of the most important that most individuals could ever make. This was certainly applicable to those refugees escaping Europe immediately after World War II.

Apart from the massive movement of people to Australia during the gold rush period of the middle 1800s, the majority of immigrants to Australia were British people who arrived mainly as assisted immigrants. For non-British settlers, the conditions were more difficult. In spite of this there was a noticeable increase in immigration, before World War II, partly caused by the creation of restrictive immigration quotas to the USA in 1921 and 1924, which redirected immigrants to other countries.

When World War II started in September 1939, the Australian government established a classification and advisory committee which divided all aliens residing in Australia into four groups:

1. Allied nationals – those persons without naturalisation belonging to Allied nations.

2. Neutral alien – people without naturalisation belonging to a neutral nation.

3. Enemy alien – people without naturalisation belonging to a nation at war with the Commonwealth.

4. Refugee alien-people who immigrated to Australia because of political or racial persecution and whose country was at war with the Commonwealth.

All aliens were kept under strict control in Australia during World War II. Those most affected were the enemy aliens who were normally kept in internment camps for some or all of the time in the war years, particularly those from Germany, Italy and Japan.

People of Czechoslovakian origin who were naturalised had the rights of all Australian citizens. Those who did not become naturalised but held a Czechoslovakian passport were treated as allied nationals with virtually no restrictions imposed on them.

In 1939, the Czechoslovakian government-in-exile was established in Britain. One of its first actions after World War II commenced was to re-establish the Czechoslovak army. Czechoslovak consulates around the world were notified of this and requested to ask all Czech nationals to volunteer for the Czechoslovak army and air force in Britain. In Australia, this was arranged through consuls in Sydney and Melbourne. The volunteers were concentrated in Sydney, put into Australian uniforms and transported with Australian troops to the Middle East, where they joined the newly formed Battalion of the Czechoslovak army in Palestine. They saw active service in northern Africa, including Tobruk.

In the history of immigration to Australia after the initial settlement of 1788, the most important milestone was World War II. In that war, Australia was threatened for the first time with an enemy invasion, from Japan, and this brought about major changes in Australian political thinking.

The Immigration Minister in 1953 stated that the danger of invasion by a determined enemy did more than all the political oratory and journalism of the preceding 50 years. It convinced the great mass of Australians that they must either populate and develop the vast continent or accept the probability of having it taken from them.

The military argument was also important and was accepted by the majority of Australian policy-makers. The demographic reason was another argument and it was based on the statistical evidence. That had shown that not enough children were born in Australia in the ten years before the war to replace the population in the next generation. This statistic also did not take into account the major loss of manpower caused by the war. The average Australian family size in 1875 included six children. This had decreased to two children in 1945. Immigration schemes appeared to offer the only solution to this serious problem in Australia.

World War II ended for Czechoslovakia in May 1945. Once the German armies had surrendered, about 90% of the country was occupied by the Russians and 10% by the Americans. In the first elections after the war, in 1946, the Communist Party became the strongest party in the country. By the summer of 1947 it remained the trend and European politics was beginning to overshadow every aspect of Czechoslovak life. This was the determination by Russia to control as much as possible of central and eastern Europe. The growth of Russian power in the country was reflected in the increasing stubbornness of the Czechoslovak Communist Party to adopt elements of Western policies to receive economic help from the West. The divide, later called the Iron Curtain, began to descend during that summer, with a barrier separating the country from any Western-organised recovery programs.

Because of the communist takeover of power, some of the people who had not been Communist Party members joined the party in an effort to keep their jobs, their income and even houses or flats. Political purges affected practically every working person. For many professionals and intellectuals, the temporary solution was to take employment in manual work and wait for the situation to improve.

Thousands did not wait for things to improve. An alternative solution was, from February 1948, to defect from the country by illegally crossing into western Germany and Austria, those countries still being under American and British occupation at the time. These Czechoslovakian defectors became known as the 'February refugees'.

Soon after February 1948, refugee camps were established in western Germany and coordination began for the aid of Czech refugees. All refugees from European countries were screened by the International Refugee Organisation, missions from immigrant-seeking countries and voluntary organisations. After they were successfully screened, an IRO eligibility was given to each refugee along with a Displaced Person's Card. They then had to wait in camps in western Germany, Austria or Italy. They received accommodation, personal maintenance items, medical care and the right to emigrate to a country selected. All costs were met by the IRO.

Between the end of 1948 and through 1949, all Displaced Persons Camps received notices detailing prospects for emigration to Australia. The short notices stated that Australia was looking for single and married immigrants up to 45 years of age. Upon arrival in Australia, immigrants would have to complete a two-year working contract.

Once prospective immigrants were medically examined and had a personal interview, the suitability of the applicant was decided. A security check was also made and the successful immigrants were notified within a few weeks about their departure for Australia. They were transported to Italy where they waited in the Embarkation Centre in Bagnoli, near Naples for a final placement aboard an immigrant ship.

Between 1948 and 1951, nearly all Czechs arriving in Australia were called 'contract immigrants'. This contract was signed in Europe before they left for Australia. On arrival, the Commonwealth employment office could direct the immigrant to any job in Australia. This often meant that highly qualified and skilled people had to work as labourers. They were under the supervision of Commonwealth authorities for the duration of two years and were issued with a Certificate of Registration.

This administrative 'red tape' was experienced by the three Sax brothers and their families, who arrived in Australia. They all left Europe from the Port of Embarkation in Genoa, Italy. John, Walter, Charlotte and Paul were on the ship *Napoli* which arrived in Fremantle, Western Australia, on the 15 October 1948. Erwin, Martha and Jane arrived in Fremantle on the *Continental* on the 23 October, 1949.

# Appendix 7

## Letter from Walter Sax to Erwin Sax

May 5, 1994

Dear brother!

Following our conversation, I am enclosing a copy of the German Bank Notice, (the original you have received from me several weeks ago) noting that U.R.O. (United Restitution Organisation) deposited your share of the claim for furniture in Hrozenkov.

Please write to the German bank, what you want to do with that money. Either mail directly to you (give the correct address) or directly to your bank (give where and your account number).

To: Georg Hauck and Son Bankers

Kaiserstrasse 24

Postfach 10 10 40

6000 Frankfurt 1

Germany

Do not forget to have your signature Notarized, and in your letter refer to your account number.

They call it: Konto NR.:-----------------

Good luck!

Here the life goes on the Californian tempo, and for going

*fishing or to Las Vegas. Every day is like Sunday.*

*I hope these lines will catch you in good health, in spite of age. Wishing you and the whole family best regards and love.*

*Walter.*

*PS – For our saw-mill the settlement was paid off more than a year ago.*

**Note:** Many years after the war ended Germany paid reparation for civilian property it had stolen, damaged or destroyed during the war. Members of the Sax family were each offered a share in the lost value of their house, furniture, machinery and the sawmill at Novy Hrozenkov. For Erwin and Martha in Western Australia the receipt of that money would have been invaluable for the financial improvement of their lives, having arrived in Australia with almost nothing.

The discussions between Erwin and Martha as to whether to accept what Erwin called blood money were apparently loud and at times angry. In the end, Erwin would not accept any money from the German government and the family went without it. It is probable that the other brothers did not have such a high-minded approach to the receipt of this justified compensation.

# Appendix 8

## Letter from Bruno Sax to Kathe Trigg

**March 1995:**

Dear Kathy,

With great interest and pleasure, I read your letter. You asked so many questions. In the book I only found the name of father's father and grandfather, but no more details. What I know and will give you is only a few pieces of information about my family. We were 11 children, five daughters and six sons. I was the youngest. My father died at the age of 53, when I was nearly 8 years old. When I was 17 years old, one newspaper looked for women who did something special in their life. Together with my sister Ruti we asked mother to tell us about her past and sent it to the paper. After time we got two parcels of books, altogether about 20. It was the prize of the third-place. We told mother the truth and she answered that you wrote what you know. If you would write what you didn't know, I would get the first prize.

We had a saw-mill, a farm with fields, a pair of horses and a good part of forest, and 11 children. When father died, it was mother who looked after it all. My brother Ernst, who studied at the University of Wein (Vienna) the second year, had to interrupt and come home to be in charge of the saw-mill. In charge of the farm and helpful on the saw-mill was brother Otto. And in charge of that was my mother. Apart from several children at school, some were in the army. We were several Jewish families in the village.

There were three sawmills in that village and ours was the oldest. All belonged to the Jews. Our relations with the population was very good and our family was really loved. Three elderly sisters were married. Each had two children and they came to grandmother for every holiday.

In 1936 I went to Prague to study medicine. In Prague, my sister Ada was employed with my brother Walter. After a while, my brother Ervin came on leave. Through Ada he met a nice woman, Gaby, and married her in 1937. They had a beautiful daughter, Jehudit (Judith). All went well, until 1939, when Hitler came to Prague. Ervin came and was of the opinion that we should leave the country. All Jews were thrown out of the University. We enquired and an illegal transport was going to Palestine. We wrote down our names: Gaby, Ervin, Walter, Jan (Johnny) and myself. Juditka was one and a half years old and was not allowed on the transport so they left her with my sister, Ruti, and grandmother with the thought that they will join us at the first possibility.

Hitler came to Prague on the 15th March, and we left on the 30th of April. We were four months on the way with three months of it on the sea. We arrived on the 2nd of September. We started to make wooden sandals, at the end we made 70 pairs daily. Three newcomers helped us. On November, 1940, we joined the British Army. In April, 1941, we fell in the German prison, where we were till 1945. We were 200-250 km from our home. So near and so far away. In 1946 we returned to Czechoslovakia and in 1948, when the communists came, we left.

Three brothers went to Australia and I joined the Jewish army and went to Israel. Brother Ervin divorced Gaby after the war. He later married Marta and in 1947 Jane was born. In Israel there was not a medical faculty. In 1949 they opened the fifth year and so I finally finished. In 1953, I married Chagit, who was a secretary of a general, the first commander of the army during the liberation, and later in charge of the Department for Science.

In 1963, together with Chagit, we went to Czechoslovakia and visited our village, Novy-Hrozenkov. Our house, which was partly destroyed, was occupied by our friend. We were walking in the courtyard and suddenly he said "I found a double wall. There was a box, full of funny things." I said that these were the Toras. My father, during the First World War, bought the Toras from three Polish Jews and the people from the neighbourhood came on holidays to pray. We took them to Israel, one of them I donated to the synagogue and on a certain holiday – Simchat tora - I dance with it.

A friend of my sister Ruti is still alive and when I am there I visited her. She was telling me about the years of occupation and how they suffered. The whole family was taken to a concentration camp in February, 1942. The village is situated in the mountains and Chagit says it looks like in Switzerland. I did not tell you all the names of our family.

Parents: Jana & Sigmund

Children: Irena, Martha, Otto, Ernst, Edith, Ervin, Walter, Jan (Johny), Ada, Ruth, Bruno

My parents had 11 children – five daughters and six sons. We have 11 grandchildren – six girls and five boys. I gave you a little of the family history and if you would like to know something about that, let me know.

With love and best regards from all of us.

Yours

Chagit and Bruno

Your grandmother told me how Jewish her family was.

Ramat Gan, March, 1995

# Appendix 9

## Letter to Jane Trigg from Bruno Sax

### May 1997

*Dear Jane,*

*We received your letter, for which I thank you very much. You wrote, that you still tire very easily. With the end of the operation and the treatment after it you cannot expect the same strong Jane as before. You have to take in the consideration now and later. The children are grown up and at least let the man look after the family.*

*Today, the 29th of April, it is 68 years since we left Czechoslovakia and 66 years since we fell in prison. A part of history.*

*In a week's time my brother Walter will come for three weeks and after this time will come his grand-daughter Jana for two weeks and together we will go back. I am looking forward to their coming. Walter was here last year and because it is difficult for me to travel to him, he will come to me. It is nice from him. He will be this year 87.*

*You are asking about our property in Czech Republic. First our brother-in-law Joseph sold after the war, during the Communist regime, all he could – the house and many other things. The forests and where the saw mill stood he could not sell. If John would be alive, he could have looked after it, but who is* looking after is the son-in-law of Joseph, husband of Ivanka. Once I met a friend and he told me, that he is doing everything that will remain to him. Once we had thoughts to take a lawyer, then we dropped it.

Now about the family. Adi, the daughter of Ruti is a soldier, she is a corporal, a nice one, and will stay in the air force another year. Now is the turn of Itamar, the son of Ifat. He will join the army next year. Now they are seven students, going to school and trying to be clever and two girls, one who will go to school this year and the other next. And about us. Hagit is working and I am passing the time, how I can, hoping for better.

Wishing you all the best, with best regards to all the family.

Yours

Hagit and Bruno

8 Habeer St.

Ramat Gan

# Appendix 10

## Letter from Walter Sax to Jane Trigg

(Date unknown)

Dear Jane,

First of all, thank you for the nice photos of your family and I can hardly believe how tall and grown-up Andrew is. It only shows how old we are getting, or already are.

I have returned from six weeks visit to Israel and am glad to be home again. Israel as you know is growing like mushrooms. The state is poor but the people have money. Very curious situation.

I hope the information I give you will help you a little in your project. Sorry I could not remember more.

Best regards to all and with love,

Walter

It is for me difficult to describe the family of Sigmund and Yohanna Sax from the start. First of all, I do not know how this couple landed in Novy Hronzenkov or what was their living income. As far as I remember we had a saw-mill, that is to say my father and his brother David together. By 1907 they had already seven children, with one who died a few days after birth.

The seventh child was Ervin. Later, approximately in 1913 another baby died, so that before World War 2 all 11 lived, were *healthy and the three oldest girls (sisters) were married. As educating the children goes, we attended some Czech, some German schools and thereafter nearly every child spent a year or two with the family relations in a bigger city. Upon returning home it was decided what next – and so Ervin and John attended a certain 'special school' for foresters and management of timber/lumber, etc. There were only two such schools in Czechoslovakia and both enjoyed a very good name. Ervin, after completely doing the above studies, became a manager of a saw-mill in Novy Hrozenkov.*

*Novy Hrozenkov had only one doctor (no hospital) and several midwives, who helped out with the home delivery and it worked out OK. To feel how they lived, go 100 years back. No electricity, hot and cold running water, telephone, autos, etc.*

*I myself wonder how one father could support so many children and accumulate the assets we had. A home with several acres of land, a small hall with a tree in the backyard, somewhere a few miles away several parcels of forest and again farming land.*

*Before the war, before we four brothers left Czechoslovakia, we gave our sister, Edith or Eva, a power of attorney and, several years later, after the Germans capitulated, we found that our dear brother in law (husband of Edith) sold whatever he could. Now their three children, who live in Czechoslovakia (now Czech Republic) are trying to get titles of what remained. None of us four brothers were interested to fight for it and stay there. Even now, Bruno and I do not want any part of it.*

*David Sax, former partner with my father, established in some town a saw-mill, but his sons-in-law were not for such a trade. I myself did not hear that David would offer Ervin to manage the saw-mill. A few years prior, after our father's death,* he (David) threw out my two brothers – Otto and Ernest – from the saw-mill, where our father was a 50% partner. It came to court, Uncle David lost, and had to leave that place. And therefore started a new saw-mill. I do not think Ervin worried about him or his property.

Going through your questions, all Saxes were born at home with the help of a midwife. There was and still is not a hospital and most probably only two doctors.

I met your mother at the end of 1933 in the capital of Moravia – Brno or Brunn (German spelling) where I served as a departmental manager after the war (in a store named JEPA) and Martha as a first sales lady (not in my department). Then in 1945/46 we were leaving by a transport from Palestine via Suez on rail to Italy. We were held up in or near Suez for several weeks because of the shortage of transportation by sea and that's where your parents hit it off.

When your parents arrived in Australia, we lived on a poultry farm (leasing it) in Tuart Hill and after a few months they moved out to the south of Western Australia, where, with John, they started a saw-mill. Because of asthma due to sheep dust your family had to liquidate that enterprise and I think started a store. The rest you know better than I.

We – John, Charlotte (wife), Paul (one year old) and I – left Prague in 1948 for Perth via Italy. We both men worked at a saw-mill in Bindoon (north of Perth) and after a few months John found a better job and left, and we had to leave, too.

I got a job as a general farmhand near Katanning. And later as a salesman in a furniture store in Perth and from there on a poultry farm in Tuart Hill. From there we left towards the end of 1952 for Canada, with the idea of going to USA. In 1956 we left for California – and the rest is history.

John lived till approx. 1954 without Jarka. He had a good job with a firm who used to deal with our family in the old Czechoslovakia and stayed in the firm to the end in the satisfactory relationship with all concerned. Jarka at the beginning lived with us in Meadford when she arrived, soon rented a little house and not long after they moved to Toronto.

I am writing this in Israel, and will mail it from the USA. In case I find something interesting in my memory bank, I will add it later. For now, good luck to you.

# Appendix 11

## Sax family notes

### Recorded by Jane Trigg from John Sax

Four brothers and Gaby, Ervin's first wife, left Czechoslovakia in 1939 for Israel.

The brothers enlisted in the British Army in Israel. They went to Tobruk after the Australians had captured it from the Germans. They were shipped to Greece where they were supposed to fight against the Italians. They arrived with no tanks, artillery or aircraft. The Italians, at that stage, controlled Abyssinia. The Germans attacked and the British attack turned to a rout. The army retreated and over 15,000 were captured, including the four brothers.

The brothers were put into work details. They went to Austria, then Germany. They ended up at Stalag VIII on work detail. Erwin and Walter were in one group, John and Bruno in another. The Russians came and liberated a section near John and Bruno. John went home and found the family home half demolished. (The timber part was gone, and the stone or brick section remained). All the British soldiers had to go to Britain to be discharged. John went last, but Erwin returned home first.

Walter and Chari were married in Britain; John and Bruno were at the wedding. Erwin was already in Czechoslovakia. All returned to Israel, then went back to Czechoslovakia. Erwin and Martha married in 1946 or 1947.

The war and evacuation from Greece: The four brothers enlisted and were in a type of Home Guard. They went to Tobruk as an occupying force, not as a fighting force. In Greece, when the army retreated to the Mediterranean, the British officers and fighting troops were evacuated first by the British Navy. The rest were to be evacuated "tomorrow", but the Germans got there first.

Erwin was a Corporal (two stripes), as was John.

There were two types of uniform that they had their photos taken in – a work uniform and a dress uniform.

Stalag VIII was divided into sections. The brothers were in two separate work details.

There were 13 children in the Sax family. Two died early, possibly at birth or shortly after. John didn't know their names. The names of the oldest five were recorded in the Jewish prayer book.

As each daughter married, the next daughter took over organising the family. Eva took over after Irene. Martha married and was excellent at looking after "the boys". When John or the others went out, their clothes were pressed and put out for them.

Irene had an 18-year-old son, Kurt, who died in the war.

# Appendix 12

# Poems by Jane Trigg

The following are poems written by Jane Trigg, nee Sax, about her Uncle Viktor (her mother's brother in Prague), a visit to Prague in January 1991, about her mother, Martha Sax, her experiences with chemotherapy, and her last writing:

### Viktor

Can this be my Uncle,
This querulous gnarled old man
In the patched, baggy pants
Who hoards the food we bring
And complains about everything?

Where is the man in the photos
My mother showed me?
The smart young man in a suit
Who worked as a clerk with the airlines?
I remember her stories about
His fastidious dress and manners.

I see nothing of her face in his,
Save perhaps the blue eyes.
Where hers were large, direct,
His are small and furtive.
Where is her strength,
Upright bearing and dignity?

They are not in this man
Who licks his knife, slurps his food
So noisily we are glad
We have eaten before him.

I see more of my mother
In my uncle's wife
And her octogenarian brother.
They too are openly hospitable,
Friendly, welcoming and do not complain
Because we can't manage rye bread
And liverwurst for breakfast.

Where has he gone,
My mother's brother?
Was it some seed within
Which changed him so completely?
Or have the years of communism,
Hard manual labour for not
Informing on a friend
Taken their toll?
Have the hard work, the years
Of scrounging for food,
Queuing for basic necessities
Twisted not only body
But also soul?

He tells us how wonderful things are,
How you can get anything here,
While his wife is delighted
To have bought carrots at the market
As a special treat.
We weep within ourselves for what is
And for what might have been.

Prague
January 1991

# Prague

*(14<sup>th</sup> January, 1991 – Rachel's fifteenth birthday)*

We have come, Rachel and I,
To visit previously unseen relations,
Intending to pay our respects
in this city of 1000 spires,
gilded statues, bridges,
buildings baroque and gothic
and its astronomical clock,
the horologe,
whose origins date back centuries.
New World intruders into the old.

We walk through colours of winter,
drab greys and browns,
flinching inwardly at
dirty evidence of the city's recent occupation.
Carefully we step
around spittle and filth
on cobbled streets.

In the coldness of an early
winter morning, we go quietly,
silently to Mass
unfamiliar at home and even more so
in this language of childhood memory.
Expecting nothing,
wanting only to please.
I find in the quiet and dark
lights gradually,
gently flickering on a full church,
people standing in side aisles.

They are mainly old, these silent worshippers
in dull coats, tea cosies, fur hats.
I admire the woman
wearing the smart red hat for
her audacity, dash of colour,
flash of life.
Ponder too the young who have come:
years of atheism have not
completely wiped the spark of faith.

I offer silent prayers for my mother
in the country of her birth
knowing her spirit is at peace:
giving thanks that I grew up
and she breathed her last breaths
where the sun shines and people laugh.

Later, encouraged by my uncle,
Rachel and I leave our written petitions
in the old Jewish cemetery
not used for 200 years.
At the grave of Rabbi Low
who supposedly answers prayers,
I write, paying tribute
To the Jewish part of my heritage;
praying, that in a world threatened by war
we will get home.

At the airport we make our tearful farewells
to my uncle and aunt
who are old and ill.
They are the almost-dead
whom we will not see again;
not in this city.

I understand for the first time
why my father has never come back.

The plane banks and climbs
Rachel and I turn our faces for home.

# Full Circle

How many times must she have sat
At my bedside, my mother
Wiping my childish forehead, holding my hand,
In this new country, far from
Relations, friends and doctors?
My mother, my brave mother.

Just as I have sat at my children's bedsides,
Wondering if the fever will abate,
The coughing cease, the breathing ease.
My task has been easier; doctors closer,
Friends nearby and my mother,
My caring mother, never far away.

And now I have become
My mother's mother, as I
Wipe her forehead, hold her hand
As she prepares for another new country
Where long lost relations will surround her.
My mother, my brave, caring, dying mother.

Perth, February 1990

# Aftermath

After chemo, my half demented
out of sync system begins
its inward twitching,
whirring, clacking and clicking;
a headlong rush into nowhere.
Insistently, incessantly I clean,
tidy, sweep, reorganise,
putting, picking, placing, pecking.
Attempts to read are met by words whirring,
whizzing, gyrating, spinning off the page.
I try to walk, stride, hike;
beaten by lethargy
which won't keep pace with desire.
Shutting my eyes in feigned sleep,
images form, re-form, skid
and slide into oblivion
only to pounce in metamorphosed form.

Only time helps;
the furious fragmented ticks
become more muted minutes,
honeyed hours and delicious days.
The petals of an inward rose
gently open and unfold;
an inward white light
fans out
spreading peace.

## Across the Street

Oft in the night I think and grieve
About the people I must leave
A left brained husband, much loved who
Is generous, organised, constant, true.

Three wonderful children, flesh of my heart
though dear (and expensive) a joy from the start.
Friends who surround, cover me with prayer
Friends who laugh and swear and share.

Loving people who fax, write and phone
Who come sit by my side so I'm not alone.
Friends bringing meals, singing a hymn
Releasing balloons, following my whim.

Then there's the beach, new every day
Kids on the shore, boats in the bay.
Seaweed and shells, dolphin at play
Lit by God's finger, showing the way.

So many things, to miss and to mourn
So much heartache which must be borne.
Then I remember the people I'll meet
When I'm called by God to this side of the street.

Thoughts of meeting my mother fill me with joy
So do tales of Dad when he was a boy.
No more secrets, evasions, lies to be told
Just two dear parents to have and to hold.

All the relatives I've yet to meet
Two sets of grandparents I'll die to greet.
They'll come from the woods, emerge from the camps
Entering my darkness, shining their lamps.

Extended family; Fiona strong and healing
Rebecca flicking suppositories at the ceiling.
They'll all be there with arms out wide
And I'll enter a new gate and step inside.

Jane Trigg Thurs 10 July 1997

# Appendix 13

## Sax Family Photo Gallery

*The brothers and Martha, visiting Israel, early 1970s*

*Sol (Solly) Sax*

*Erwin and Martha Sax, at their home in Rossmoyne, Perth, WA*

*Walter Sax*

*Jarmila/Jarka Sax*

*John Sax*

*Robert Sax (Walter's son) and his children, David and Sarah*

*Paul Sax (Walter's son)*

*From the left: Bruno, John, Erwin and Walter, in Singapore*

*Grandmother Jana Sax in her vegetable garden at Novy Hrosenkov*

*Eva's daughter Evanka, husband Milan,
son Milan and daughter Barunka*

*Soldier Erwin Sax*

*Sol Sax and father John, at Sol's wedding to Domonique, Canada*

*Bruno and Chagit Sax, with daughters Ruti and Yifat*

*Mother Jana Sax (centre) and four of her older daughters*

*Jane Sax at her wedding to Geoff Trigg, and her father Erwin Sax*

## About the Author

Geoff Trigg is a retired local government engineer, born in 1950, in Warrnambool, Victoria, with a strong interest in his own family's history. His professional career left him little time to research his first wife's family history until retirement. Increased connections and detailed information from her extended family in Israel, Canada and the United States of America brought together a combination of skills and passion to include all available information regarding these extraordinary men in one book for wider family use and study.

Geoff's interest in Australian and European history, conditions faced by immigrants to Australia from post-war Europe and the disaster to the Jewish people caused by the Holocaust was focused by his wife's written memories and stories about her father and his brothers. This was expanded with the information and photos supplied from her cousins and uncles.

This is Geoff's second book. His first book covered the life and times of his Irish great-great-grandfather, John Stephenson Henry.

www.ingramcontent.com/pod-product-compliance
Lightning Source LLC
Chambersburg PA
CBHW041956080526
44588CB00021B/2754